Enterprise Computing with Objects

The Addison-Wesley Object Technology Series

Grady Booch, Ivar Jacobson, and James Rumbaugh, Series Editors

For more information check out the series web site [http://www.awl.com /cseng/otseries/] as well as the pages on each book [http://www.awl.com/cseng/I-S-B-N/] (I-S-B-N represents the actual ISBN, including dashes).

David Bellin and Susan Suchman Simone, *The CRC Card Book*
ISBN 0-201-89535-8

Grady Booch, *Object Solutions: Managing the Object-Oriented Project*
ISBN 0-8053-0594-7

Grady Booch, *Object-Oriented Analysis and Design with Applications, Second Edition*
ISBN 0-8053-5340-2

Alistair Cockburn, *Surviving Object-Oriented Projects: A Manager's Guide*
ISBN 0-201-49834-0

Dave Collins, *Designing Object-Oriented User Interfaces*
ISBN 0-8053-5350-X

Bruce Douglass, *Real-Time UML: Developing Efficient Objects for Embedded Systems*
ISBN 0-201-32579-9

Desmond F. D'Souza and Alan C. Wells, *Objects, Components, and Frameworks with UML: The Catalysis Approach*
ISBN 0-201-31012-0

Martin Fowler with Kendall Scott, *UML Distilled: Applying the Standard Object Modeling Language*
ISBN 0-201-32563-2

Martin Fowler, *Analysis Patterns: Reusable Object Models*
ISBN 0-201-89542-0

Peter Heinckiens, *Scalable Object-Oriented Database Applications: Design, Architecture, and Implementation*
ISBN 0-201-31013-9

Ivar Jacobson, Maria Ericsson, and Agenta Jacobson, *The Object Advantage: Business Process Reengineering with Object Technology*
ISBN 0-201-42289-1

Ivar Jacobson, Magnus Christerson, Patrik Jonsson, and Gunnar Overgaard, *Object-Oriented Software Engineering: A Use Case Driven Approach*
ISBN 0-201-54435-0

Ivar Jacobson, Martin Griss, and Patrik Jonsson, *Software Reuse: Architecture, Process and Organization for Business Success*
ISBN 0-201-92476-5

David Jordan, *C++ Object Databases: Programming with the ODMG Standard*
ISBN 0-201-63488-0

Wilf LaLonde, *Discovering Smalltalk*
ISBN 0-8053-2720-7

Lockheed Martin Advanced Concepts Center and Rational Software Corporation, *Succeeding with the Booch and OMT Methods: A Practical Approach*
ISBN 0-8053-2279-5

Thomas Mowbray and William Ruh, *Inside CORBA: Distributed Object Standards and Applications*
ISBN 0-201-89540-4

Ira Pohl, *Object-Oriented Programming Using C++, Second Edition*
ISBN 0-201-89550-1

Terry Quatrani, *Visual Modeling with Rational Rose and UML*
ISBN 0-201-61016-3

Yen-Ping Shan and Ralph Earle, *Enterprise Computing with Objects: From Client/Server Environments to the Internet*
ISBN 0-201-32566-7

David N. Smith, *IBM Smalltalk: The Language*
ISBN 0-8053-0908-X

Daniel Tkach and Richard Puttick, *Object Technology in Application Development Second Edition*
ISBN 0-201-49833-2

Daniel Tkach, Walter Fang, and Andrew So, *Visual Modeling Technique: Object Technology Using Visual Programming*
ISBN 0-8053-2574-3

Available Summer/Fall 1998

Grady Booch, James Rumbaugh, and Ivar Jacobson, *Unified Modeling Language User Guide*
ISBN 0-201-57168-4

Ivar Jacobson, Grady Booch, and James Rumbaugh, *The Objectory Software Development Process*
ISBN 0-201-57169-2

James Rumbaugh, Ivar Jacobson, and Grady Booch, *Unified Modeling Language Reference Manual*
ISBN 0-201-30998-X

Enterprise Computing with Objects

From Client/Server Environments
to the Internet

Yen-Ping Shan
Ralph H. Earle

ADDISON-WESLEY

An Imprint of Addison Wesley Longman, Inc.

Reading, Massachusetts • Harlow, England • Menlo Park, California

Berkeley, California • Don Mills, Ontario • Sydney • Bonn • Amsterdam

Tokyo • Mexico City

The publisher offers discounts on this book when ordered in quantity for special sales.

For more information please contact:
Corporate & Professional Publishing Group
Addison Wesley Longman, Inc.
One Jacob Way
Reading, Massachusetts 01867
(617) 944-3700

Library of Congress Cataloging-in-Publication Data

Shan, Yen-Ping.
    Enterprise computing with objects : from client/server environments
to the Internet / Yen-Ping Shan, Ralph H. Earle.
        p.   cm.—(The Addison-Wesley series in object-oriented
software engineering)
    Includes bibliographical references and index.
    ISBN 0-201-32566-7
    1. Object-oriented methods (Computer science)   2. Client/server
computing.   3. Internet programming.   I. Earle, Ralph H.
II. Title.   III. Series.
QA76.9.035S53   1998
005.3'76—dc21   97-35568
                                                                      CIP

ISBN 0-201-32566-7

1   2   3   4   5   6   7   8   9—MA—0100999897
First printing, December 1997

To my parents, my wife Ke-Jen, and my son Stephen.
—YPS

To my parents Virginia and Morris.
—RHE

Contents

1.
Client/Server Computing

2.
Object Technology

3.

Integrating Object Technology
with Enterprise Systems

4.

Object-Oriented Clients

5.

Object-Oriented Servers

6.

Object-Oriented Glue

Contents

7.

Object Persistence and Sharing

10.

Performance

11.

The Scaleable OO Enterprise System

12.

Security

13.

Business Systems

14.

Some Conclusions and Predictions

Preface

Enterprise computing has embraced client/server environments and is now reaching into the world of the Internet. In our view, one key to the success of this evolution is object technology. By enterprise computing, we mean the development, deployment, and maintenance of the information systems required for survival and success in today's business climate. With its modular approach to development, object technology addresses many of the key issues of enterprise computing. It is good at managing complexity, making software components available for reuse, and managing changes, such as the rapid evolution of the World Wide Web.

As enterprise systems evolve in the direction of the Internet, our view is that enterprises can leverage what they already know about client/server technology and object technology. *Enterprise Computing with Objects'* purpose is to take enterprise systems from where they are today and show how objects can help move them into the 21st century. In so doing, we focus on client/server architecture, which introduces order to enterprise systems and promotes understanding of enterprise computing in the past, present, and future.

The synergy of object technology and client application development has already fueled the first generation of client/server computing. In the process, it transformed the face of human-computer interaction, giving us graphical user interfaces (GUIs) and object-oriented user interfaces (OOUIs). Now client/server technology is moving into another generation. The World Wide Web has introduced a new and pervasive user interface platform and object technology has expanded out of its client-only role. We are facing a transition with a profound impact on existing information systems, as well as on systems yet to be constructed.

Technological advancement always produces confusion, risks, and opportunities. There is great value in understanding the essential elements of the technology (as opposed to the incidental ones). Notice that we say the value is in *understanding* rather than *knowing.* People can know dozens of buzzwords and hundreds of implementation details, but if they do not have a fundamental understanding of how and why the pieces fit together, their knowledge will soon become obsolete. Simply knowing the details of today's systems does not imply an understanding of tomorrow's systems. However, a person who truly understands today's systems can leverage that understanding to quickly grasp new technologies and trends as they come along.

This book is an architectural overview and a digest of essential topics, covering a broad and complex subject as quickly as possible. Our goals are to present the client/server models that govern the implementation of enterprise information systems and to show how object technology fits into these models. By focusing on what strikes us as intrinsically true about this union, we describe and clarify the architectural concepts that make today's and tomorrow's systems possible. We separate what is essential from what is incidental so that as products continue to evolve, the book will continue to have value.

Such a book could easily run over a thousand pages. However, because your time is precious, this book distills and filters the information so that a busy professional can receive the maximum benefit in the shortest amount of time. We do not attempt to provide comprehensive evaluations or recommendations of products. Although we include many details of products and systems, we use these to illustrate our concepts and ensure linkage between our concepts and the real world. Because we cannot cover everything in detail, we include comprehensive references that point the reader to more detailed information sources.

What Readers Can Hope to Gain

En route to understanding enterprise computing with objects, readers will gain a clear picture of different types of clients, servers, and the software "glue" that holds systems together. They will also come to understand why object technology was introduced to enterprise computing and where the combination is heading. They will learn how objects can be introduced into various implementations, as well as the benefits and drawbacks of each case.

After reading the book, readers should be able to better see through the marketing hype surrounding both object technology and enterprise computing, and they should be able to focus on the essential architecture issues relevant to solving real-life business and computing problems.

The World Wide Web is, of course, the fastest growing area of computing, and object technology has profound implications for the Web. In reading this book, readers can gain an understanding of how enterprises can leverage their client/server and object expertise to create effective Web-enabled systems.

Who This Book Is For

The book is aimed primarily at technical professionals, such as application developers, systems analysts, managers, and system architects. However, other technical professionals can benefit from the book, as can students of computer science, management information systems, and computer engineering. Nontechnical managers can benefit from our general overview of concepts and concerns that affect their computing systems. Our global view of object-oriented client/server computing can show many kinds of professionals how their work fits into a larger context. This kind of technical understanding can be valuable in helping people reach their career goals.

We assume that readers do not necessarily have prior application programming experience. At the same time, readers who are subject experts in object technology, client/server computing, or the Internet will benefit from seeing how concepts they are already familiar with can fit with concepts from the other areas we discuss.

Although the book is potentially valuable for programmers, it is not a programming manual or a "hands-on" guide. Rather, it can help programmers gain a high-level architectural understanding of areas they may be less familiar with.

Structure

The book starts with the basic concepts of client/server computing and then gives a brief overview of object technology. Once this groundwork is established, we look at a series of possible approaches for incorporating objects into enterprise computing systems. We go on to look at architectures for the three main client/server components—client, server, and glue—and for each component, we discuss object implementations, both current and projected.

After looking at object persistence, we examine the ways enterprises can leverage their existing knowledge base to move their information system onto the Internet and the World Wide Web. We follow this with an examination of the development tools that make end-to-end enterprise and Internet development possible. Finally, we examine the universal issues critical to successful deployment of OO enterprise systems, whether in a traditional client/server environment or on the Internet: performance, scaleability, security, groupware, and business engineering. The concluding chapter offers a summary and a direction for the future.

Using this Book

Although this book is meant to be read from cover to cover, it can also be used in less structured ways. Summaries at the end of each chapter offer a digest of the essentials for easy reference. The glossary provides a comprehensive list of the terms used in this book. Sidebars provide more in-depth looks at related topics. Readers who are already familiar with object technology and client/server concepts can skip over the introduction of those subjects and go straight to the later chapters. Readers interested in specific topics can navigate by using the table of contents and the index. The comprehensive list of references provides a jumping-off spot for further research and study.

Conventions

For ease of reference, the book uses a two-column format. The sentences in the left column summarize the key points in the text. These summaries are not intended to be read sequentially. Instead, readers can use them to quickly review what they have read or to skim to find relevant information. Also, by quickly scanning the summary sentences above and below a section, a reader who jumps into a section can quickly establish the context for reading.

Sidebars

Sometimes a topic strikes us as interesting or relevant and needs further treatment, but it does not seem to fit into the immediate discussion. We have included these topics in sidebars like this one. Sidebars tend to cover related technological issues. They can also cover our own opinions or speculations on a subject.

The book contains a large number of figures to illustrate technical concepts, system configurations, and other items of interest. We use the following conventions to denote the different components of enterprise systems.

Database

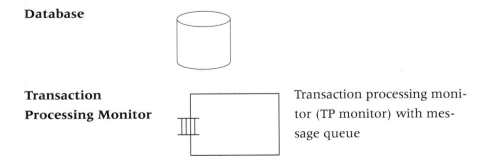

Transaction Processing Monitor

Transaction processing monitor (TP monitor) with message queue

Programs

Traditional 3GL program written in a non-OO language, such as Assembler, C, and COBOL

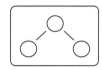

OO program, using connected circles to depict objects and their references to each other

Executing Programs

Executing programs are depicted as programs inside an executing environment, as in the following two examples:

3GL program executing inside a TP monitor

OO program executing inside a database.

Acknowledgments

Many people have helped us with this book. Although it is impossible to thank all of them, we will try.

To our reviewers, for their numerous helpful and insightful comments: Mark Landry, Lloyd W. Taylor (DIGEX, Inc.), Dayle Woolston (ObjectSelect LC), and especially Sandeep Singhal (IBM). To Hayden Lindsey, whose early work and discussion inspired Chapter 9.

To our IBM managers who encouraged us along the way: Danny Sabbah, Greg Clark, Steve Robinson, Bob Gilliam, and Susan Wallenborn.

To many friends, mentors, and colleagues in and outside IBM from whom we have learned so much in numerous discussions and exchanges over the years. We list them in alphabetical order: Jim Adamczyk, Sam Adams, Rich Arcuri, Ken Auer, Roger Barney, Brian Barry, Elias Bayeh, Andrew Bear, Toufic Boubez, Ian Brackenbury, Paul Buck, Rose Bynum, Tom Cargill, Kevin Cattell, Dan Chang, Virginia Clark, Ed Cobb, John Cook, William Cook, Paul Cotton, Brad Cox, Jerry Cuomo, Mike Conner, Mark Day, John DeBinder, Scott de Deuge, Rick DeNatale, Jim des Rivieres, John Duimovich, Cort DeVoe, Dave Ehnebuske, David Fallside, Walter Fang, Don Ferguson, Karl Freburger, Bjorn Freeman-Benson, Chris Gerken, Tom Glover, Eric Gold, Adele Goldberg, Jim Gray, Delores Hamilton, Bernard Horan, Paul Huffman, Don Hyde, Keith Jones, John Kellerman, Phil Kerklo, Dennis King, John Knapman, Mitchell Kramer, Marie Lenzi, Dan Lesage, Frank Leymann, Rui-Ji Ling, Mary Loomis, John Lord, Larry Loucks, Lou Mamo, Skip McGaughey, Jeff McAffer, Jim Mickelson, Mike Milinkovich, Tom Morgan, Pat Mueller, Lee Nackman, Martin Nally, Binh Nguyen, Bruce Neuchterlein, Scott Penberthy, Larry Poe, Phil Proudfoot, Jim Rhyne, Dieter Roller, Jim Russell, Arthur Ryman, John Rymer, Danny Sabbah, Jim Salmons, Timo Salo, Marc-Thomas Schmidt, Harm Sluiman, Larry Smith, Rod Smith, Alan Snyder, Andy So, Jane Stanhope, Barry Stevenson, Tony Storey, John Sweitzer, David Taylor, Ruth Taylor, Dave Thomas, Dave Thomson, Jim Thompson, John Tibbetts, Ava Vanyo, Dave Wallace, Alan Warren, Bill Waskom, Chris Weatherly, Mark Wegman, Mike West, Mike Wheatley, Don Wildman, Rob Will, Tim Wolf, Al Woolfrey, Lun Xiao, and Al Zollar.

To Tom Love, who encouraged Shan to create the book.

To the thesis advisors at the University of North Carolina, especially John B. Smith and Fred Brooks, who taught Shan, among many other things, the discipline of writing ten minutes every day, no matter how great the workload at the time. Without this discipline, the book, which took five years to finish, would not have been possible.

Special thanks to our editor, Carter Shanklin, and to the other people at Addison Wesley Longman who made this book possible: especially production coordinators Jacquelyn Young and Melissa Lima; copy editor Arlene Richman; editorial assistants Rachel Beavers and Angela Buenning; also to the book production people at NK Graphics: especially Tonnya Norwood, Dawn Nebelski, Nancy Howard, and graphic artist David Ziarnowski.

To our families, who have been steadfast supporters throughout this long journey, for their invaluable love and understanding.

Foreword

There is no turning back. The moment the first PC landed in a corporation, the stage was set for what we are beginning to realize today: distributed heterogeneous object computing.

Typical of evolution, it began quietly and slowly. Then, in the first half of the 1990s, the process began to pick up. Superficially enough, we began replacing primitive, character-based forms with GUI front ends. But the work was crude and had no impact on the corporate bottom line. It was indeed the corporate "R&D" of what we are now experiencing. However, much more needs to be understood than simply how to scrape a screen.

When we talk about enterprise-level client/server, we are not talking about replacing 3270 interfaces to CICS or IMS systems with a GUI front end. We are talking about a fundamentally more significant progression in software development. We are headed towards systems, not applications, that communicate across many, many (several hundred) servers and many more (possibly tens of thousands) clients. These mega-networks typically include elements of the mainframe, the Internet and the World Wide Web, and can occur within and among large, medium and small companies.

Enterprise-level systems will be the life blood of organizations 5 to 10 years from now, and the companies that understand this today will be those that come out on top in the next decade. To accomplish this we need to understand not only the technology, but also the business that the technology supports.

The technology appears to be difficult and is more complex than it has ever been for several reasons. First, we are trying to do some very sophisticated things. Instead of attaching two things linearly, we are hooking up many things multi-dimensionally. *N*-tier is not linear! Second, and far more significantly, we need to understand the technology as well as the business that the technology supports, as we try to connect technologies and software that were deliberately architected to be independent. We now want all of our mismatched proprietary technology to play together nicely. This is the part that is **hard;** this is the part that is expensive!

Enterprise-level software development is not as cut and dried as some manufacturers lead us to believe. It can be quite complex and daunting if you don't see the broad perspective of the terrain. Likewise, enterprise development is not what has been traditionally thought of as client/server computing. So, how do we get there and keep our sanity? For starters, we must manage complexity. Understanding the multiple and various pieces is the place to begin. Next, we need to know how the pieces fit together. And most importantly, we must learn to keep the pieces separate. *Enterprise Computing With Objects* articulates all of the pieces independently and explains them clearly and concisely. The authors describe how each of the pieces fits together, all the while maintaining its independence.

I've worked with enterprise-level systems since 1970. I've been working with object technology since 1988. Object technology is probably the single most significant element available today for the management of such complexity. All application areas are ripe for object technology. Since things in nature exist as objects, there are no intrinsically object-oriented applications. Objects can be thought of as data and the appropriate behavior for that data, compacted in a single package. These packages cruise the Net and explode at your viewpoint of choice. With this image in mind, it is not much of a leap to comprehend that objects are much more nimble and viable in a network environment than our old 50,000 line monolithic procedural dinosaurs. The multi-dimensionality of objects is form following the function of distributed enterprise-level systems including web and inter/intra/extranet components.

This all can appear a bit daunting. However, I find rejuvenating old and new legacy software into distributed environments to be most exciting. We are breaking free of the constraints of the singular centralized environment. Never again will we build a system for a single user in a homogeneous environment; not if we are lucky. In *Enterprise Computing With Objects,* Yen-Ping Shan and Ralph Earle have provided readers with essential information and tools to launch us beyond the year 2000, into the world of heterogeneous systems running on disparate machines located all over the world.

Marie A. Lenzi
Non-practicing developer
Editor-in-Chief, DOC

1

Client/Server Computing

Enterprise computing involves the development, deployment, and maintenance of the information systems required for survival and success in today's business climate. In discussing enterprise computing, client/server computing is the natural place to begin because it has been one of the core elements of enterprise computing for the past five years. Furthermore, the concept of client/server computing is a general one, which can be used as a framework to discuss past, present, and future enterprise computing subjects. This opening chapter establishes client/server concepts as the fundamental concepts that will apply to the rest of the book. In a like way, Chapter 2 establishes the fundamental concepts of object technology, so that we can begin to see how object technology and client/server computing interact—currently and potentially—in the evolving world of enterprise systems.

Enterprise computing involves developing, deploying, and maintaining business information systems

Client/Server Concepts

The basic concepts we start with are *client, server, glue,* the *logical client/server model,* and *client/server layers.* In most cases, we use the terms *client* and *server* in their commonly understood sense, as defined below. In addition, we use the concept of *glue,* which can be considered the / in client/server. Later chapters contain detailed discussions of all three concepts.

The Client

Client usually refers to the front end of the client/server system, the component with which a user interacts. In most systems, the client has responsibility for presentation management (typically GUI management) and some application logic. Most clients reside

Clients include presentation management and some application logic

on a personal computer that also runs desktop applications, such as a word processor and a spreadsheet. Generally, the client contains the application logic relevant to the presentation management. In some architectures, such as a client that front-ends a database server, the client may contain the entire application logic.

The Server

Servers provide shared resources

Server usually means the entity that provides shared resources, such as a database, that can be connected to multiple clients. The server generally runs on a larger-class machine than the client (for example, a mid-range or mainframe computer).

We approach servers from an architectural perspective

One approach to servers is the **functional** approach, to look at them in terms of what they do: There are file servers, print servers, database servers, and so on. Many books and articles are available on this functional perspective. The approach we take, however, is **architectural.** We want to establish a clear architecture model that can be used to examine and understand a wide range of issues. Our architecture model views servers as either procedural or object-oriented, and we view them falling into three categories: transaction servers, database servers, and native servers, which we discuss in Chapter 5.

The server architecture model remains valid as server functions evolve

While the functions of servers continue to evolve, we anticipate that our taxonomy of server architecture will remain valid. In this way, the user can benefit from the taxonomy even when faced with new technology.

The Glue

Glue includes plumbing, programming model, and development tools

As long as a client and server are cooperating to complete a task, they need to communicate with each other. The **glue** makes this possible. Our concept of glue includes three aspects: the low-level **plumbing** (TCP/IP, for example), the programming model, and the application development tools supporting the programming model. Glue can be categorized according to the level of communication it makes possible. Client and server components can communicate with each other at the level of common buffers, common middleware, or a common language. Chapter 6 discusses these topics in detail.

The Logical Client/Server Model

The client/server relationship can also be viewed as a logical one. It represents a paradigm in which elements of a computing system request services from each other in order to complete one or more tasks. The requesting element is the client, and the elements that provide services are the servers. In this model, the roles of client and server are not fixed. A server can request other elements of the system to help it fulfill a request, in which case the server is also acting as a client. For example, a PC client can request a print server to print a job. The server, in turn, can request a printer to carry out the work. The print server acts as a server to the PC client and as a client to the printer.

In the logical client/server model, components request services from each other

In other words, the configuration of a single server communicating with multiple clients is merely a convenient way of understanding the client/server paradigm. The paradigm does not define the roles required in any given system, nor does it imply any actual software or hardware architecture restrictions. People associate *client* with the UI and *server* with shared resources because that represents the most commonly used client/server implementation scheme. In a networked environment, however, the logical client/server model allows the following possibilities.

The model does not dictate fixed roles for system components

- Servers can connect to one or more clients.
- Clients can communicate with multiple servers.
- Client-client or server-server communications are possible.

- Communicating partners can have a peer relationship or a master/slave relationship, depending on the application semantics.
- Client and server elements can exist on distinct physical machines or on the same machine

The logical client/server model has useful similarities to the object model

The logical client/server model turns out to be very similar to the object technology paradigm. At the object interaction level, objects request services from other objects to complete a task, just as clients request services of servers. The similarity of the two paradigms makes it easy to combine the two technologies and bring the benefits of both to the software developer.

Normally, we use the terms client and server in their conventional sense. In cases in which we discuss system components in terms of their place in the logical client/server model, it is self-evident from the context, or else we point it out.

Client/Server Layers

This book focuses on the application layer of client/server computing

Client/server computing occurs at three levels in a computing system: application, system services, and hardware. This book focuses on the application level, which we believe is the layer most relevant to object technology. To understand the differences between these vertical levels, or layers, look at the perspective shown in Figure 1-1.

The hardware provides the underlying layer

The lowest layer consists of the **hardware elements** of client/server computing: computers, printers, networking hardware such as routers, and other related devices.

System services include software that controls the hardware

The **system services** layer encompasses the operating system, networking software, system management, file system, database services, UI library, and so on. It includes all software used by the application layer to control the hardware.

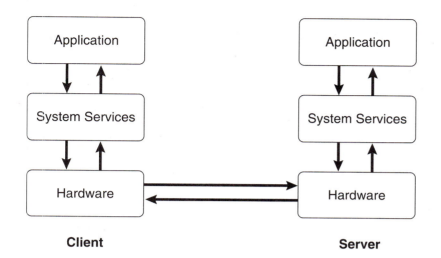

Figure 1-1 The three layers of a client/server system

It is often generic, reusable, and not specific to any application domain.

The **application** layer is the software that "runs" on top of the system services layer. These application programs differ from domain to domain. A useful way to understand the difference between the system layer and application layer is to consider the user. At the application level, the "user" tends to be a real human being on the client side. In contrast, the "user" of system services is generally an application program.

The application layer runs on top of the system services layer

Although the actual physical communication takes place at the hardware level, the client/server paradigm holds true at all three levels. For example, a system service element can request services from other system service elements just as a client application can request services from a server application.

The client/server paradigm holds true for all layers

Although the boxes in Figure 1-1 are all drawn the same size, not all system elements do equal amounts of work. For example, in a 3270 terminal or X Windows client configuration, the client side

System elements do varying amounts of work

does no application processing. From the perspective of the application layer, the server side does all the work.

We do not cover topics related to the hardware and system services layers

As we have pointed out, this book focuses on the application layer. Many good discussions of the hardware and system service layer are available. Therefore, we do not cover the following topics, except when a high-level discussion of them is relevant to object-oriented client/server computing.

- Hardware
- Networking infrastructure (LANs, WANs, TCP/IP, SNA, NetBIOS, and so on)
- Customary system services, such as printing and shared file systems

Client/Server Architecture Models

Many factors contribute to confusion in client/server models

Existing client/server architecture models can be confusing and contain overlapping terminology. This is due in part to the fact that they do not always separate the concerns of the hardware, system, and application layers. It is also due in part to the historical development of client/server systems from relatively simple host-terminal configurations to the complex configurations available today. It does not help that all the stages of client/server evolution are still in use, sometimes even coexisting on the same system.

We examine the relationship between client/server architectures

Rather than discuss the different architectures from a historical perspective, we will look at them in terms of their relationship to one another. To take a systematic look at the architecture models, we need to consider the basic functional elements of a typical application: presentation, logic, and data.

Presentation, Logic, and Data

As you can see in Figure 1-2, a typical application, client/server or not, includes elements that represent presentation, logic, and data. Every application that interacts with a user needs a presentation component to handle the user interface. As long as an application has effects that need to persist over time, a data element is required. As long as an application has to manipulate data or user input, it needs a logic element.

Presentation, logic, and data are the basic elements of any application

A text editor that runs on a stand-alone PC is a non-client/server application that offers a good example of these three application elements. Its user interface handles the user's keyboard input; its logic can then process the words, sentences, paragraphs, and other units of information. It can store the result of the editing to a file, which then becomes persistent data.

A text editor is a non-client/server example with all three elements

An order entry application provides a typical client/server example: The presentation element on the client allows the user to enter orders and requests the logic element on the server to process them. The logic element updates the server database that keeps records of the transactions.

An order entry application is a client/server example

There are exceptions to the three-element rule. Some applications may not have the presentation element. For example, an embedded application may not have any real human user and thus does not need a presentation element. Other applications, such as a cal-

Some applications may not have all three elements

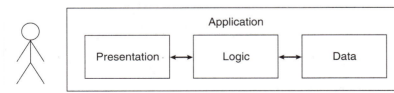

Figure 1-2 Elements of a typical application

culator, may not have a data element because no persistence is required. However, it is hard to conceive of any application without a logic element. No matter how trivial an application is, it always requires some logic. Even for a file system that mainly concerns itself with data, logic controls the data access and synchronization.

Partitioning the System

Systems can be partitioned according to a number of topologies

Once it is clear that an application consists of three basic functional elements, we can consider partitioning the application so that its elements can run on different computers. It turns out that there are a number of possible models, each of them suited to different purposes. A traditional way of seeing these models is the set of five logical topologies developed by the Gartner Group (Figure 1-3). (Note that what the diagram calls "application," we refer to as "logic," and what the diagram calls "data management," we refer to as "data.")

a) **Distributed presentation** is a server-heavy configuration in which the client is responsible for only a portion of the UI. Some examples are the X Window System, traditional 3270-type host-terminal systems, and simple Web browsers that render only HTML (that is, no plug-ins and applets). We will

Figure 1-3 Five client/server topologies

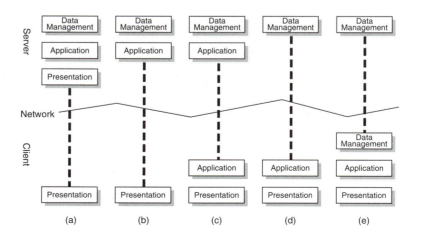

discuss partitioning issues related to the Web and the Internet in detail in Chapter 8.

b) **Remote presentation** means that the client is responsible for the entire UI but not for any application logic or data function. The technique of **screen scraping** creates this kind of configuration by building a sophisticated GUI in front of an existing host system.

c) **Distributed function** means that the application logic is split between client and server. There are a number of ways of doing this, including distributed transaction servers, remote procedure calls, stored procedures in databases, and (on the Web) Java applets and downloaded ActiveX components.

d) **Remote data access** puts presentation and application logic on a client that retrieves data from a remote database. For example, remote data access might use SQL APIs to make calls to a relational database. This is an example of **fat client** architecture, in which the client is heavy on logic.

e) **Distributed database** splits the data management function between the client and one or more servers while the application logic and UI components remain on the client. One example is IBM's Distributed Relational Database Architecture (DRDA). Webcasting that leverages "push technology" is another.

It can be confusing to keep up with these different system topologies, not to mention all their permutations and combinations. An alternative way of seeing the possible client/server splits is to consider presentation, logic, and data as a three-part application continuum, as in Figure 1-4.

Partitioning is a way of deciding where to slice the application continuum

The five labeled arrows in Figure 1-4 correspond to the five topologies in Figure 1-3. In the figure, partition points (a), (b), and (d) are less flexible than (c) and (e). This is because their interface protocols specify exactly what kinds of components can reside on either side of

Some partition points are more flexible than others

**Figure 1-4 Typical
client/server parti-
tion points**

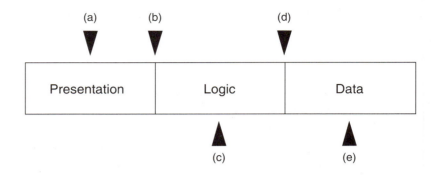

the partition and what data can flow between them. The software protocol rigidly determines the partition points, leaving no leeway for the application developer. For example, X Windows precisely defines the UI events and drawing commands that flow between client and server, as well as the required processing. Similarly, SQL provides a well-defined partition for remote data access.

Both distributed function (c) and distributed database (e) allow the developer to decide where the partitioning point should fall in the spectrum. This gives a greater amount of freedom for application designers to decide how they want to split the logic and data elements across the network.

Partitioning is based on hardware, enterprise needs, and the application itself

Rather than prescribe a set of distinct topologies, Figure 1-4 suggests a continuum of ways to partition an application, depending on the system hardware topology, the needs of the enterprise, and the nature of the application itself. This view of partitioning applications emphasizes the flexibility possible within the client/server model.

Two-Tier, Three-Tier, and *n*-Tier Architectures

"Multi-tier" can refer to hardware, operating system, or software function

The idea of two-tier and three-tier architecture can be a bit confusing because both terms can refer to either the hardware or the software configuration of a system. The more restrictive definition is from a hardware platform perspective. A **three-tier** hardware architecture involves three classes of machines: The client is usually a PC; the middle tier is usually a workstation server or a minicomputer; the back end is usually a mainframe. A **two-tier** hardware architecture generally involves only the client and either a middle-tier server or a mainframe.

Sometimes, though not as often, people consider the tiers of a system to represent the different software platforms it contains. From this perspective, the client tier generally runs Windows, MacOS, or OS/2. The middle tier runs UNIX, Windows NT, or OS/400. The third tier runs operating systems such as MVS, CICS, or IMS. Again, a two-tier system would include only two of the platforms.

From a software architecture perspective, the three tiers are presentation, logic, and data. This is the perspective taken in this book. In a typical enterprise computing environment, as shown in Figure 1-5, a PC handles the UI, a workstation server or minicomputer server executes the business logic, and a mainframe machine runs the database.

In software function, the three tiers are presentation, logic, and data

It is possible for two or more elements to run on the same machine. For example, Figure 1-6 shows a configuration that is physically two-tier but logically three-tier, in which the presenta-

Two or more elements can run on the same machine

Figure 1-5 Typical three-tier architecture

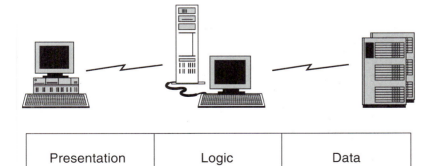

Presentation	Logic	Data

Figure 1-6 Logically three-tier but physically two-tier

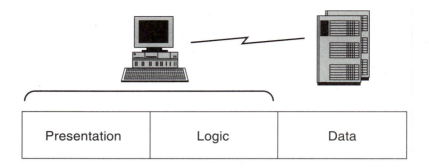

Presentation	Logic	Data

tion and business logic both run on the PC, and the database runs on the server.

N-tier systems split physical tiers across the network

Some systems take the partitioning of applications one step further and split one or more of the tiers across the network. For example, a distributed database service, Figure 1-4 (e), enables an enterprise's database to run on multiple types of machines and still present a logical view of a single database to the application logic that accesses the database. A distributed function service, Figure 1-4 (c), allows the middle tier that runs the business logic to be partitioned and run on multiple machines. In such cases, the partition points are not just at the presentation/logic or logic/data boundary. Partitioning can occur almost anywhere inside the logic or data section. Physically, the application can run across four, five, or even more machines (tiers); hence the name ***n*-tier.** Figure 1-7 shows a logical three-tier architecture that has four physical tiers because the business logic is partitioned.

An environment can mix two-tier, three-tier, and n-tier architectures

Note that it is completely possible, and even likely, that you can have an environment with two-tier, three-tier, and *n*-tier architectures mixed together. For example, a client program may access a database directly (two-tier), invoke a transaction that runs on the middle tier, and execute logic that is partitioned between it and a third server, which eventually accesses the database (three-tier).

Figure 1-7 Logically three-tier but physically four-tier

Presentation	Logic	Data

Distributed Computing and Concurrent Computing

In understanding what client/server computing is, it is helpful to understand two related concepts: distributed computing and concurrent computing. Although there is a great deal of overlap between the definitions of these two terms and the definition we are using for client/server computing, none of the terms are synonymous, and the differences can be instructive.

Distributed and concurrent computing are related to client/ server computing

We define **distributed computing** as computation on multiple machines utilizing computing resources that are distributed across a network. In other words, it is an all-encompassing category of which our client/server model forms a subset. Other forms of distributed computing, such as the peer-to-peer model, do not require a distinction between client and server.

The client/server model is a subset of the distributed model

A distributed system is not the same thing as a concurrent system, although the two models have significant overlap. In **concurrent computing,** several elements of a program execute in parallel. Usually, this implies a computing system with multiple CPUs executing program elements concurrently. (Multiple independent threads on a single processor can simulate the effect of true multiprocessor hardware. However, for simplicity's sake, our discussion will not include this case.)

Distributed computing bears comparison to concurrent computing

Shared Features of Distributed and Concurrent Systems

Concurrent systems share several key features with distributed systems (and their subset, client/server systems).

Both deal with issues of concurrent execution

- Both deal with the issues of programs running concurrently, either in CPUs distributed across the network or in concurrent CPUs in the same system. Many programming techniques are shared between the two systems, particularly synchronization techniques, such as semaphores and monitors.

Both deal with cross address space communication

- Both deal with the issue of communication across multiple address spaces. A distributed system needs to have programs on either side of the network boundary (thus, the address space boundary) communicate with each other. Concurrent systems also deal with multiple address spaces. In a concurrent system with a **messaging architecture,** programs communicate by sending messages that cross address space boundaries. In a concurrent system with a **shared memory architecture,** programs read and write into shared system memory. Information crosses the address space boundary when it moves between shared and private memories.

Differences between Distributed and Concurrent Systems

Distributed and concurrent systems also have significant differences. (Of course, any node in a distributed system can contain a concurrent system, so the two are not mutually exclusive.) Remembering that client/server systems are a kind of distributed system, the following discussion introduces additional characteristics of our client/server model.

Distributed systems support more dynamic system configuration

- **Dynamic configuration** The configuration of a distributed system is more dynamic. Arbitrary and voluntary changes in system configuration can occur, unrelated to system failure. For example, it is routine for new users and computers to connect to the network and for existing users and computers to disconnect. New networks can even be attached while the entire distributed system is executing. In contrast, concurrent systems rarely experience such dynamic reconfiguration; it's hard to install new CPUs to a multi-CPU machine while programs are running.

- **Platform heterogeneity** A system distributed across a network is very likely to involve heterogeneous platforms. Platforms can vary according to CPU type, operating system type, or other infrastructure elements, such as the transaction processing monitor used. Concurrent systems are generally more homogeneous.

  Distributed systems tend to exist on heterogeneous platforms

- **Networking** The network introduces additional differences. Network latency makes communication slower between nodes in a distributed system than in a concurrent system. With wide area networks, latency is often several orders of magnitude greater than the time required for local messaging. Concurrent system developers often focus on increasing the concurrency; distributed system developers often must focus more on reducing the amount of network traffic and latency.

  Performance over networks is a major issue for distributed systems

- **Network or component failure tolerance** This is another differentiator. It is common to have a portion of the network inaccessible while the remainder of the distributed system continues to function. That is, a portion of the distributed system may be in trouble while other parts are still operative. In contrast, many concurrent systems (outside the fault tolerance area) tend to start and stop as a single unit.

  Partial failure tolerance is also an issue

The characteristics of client/server computing that we have introduced in this chapter create a context for the OO and enterprise computing issues that we discuss throughout this book.

Summary

In discussing enterprise computing, client/server computing is the natural place to begin because it is one of the core elements of enterprise computing. Although we normally use the terms *client* and *server* in their popular sense, some of our discussion is based on the logical model, in which "client" indicates the component that requests services and "server" is the component that provides services. Such a logical client/server model is similar to the OO paradigm and can facilitate the introduction of object technology into client/server systems.

Although the client/server paradigm holds true for the hardware layer, system services layer, and application layer of a system, this book focuses on the application layer.

The basic functional elements of any application are

- Presentation
- Logic
- Data

The three elements exist on a continuum. This continuum can be partitioned at many different points. The multiple-split points allow us to map an application to run on two, three, or more physical tiers (two-tier, three-tier, or *n*-tier).

Client/server computing is a subset of distributed computing. It inherits many critical aspects of distributed computing, such as concurrent processing, crossing of address space, dynamic system configuration, heterogeneous platforms, network-driven performance and failure issues.

2

Object Technology

Object technology represents a paradigm shift in the way we develop and use computer software and, thus, in our approach to enterprise systems. Fortunately, the underlying concepts are relatively straightforward. This chapter introduces the most important terms and concepts of object technology.

Because our introduction to object-oriented concepts is brief, you might discover you would like a more comprehensive overview of the subject. Many good books are available on the subject, such as Grady Booch's *Object-Oriented Design with Applications* and David A. Taylor's *Object-Oriented Technology: A Manager's Guide*. On the other hand, if you are already familiar with object technology, you can skip to the next chapter.

Object technology represents a paradigm shift

A Typical OO System

The basic idea behind object technology is to make computer software behave more like the things and activities it models in the real world. To use a familiar example, let's look at a videotape rental store. The store contains many hundreds of similar objects— videotape cassettes. Customers look at the videotapes on the racks, read the backs of the boxes, take their selections to the clerk, and check them out.

Object-oriented software models real-world objects and activities

Meanwhile, the clerk uses a software system to track the flow of the tapes and check for special conditions, such as whether customers owe late fees. The software might be a traditional procedural program that creates database entries for the checked-out tapes based on other database entries for the tape inventory and

Example: a video store's traditional program is useful but not flexible

customer accounts. This kind of software is extremely good at what it does. However, it is not very flexible. Because it is based around a fixed set of procedures, the only thing it can do is execute those procedures and work with their results. If the procedures change or new procedures are added, a thorough overhaul of the software may be needed.

An object-oriented program is based on objects, not procedures

In contrast, an object-oriented program is based around the objects—the videotapes—themselves. The system contains a software object representing each physical videotape. Each object maintains a record of its own properties, such as title, length, rating, acquisition date, and checked-out status. These videotape objects track the customers who check them out and provide reports on request.

Objects keep track of the procedures that can act on them

In addition, each videotape object provides procedures that can act on its properties. These include simple procedures, such as reporting its title or checked-out status, or complex procedures, such as recommending inventory changes based on check-out frequency.

Objects can report their own status

In this system, rather than update a data table when a tape is checked out, the clerk's software tells the object representing the tape to change its status to "checked out." One way to create a report of checked-out tapes is to ask each videotape object to report its status and collect the ones that indicate they are checked out.

In a procedural system, a new feature might require extensive system redesign

The most visible advantage of such an object-based system is flexibility. For example, let's say that the video store wanted to install display terminals for its patrons to read capsule reviews of the videotapes in stock. In a traditional system, adding such a feature would require creating a new program to store the reviews. It would be difficult to integrate the review program and the inventory control program. This might make it difficult to keep up with reviews of new videotapes as they enter the system or older tapes as they are retired.

In contrast, an object-oriented system can add "review" to the properties stored in each videotape object and add a small generic procedure that enables customers to access each video's review. In this way, the review capability is a simple extension to the existing system. After a customer asks a videotape object to display its review, she can go on to ask whether the tape is in stock, without having to switch to another program.

In object-oriented systems, new features can be extensions to the existing system

Object-Oriented Concepts

Our video store scenario shows a few of the capabilities of an object-oriented software system. The object model results in far different software than a traditional procedural model does. Essentially, the object model yields a system full of objects that request information and services from one another and inform one another of the results. Typically, a graphical user interface enables users to set the system into action by initiating the first request, and it notifies users when the system has accomplished the given task.

Objects request information and services from one another

The advantages of this model arise from a single premise: An object-oriented system can model real-world activities more closely than a procedural system can. To understand how the system works, it is necessary to understand objects, messages, and their related concepts.

Object-oriented systems model the real world

Objects The basic concept in object technology is the **object** itself. An object is a self-contained bundle of software with an identity that is unique among objects in the system. Each object consists of

Objects consist of variables and methods

variables that store data and **methods,** or procedures, capable of acting on the object's variables.

An object encapsulates its variables

Figure 2-1 shows a typical notation for an object. The variables are shown as items in the middle of the "donut," and the methods are shown forming the ring of the donut itself. The object **encapsulates** its variables, and it is only through sending messages to the object's methods that another object can access the contents of the variables.

Variables can be of different data types

Variables These can be numbers, character strings, or other data types. Most object-oriented programming languages provide a rich set of data types. However, one of the great strengths of object technology is that programmers can define their own data types by combining existing ones.

Programmer-defined data types are treated as if they are native to the system

These so-called **abstract data types** can be extremely complex and can be specific to the system's purposes. For example, our videotape objects could contain a variable called "review" to hold a sample review of the tape. This variable's abstract data type could include specifications of author's name, periodical, date, and review text. The advantage of object-oriented languages is that they treat user-defined abstract data types as if they had been built into

Figure 2-1 A typical notation for an object

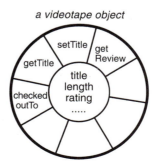

a videotape object

the language (often as classes), with access to all of the language's services and capabilities.

Compound Objects Variables can also contain references to other objects, enabling one object to act as if it contained other objects. For example, the video store is likely to have a number of sections, such as a humor section. This section would be represented in the software by a "humor section" object, which would "contain" the objects representing individual humor videos. The humor section object is a **compound object** because it contains other objects. Compound objects can be quite complex. In fact, the entire store can be represented by a video store object, which would contain all the other objects in the system, including the section objects. For purposes of organization, we could establish a containment hierarchy for the objects in the system—for example, the video store contains sections, the sections contain videotapes.

Compound objects are composed of other objects

Compound objects model the way the real world works. A complex piece of technology, such as a computer, is really a compound object assembled out of many components, each of which can be a compound object, too. Sometimes, it is most useful to treat the computer as a single object; sometimes it is more valuable to work at the level of its individual components. The same is true for object-oriented software. Certain procedures affect the video store as a whole, or sections within the store; other procedures affect elementary objects, such as the individual videotapes. Object-oriented software can address an object at the right level of complexity for the task at hand. In this way, object-oriented systems exhibit scaleability and a great capacity for managing complexity.

Compound objects model the way the real world works

Methods In addition to its variables, an object contains **methods.** Simply put, these are the procedures that enable other objects to access variables and perform operations on them. Although some methods can be complicated, most objects tend to have simple,

Objects use methods to request services or access another object's variables

straightforward methods. Objects typically have "get" and "set" methods for most variables. These methods enable other objects to set or request the value of a variable.

Methods do such things as setting and reporting the values of variables

For example, each of our videotape objects has "get" methods for such variables as title, review, date, and length. The videotape objects do not have "set" methods for these variables because the title, review, date, and length of an existing video are not likely to change. For variables that do change, such as "Date checked out" and "Customer of record," the videotape objects have both "get" and "set" methods.

They also perform calculations

In addition, each videotape object can have methods that perform operations on one or more variables, such as "Calculate days checked out," "Calculate frequency of checkout," and "Report when overdue." The number and scope of the methods are up to the application designers.

Objects can model the everyday business operation

Business Objects So far, we have been using the example of a videotape object because it clearly shows the relationship between a real-world object and its software representation. However, our video store system could contain numerous **business objects,** too. For example, customer objects can store and report such data as their names and addresses, as well as what videos they had checked out. Clerk objects, corresponding to store personnel, can receive input from the real clerk at the hardware I/O device and transmit requests to the other objects in the system. The clerk objects can track the customer transactions each real-life clerk performs.

The design phase determines what the objects need to model

In object-oriented programming, the initial design phase is important. This is when the system designers decide which objects in their business environment need to be modeled by software objects, and which methods and variables each software object requires. For example, depending on your business or the OO methodology you adopt, you might find that you want to define a class of Transaction objects, or you might find that all transactions could be handled by methods and variables in another class of objects, such as the Customer class.

Classes The system we have been describing presents a world full of objects, each with its own personality and behavior. This reflects the real world. With so many kinds of objects, it also reflects the chaos we sometimes find in the real world. We make sense out of the real world by thinking of objects in meaningful categories, with predictable properties and behaviors. For example, we expect all places in the category called "restaurants" to have menus and a means for ordering meals. Such meaningful categories are essential in the object-oriented world too.

Classes provide objects with organization

The main mechanism for bringing order to objects is the **class.** A class is a template for objects, which contains the methods we want our object to have plus data-type definitions for its variables. For example, videotape is an obvious class for our video store system. The videotape class defines the data types and behaviors we expect of any videotape object. Using the videotape class as a template, we then create **instances,** the individual objects of each class. The instances of videotape might include objects with such names as *Jurassic Park, Star Wars,* and *The English Patient.* These objects would each have different values for their variables, but they would share the behaviors and overall structure defined by the videotape class.

A class is a template for creating object instances

Classes add reusability to object-oriented systems. The methods and data structures are typically defined in the class itself, not in the instances. Each instance contains only the values of its own variables, plus a reference to the resources that all the instances of the class share, such as their methods.

Methods and data structures are defined in the class, not the instance

To change every in-
stance of a class, you
need only change the
class itself

Thus, if we want to extend our system to include review capabilities, we only have to make a single set of changes at the class level. We can add a new variable with the abstract data type of "review." This data type's primary purpose is to provide a text container for the review. We can also add new methods to input and display the review. Adding this new functionality in a single place—the videotape class—automatically makes it available to every instance of that class.

A subclass inherits
the methods and
variables of its su-
perclass

Subclasses and Superclasses Let's say that we have a special category of videos, such as corporate training videos. They share many properties with the existing videotape class, but they have additional properties that they share only among themselves, such as a different fee structure. Rather than define independent videotape class and training tape classes, we can define training tape as a **subclass** of videotape. This means that training tape **inherits** all the properties of videotape so that they are simply referenced rather than repeated. As far as system users are concerned, training tape has the same variables and methods as videotape and may have additional variables and methods of its own. If training tape is a subclass of videotape, then videotape is a **superclass** of training tape.

An object includes
methods defined in
all of its superclasses

When an object receives a message to perform one of its methods, it first checks to see whether the method is part of its definition. If the method is not found, the object checks the definition of its immediate superclass, then that class's superclass, and so on. In this way, each unique method needs to be defined only one time in a system.

OO languages can
use single inheri-
tance or multiple in-
heritance

Some object-oriented languages, such as Smalltalk, define a **single inheritance** mechanism—that is, each subclass inherits its data types and methods from just one superclass. Other languages, such as C++, provide **multiple inheritance,** which means that a subclass can inherit from two or more superclasses. For example, a training tape that is unusually funny, such as the John Cleese business management tapes, might inherit properties and behaviors from both the training tape class and the humor tape class.

When we define a subclass, we tend to add new methods and variables that differentiate it from its parent class. We can also **override** existing methods. For example, the training tape class probably inherits most of its methods from the videotape class, but it might define a new method for "Calculate late fee" that would override the method provided in its superclass. Overriding is an example of an important object-oriented concept, known as **polymorphism.**

A subclass can add new methods or redefine existing methods

Polymorphism This concept enables a single message name to trigger different processing, depending on its context. The great advantage is that an object requesting a service does not have to know anything about the internals of the object that provides the service. We can request an ordinary videotape to calculate its late fee, or we can request a training tape to calculate its late fee. Each object calculates the fee in a way appropriate to its type. It does not matter that the two tapes use different methods to calculate their fees. As business conditions change, if we want to revise one of the calculation methods, we can do so without any impact on the other calculation methods.

Polymorphism allows a single name to represent different processing in different contexts

Virtual Machine and Garbage Collection

The **virtual machine,** also known as the **bytecode interpreter,** is a mechanism to support portability. In a typical virtual machine environment such as Java or Smalltalk, the source code is compiled into bytecodes designed to be executed by the virtual machine. **Bytecodes** are a machine language for an abstract machine (hence the word *virtual*). They are interpreted by the virtual machine (normally a piece of software) on each system that supports the language. Virtual machines are implemented in such a way that they present the same functionality and system interfaces to the bytecodes no matter what operating system the virtual machine actually runs on. Essentially, the virtual machine makes all the different hardware machines and operating systems look the same to the bytecode. A piece of source code needs to be compiled into only one set of bytecodes, which can then run on all platforms that have the appropriate virtual machine support. The virtual machine itself is not portable because it has to use the underlying operating system services to execute the bytecodes. The figure below

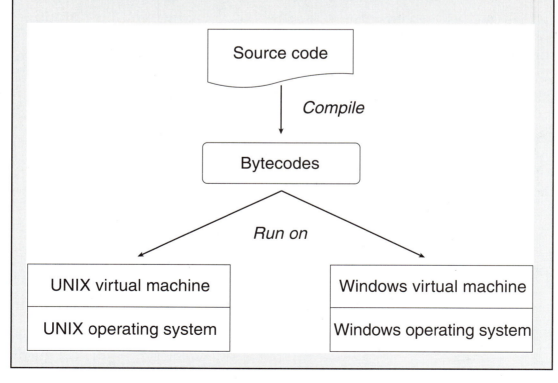

shows a piece of source code compiled into a single set of bytecodes that can be executed by both a Windows virtual machine and a UNIX virtual machine.

Because the virtual machine completely isolates the application from the underlying operating system, it can be used to support security. The bytecodes can not get anything done without going through the virtual machine. Therefore, the virtual machine can serve as a control point where unsafe operations can be blocked.

Note that languages such as Java and Smalltalk can also be implemented without a virtual machine. In fact, some optimizing implementations compile the source code directly to the specific underlying machine instructions. Such an approach attempts to trade portability for performance. Because the bytecode representation is often several times more compact than the machine instruction representation, compiling the source to machine code can produce a large executable footprint. It is no wonder that applets, which require portability and compactness, are not compiled to machine instructions.

A language can support automatic memory management by having a **garbage collector** run in the background to track object references. When an object no longer has any references to it (and thus cannot be used by anyone anymore), it can be removed from the system, although its actual removal may be delayed until an appropriate time. We use the phrase *can be removed* because garbage collection is often triggered under specific circumstances, particularly if more space is needed or the system is idle. A program may exit without running out of space or having any idle time—and so never need to perform garbage collection. With automatic garbage collection, a programmer does not have to do anything to trigger the return of space. The system takes care of that; in this way it removes the complexity associated with writing application code to manually manage the allocation and de-allocation of objects.

Automatic garbage collection also prevents common programming errors, such as **memory leak** and **dangling references.** In systems such as C++ that require manual deletion of unwanted objects, you can forget to do the deletion. If that occurs, it can hinder system performance because useless objects are occupying space needed for doing real work. It can even bring down the system if all the free memory runs out.

> **Dangling references** occur when you delete an object prematurely while other objects still hold references to it. Those references are now "dangling" since they refer to space that the system considers free. If the system allocates the space to a new object, the dangling reference now refers to something completely different from what the other objects think it refers to. If other objects use the values in that space as if they belong to the deleted object, serious problems, which are often difficult to detect, can occur.

Classes inherit behavior according to hierarchies

Class Hierarchies Superclass-subclass relationships are expressed in terms of **class hierarchies.** Languages such as Java and Smalltalk define a single class hierarchy, based on a fundamental "Object" class, from which all classes inherit behaviors common to all objects. A class hierarchy for a video store system might look, in part, like Figure 2-2.

Subclasses define different methods as needed

In this hierarchy, the VideoStore class has two subclasses: MainStore and BranchStore. They share many of the same methods, but for areas in which their procedures differ, they can define different methods, or one of them can override a method it inherits from the VideoStore superclass. For example, MainStore might have a set of accounting procedures defined in its methods while BranchStore's accounting methods might send its data to MainStore for processing.

C++ makes multiple hierarchies possible

In C++, you can define multiple hierarchies, each with its own top-level class or classes. For example, one hierarchy can define user interface objects, such as windows, fields, and buttons, and an-

Figure 2-2 A class hierarchy for the video store system

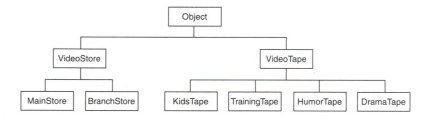

other hierarchy can define bookkeeping objects, such as purchase orders and bills of sale.

Hierarchies bring a sense of order to the mechanism of inheritance. When an object is asked to implement a method, it always attempts to locate the method in its own definition first, then it traces the path up the hierarchy until it locates a definition for that method. In this way, the most specialized definition of the method is always applied.

Hierarchies bring order to inheritance

Messages Now that we have a system full of objects, classes, and class hierarchies, we have to provide it with a mechanism for getting things done. The mechanism that enables objects to do things is the **message send.** In its simplest form, a message send consists of the identifier of an object and the name of a method defined in that object (or in one of its superclasses). For example, in a video store system written in Smalltalk, a clerk could send a message such as the following.

Messages enable objects to get things done

```
jurassicPark checkedOutTo
```

This message tells the receiving object to perform the activity defined in its `checkedOutTo` method. The receiving object then returns the name of the customer who had checked out *Jurassic Park* to the sending object.

A message can also include parameters. For example, the clerk could send the message

A message includes a method and optional parameters

```
jurassicPark checkedOutTo: JBSmith
```

In a C++ system, the same message might look like

```
jurassicPark.checkedOutTo(JBSmith)
```

In either case, when the Jurassic Park object receives the message, it adds the customer identified as JBSmith to its customer variable, as seen in Figure 2-3.

Objects answer messages with return values

Messages generally require a response of some kind from the receiving object. This response is usually called a **return value.** The return value can be the contents of a variable, the result of a calculation, or simply a confirmation that the requested action actually occurred.

Figure 2-3 A message send from one object to another

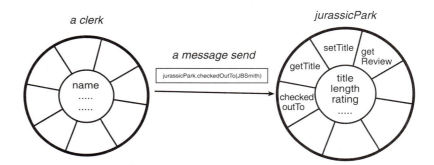

Some Object Terminology
(in alphabetical order)

Class: A template for defining an object, with its attributes defined as variables and its behavior defined as methods. A class can be used to create instances of itself, all of which have the same methods but can have different variable values.

Class hierarchy: A tree structure defining the inheritance relationship between classes. A class can have subclasses down the hierarchy from itself and superclasses up the hierarchy. A class inherits the methods and variables of its superclasses. In systems supporting multiple inheritance, the inheritance relations can form a lattice instead of a tree.

Compound object: An object composed of one or more other objects. For example, a dialog box is a compound object made up of text entry fields, buttons, list boxes, labels, and so on.

Encapsulation: The practice of hiding and protecting an object's data and internal implementation details. Another object can access the data only through methods available from the object's interface and cannot access the private methods used in the internal implementation.

Inheritance: A mechanism that enables one class to share the methods and variables of another. A subclass inherits from its superclasses in the class hierarchy. Some OO languages, such as C++, have multiple inheritance, which enables a class to inherit from two or more superclasses.

Instance: A single object that is defined by a particular class. One class, such as Customer, can have multiple instances in a single OO program.

Instance variable: A container for data within an object.

Message: A request from a sending object for the receiving object to perform a behavior. Normally, a message consists of the name of the receiver's method that calls the desired behavior and can include a set of parameters and a return value.

Method: A defined behavior that an object can exhibit, given a name on the object's interface, by which other objects can request that behavior. (Also referred to as a *member function*.)

Object: The basic building block of object technology. A self-contained software component that includes variables for storing data and methods that can act on the data.

Polymorphism: The ability for a message to invoke different behaviors (methods) depending on the class of the receiver. Subclasses can define methods with the same name but different behaviors from their superclasses. Because of polymorphism, a sending object does not have to know the implementation details of the behavior it requests.

> **Subclass:** A class that inherits its methods and variables from a class above it on the class hierarchy. A subclass can define additional methods and variables of its own, or it can override the inherited methods from the superclass.
>
> **Superclass:** A class whose methods and variables are inherited by a class below it in the class hierarchy.

Object-Oriented Languages

C++ is a hybrid language

The three most commonly used object-oriented languages are C++, Smalltalk, and Java. The major difference between them lies in their underlying design and implementation. C++ is a hybrid language, based on the procedural C language. As such, it can be used in procedural or object-oriented programs. Like traditional procedural languages, it is a compiled language. It fits easily into programming environments in which the C language is used extensively. It is also good at addressing runtime performance issues.

Smalltalk is a pure OO language

Smalltalk, on the other hand, is not compiled. Instead, it is dynamically translated. It is a pure OO language in that everything is an object, and as such, its programming model is relatively simple. It provides the benefit of rapid prototyping and development, at the expense of some runtime performance. It is a good language for introducing object-oriented programming.

Java was designed specifically for the World Wide Web

Java, a more recent addition to the list of object-oriented languages, is quickly growing in popularity. It is an object language that combines qualities of both Smalltalk and C++. At the syntactic level, it feels like C++, but features like single inheritance, no pointers, a virtual machine for portability, and automatic garbage collection make it feel more like Smalltalk at the semantic level. It has become famous as a language for programming on the World Wide Web. However, it can also be used as a general-purpose programming language.

Separation of Interface and Implementation

Object systems, such as Java, CORBA, and OO COBOL, have adopted the notion of separating the interface from the implementation of a class. The interface contains the declarations of a set of methods and their semantics. This is all that the user needs in order to send messages to any object supporting the interface and, thus, make use of that object. For example, the clerk object needs to know only that the videotape object supports the method "checkedOutTo" in order to send messages to it. No implementation details are disclosed with the interface.

Users of an object need to know the interface, not the implementation details

The developers of the video system can choose whatever way they please to support the interfaces with real implementation classes. A single interface can be supported by multiple implementation classes and a single implementation class can support multiple interfaces. Figure 2-4 shows a case in which two classes implement the same Videotape interface.

Multiple classes can implement the same interface

The two classes have different ways of organizing and storing their internal states. The class on the bottom is the one we described on page 20. The class on top represents videotapes on loan from another store, which keeps all the information in a "tapeInfo" database and uses each videotape's ID variable to look up the associated information. Ordinary users can go through the Videotape interface to retrieve information about instances of either type of videotape class. They do not have to know that the information is stored

Classes supporting the same interface can have different internals

Figure 2-4 Separation of interface and implementation

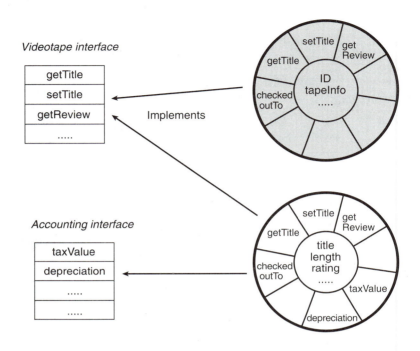

Videotape interface

getTitle
setTitle
getReview
.....

Implements

Accounting interface

taxValue
depreciation
.....
.....

differently in each class or even that two implementation classes exist.

A single implementation class can also support multiple interfaces

The class at the bottom also implements the Accounting interface, which is used by the store's accounting department to process tax returns. From an accounting department's viewpoint, they are dealing with assets. Whether an asset is a humor videotape or a drama videotape is not important. They only deal with the functionality defined by the Accounting interface. The class on top does not support the Accounting interface because it represents assets belonging to another store, which should not take part in accounting calculations for this store.

Interfaces can have inheritance relationships and form hierarchies with each other. With strong separation between the interface and the implementation classes, the interface hierarchy does not have to correspond to the implementation class hierarchy. In fact, Java allows multiple inheritance for the interfaces but only single inheritance for the implementation classes.

Interface hierarchy does not have to correspond to implementation hierarchy

The interface serves as the contract between the users of an object and its implementation. Separation between the interface and the implementation further strengthens the encapsulation of an object system and better enables it to deal with changes. For example, the developer of the video store system can change the videotape implementation class hierarchy completely (and even rename everything) without requiring any code change to the user objects (the clerks), as long as the interfaces remain intact.

Separating interface and implementation strengthens encapsulation

Object Databases

Objects are not easily stored in traditional databases. A typical object-oriented system contains a wide variety of objects, all highly specialized and different from one another, and all subject to change. Hierarchical and network databases provide rich data structures but are not flexible enough to adapt to the rapidly changing nature of objects. Relational databases are more flexible, but they are best at storing data having relatively fixed formats. One solution to this problem is to add a layer of software to traditional databases that converts objects into simpler structures that the database can then handle.

Traditional databases encounter difficulties when storing objects

However, the process of dismantling objects and reassembling them is not efficient. One solution is to design a database that stores objects intact. Such a system is known as an **object database management system** (ODBMS). Often an ODBMS can store the code, as well as the data, for the objects. It organizes the

An ODBMS stores and organizes objects

objects it contains in terms of composite structures, in which a structure consists of a compound object that contains other objects by means of referencing them. In this way, an ODBMS can contain any number of alternative structures through which to reference, understand, and retrieve the data it contains. Note that an object system does not have to use an ODBMS. In fact, many of the existing object systems do not. We return to the subject of ODBMSs when we discuss object persistence in Chapter 7.

Frameworks

An OO framework defines the interaction among system components

A **framework** is a set of protocols (interfaces) and their corresponding code that define the interaction among the components in a system. By providing new components to plug into the framework, developers can quickly customize a system. A framework captures a flexible system design. (As an analogy, a railway system is similar to a framework. By plugging and unplugging rails, old routes can easily be modified and new routes can be built.)

A framework is often implemented as a class library

In object technology, components are represented by objects, and the protocols defining their interaction are represented by the messaging signatures of the participating objects. Usually, a framework is provided in the form of a class library.

Some additional considerations regarding frameworks are:

- Implementation inheritance is not essential to a framework. Remember the strong separation between interface and implementation class? The first concern of a framework is the protocol. Implementation inheritance is not the only way to conform to a protocol.
- Client GUI construction uses frameworks extensively. This subject is discussed in the next chapter.
- Rapid prototyping results from a combination of frameworks and reusable components.

- Evolving a framework is costly. A deployed framework contains a great deal of application code that depends on the protocols defined by the framework. Evolving a framework often involves changing these protocols. Because the protocols represent the encapsulation boundaries between objects, changing them requires rewriting all the code that references them. This is similar to changing the APIs of a procedural library, which has always been costly.

Using the Object Model

A traditional development project begins with gathering requirements for the tasks that need to be performed. In contrast, an object-oriented development project often begins by studying the aspects of the business that need to be modeled in order to perform the required tasks. The object model is inherently reusable. If the business is modeled well, then the objects developed to solve one set of problems can easily be adapted to other purposes.

OO development often begins with modeling

For example, the task at hand might be to redesign your billing system. In modeling the way you handle billing, you are likely to decide that a Customer class is necessary, with methods and variables that reflect real-world aspects of your customers, such as names, addresses, and account records. You are likely to create and store instances of that class for all of your customers. Once the system is populated, you could then use your Customer instances for a variety of purposes, such as promotional mailings and tracking sales calls.

Well-designed classes can fulfill a variety of purposes

Advantages of the Object Model

A computer system can be only as good as the people who develop it, and it is just as easy to write a bad OO program as it is to write a bad procedural program. Nevertheless, certain key qualities of the

OO advantages are based on encapsulation and reusability

object model can lead to great advantages in programming. In particular, advantages can come from the principles of encapsulation and reusability.

Advantages of Encapsulation

Encapsulation means hiding an object's internals

Encapsulation is the principle of hiding an object's internal implementation so that it is accessible only through the methods exposed on an object's public interface. It can be useful for

- Protecting data
- Managing complexity
- Managing change
- Integrating legacy systems

Encapsulation makes it hard to access data by accident

Protecting Data In an encapsulated system, data is available only for specific purposes and only when requested through the methods of the object it belongs to. It is difficult to access data by accident. The rest of the system does not need to know of the existence of any data unless or until it has a specific use for that data.

A complex system can be concealed behind a simpler public interface

Managing Complexity In the same way, encapsulation tends to hide the complexity of the system. The use of compound objects helps conceal complex systems behind the public interface of a single compound object. A large procedural program can be encapsulated and viewed as a single object so that, however complex its internal workings, the rest of the OO system can address it through a clearly-defined public interface. This interface can consist of a relatively simple set of methods. It is easier to incorporate new extensions to the system or scale the system to tasks with an increasingly larger scope because the complexity can be hidden at any level.

Object internals can change radically with minor effect on the rest of the system

Managing Change The same principle also helps in managing change. If an object's internals are hidden from the rest of the system, that implementation can be changed radically without affecting the rest of the system. As long as an object's public interface—the names, signatures, and semantics of its accessible methods—remains the same, there is never a ripple effect from changing the procedures behind those methods. Problem determination is easier because problems are limited to the objects that have changed. In procedural code, a change to one portion of the code can have effects in seemingly unrelated portions. Encapsulation makes this problem a thing of the past.

Integrating Legacy Systems With object-oriented techniques, you can encapsulate an entire application and, on its public interface, only expose methods for handling inputs and outputs. In this way, other parts of the system treat the legacy application as a single object. Applications in languages such as COBOL and C can be **wrappered** and integrated piecemeal into an OO environment. This use of encapsulation enables you to introduce new OO applications into your existing system gradually, to minimize the risk and maximize the increasing skills of your OO development and implementation teams.

You can wrapper a legacy system with a single object

As better implementation components become available for particular functions, the system can also be upgraded in a piecemeal fashion. For example, you can replace a wrapped legacy application with an OO implementation while keeping the wrapped object interface. Upgrading a system can be done by extending the current system rather than by overhauling it.

Wrappering helps to extend the current system rather than overhaul it

Advantages of Reusability

When we talked about inheritance, we could see that subclasses reused the method and data definitions of their superclass. And we saw that, through referencing, hundreds of instances of the same class could reuse the single set of methods defined for that class. There is another important way that OO development leads to reusability—namely, by creating classes and class hierarchies that

OO development creates reusable classes and hierarchies

can be reused in one program after another. Reusability helps to enable

- Faster development
- Higher quality
- Reduced cost

Existing objects can be used in different programs for different purposes

Faster Development Another look at the video store will show us how reusability can speed development. When we set up the basic store system, we might develop Customer objects to participate in our check-in/check-out functions. Later on, we might decide to add a facility for promotional mailings. It turns out that we can use the existing customer objects for this new function because they already contain most of the necessary information. Developing the new function is simply a matter of developing the new mailing list object that requests the customer names and addresses and then processes them. This mailing list object can, in turn, be subclassed and used for a variety of mailing purposes as the business expands.

Reusable objects are already tested and proven

Higher Quality When you build a system out of reusable objects, you are working with code that has already been tested. By reusing existing objects, application developers are able to concentrate more on the new functions instead of the lower-level components. Debugging is also easier because individual defects generally do not have implications throughout the system. As a company builds up an inventory of proven high-quality objects, the overall quality of their software improves.

Using existing parts saves time and money

Reduced Cost The development of proven, high-quality objects also works to reduce the cost of software development. Developers can assemble new applications out of existing parts, saving the time and cost it would take if they rewrote the function from scratch.

In many cases, it is cheaper to buy code than to develop it. With reusable objects, companies can purchase proven objects that contain all the functionality they want, in much the same way as they might otherwise purchase a software program that contains the required functionality. As more companies come into the business of providing class libraries and other forms of reusable objects, application development can become more a matter of selecting available classes that fill your needs than of building everything from the ground up.

Companies can purchase proven objects

Some OO Concerns

Because OO is still a maturing technology, it raises some of the same concerns as any emerging technology. For example, how much tool and language support is actually available, and how stable is this support? What standards (COM, CORBA, or JavaBeans) ensure that OO components will be interoperable? These issues are being addressed on an ongoing basis, and we touch on them later, as they become relevant to our discussion.

OO raises certain concerns

Performance is a concern that is particularly relevant to OO. With the addition of encapsulation and polymorphism, overall system performance suffers a bit because more indirection is required and the system must do more work. However, the gain often outweighs the loss because every year programmer time becomes more and more expensive (in both cost-to-hire and time-to-market) and machines get faster.

OO systems often pay a performance overhead

Objects offer no free lunch. The more work required and the more flexible the system, the slower it will perform. However, technology providers continue to push the boundaries of performance. For example, as compilers advance, they can better optimize OO programs. Also, the OO infrastructure is steadily improving—for example, automatic garbage collection now generally incurs less

Technology providers continue to work on performance enhancements

overhead than earlier methods of storage management. Without automatic memory management, each programmer needs the high skill levels required to write memory management code. Not only is this error-prone, but ordinary programmers cannot do as good a job as a garbage collector that has been tuned over the past decade.

OO can have a steep learning curve

Conversion to Object Technology OO programming requires new skills, and the learning curve is usually steep. A typical developer might take at least four to six months to become proficient and productive in OO programming. Design and architecture skills take even longer to mature.

On Balance

Object technology is no panacea

Clearly, object technology offers many benefits to the enterprise computing world, particularly in reducing development time and cost, improving application quality, managing complexity, and integrating legacy systems. But OO is no panacea. The issues associated with frameworks, performance, and conversion are very real.

Object technology is a means, not an end in itself

On balance, it is probably best to see object technology for what it is—a development technique. Given the complexity of today's systems, it is a technique with great potential, but the danger lies in seeing object technology as an end instead of a means. It's not a place to get to, simply a way to get there. Nobody should adopt OO programming simply because of what it is. They should adopt it because it helps in their situation, such as in developing client/server applications.

Summary

Object technology represents a paradigm shift in the way we develop and use computer software.

- It models real-world objects and activities.
- Programs are based on objects, not procedures.
- New features can be introduced as extensions to the existing system rather than require extensive system redesign.
- Objects separate their external interface from their internal implementation.

Of the three major object-oriented languages, C++ provides high performance and backward compatibility with C; Smalltalk enables rapid prototyping and development; and Java's wide portability is valuable on the World Wide Web and in ordinary development.

OO programming offers many advantages.

- Encapsulation
- Better management of complexity
- Better change management
- Extension of current system rather than overhaul
- Reuse

Objects also raise issues such as performance and conversion strategies. On balance, it is best to view object technology as a means to develop applications, not as an end in itself.

3

Integrating Object Technology with Enterprise Systems

Object technology can enhance enterprise system development in many ways. The approach to introducing objects into a system depends on the system itself and the degree to which the system architects, planners, and administrators want to objectify it. This chapter provides a general overview of the approaches; later chapters look at some of the more important techniques in greater detail.

These are several different approaches to introducing object technology

In all cases, the key question is what to make into objects. This question is answered by four possible approaches.

The key question is what to objectify

- Objectify individual modules of a conventional system.
- Objectify the conventional architecture model.
- Use an OO language within an objectified conventional architecture model.
- Objectify an entire system without the conventional program-based architecture.

In practice, it is unlikely that you will see any of these approaches in a pure form. Most organizations evolving toward object technology practice some combination of them.

Most organizations combine the four main approaches

Objectifying Individual Modules

One advantage of using object concepts with conventional system architecture is that organizations can start working with object technology immediately, without a great commitment of resources. A disadvantage is that without OO architecture, the effects and, therefore, the benefits of object technology are necessarily limited.

Introducing OO concepts to conventional architecture is manageable but limited

This approach is a typical first step

This approach is a typical first step for an organization interested in adopting object technology. It enables the organization to adopt object technology gradually and in a staged fashion. Most production systems of any complexity would need to follow this gradual approach.

An OO language brings some benefits to existing system architecture

The most practical way to bring OO benefits to an existing system architecture is to begin incorporating an OO programming language, such as C++, Smalltalk, or Java, into individual modules of the system. Instead of using a conventional third-generation language, such as C or COBOL, the developer uses an OO language to implement the internals of new (or existing) programs.

Developers can use OO to implement the internals of new programs

Figure 3-1 shows a structure of programs that interact within a system. Note that while several of the programs are 3GL, written in third-generation languages (3GLs), one program is OO. However, the OO characteristics stop at the program boundary. The programs treat each other as 3GL modules when they interact, even when two programs written in OO languages interact with each other. In other words, the system architecture remains conventional.

An organization can start small with this approach

System development using this approach is itself modular and encapsulated. This can be an advantage for an organization that is interested in OO development but not yet sure how much effort to devote to it. The approach also enables individual developers to

Figure 3-1 Objectifying a module within a conventional architecture

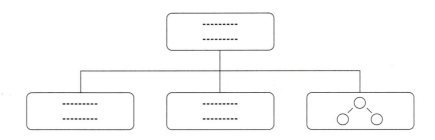

master the learning curve in a controlled setting. An organization can start with a relatively small-scale pilot program, and as developers become comfortable with OO techniques, more of the system can be objectified. In this way, when the time comes for objectifying mission-critical programs, the needed skills will be in place and so will a useful track record in OO development.

Objectifying the Conventional Architecture Model

A second approach takes the architecture of the system and objectifies it, as shown in Figure 3-2. This scenario is not concerned with program internals but only with the client/server architecture that enables the programs to interact. The programs themselves can be either procedural or OO. For the time being, we assume that they are procedural, which enables us to look at the architecture in isolation. In the third approach, we consider the implications of objectifying both the architecture and the programs it contains.

The architecture itself can be objectified

Bringing object concepts into the client/server architecture model enables us to express communication between programs in terms of objects messaging with each other. As far as any program in the system is concerned, all the other programs now become objects that are capable of sending and receiving messages. This scenario enables developers to use OO analysis and design methodologies,

Programs can become objects that send and receive messages

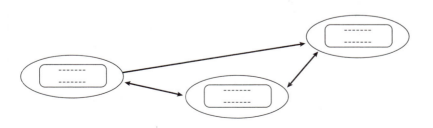

Figure 3-2 Objectifying the architecture model

particularly if the business domain leads naturally to an OO domain model.

Developers can provide OO interfaces for conventional programs

Developers can implement an OO architecture by providing OO interfaces to entire programs so that input to and output from the programs takes place in terms of messages that call the methods available on the new OO interface. OO programming languages are often employed to specify the OO interface and to do the mapping from OO messages to the procedural implementation. This offers a good opportunity for using OO/procedural hybrid languages, such as C++ or OO COBOL.

The system views a wrapped program as a single object

This technique is sometimes called **wrapping.** Wrapping a conventional program encapsulates it with an object interface: although the program's internals remain unchanged, the system now views the program as a single object. Of course, the objects are likely to be coarse-grained and include a great deal of functionality. This technique is appropriate for the many complex legacy programs in COBOL and other languages, which cannot be easily rewritten.

For example, to return to the video store example of the previous chapter, a videotape object that receives the message `checked-OutTo: JBSmith` might not actually store `JBSmith` in an instance variable. Instead, it might invoke a COBOL transaction that runs on a mainframe server to update a database record. The object user does not see the COBOL transaction because it is wrapped by the videotape object. The videotape object presents an OO view of the old 3GL world.

Legacy programs can function undisturbed while the system is objectified

Wrapping enables the legacy portion of an existing system to function without interruption while other pieces of the system are being objectified. (For example, 3270 terminal access to an IMS database could continue to run within a new OO application.) In addition, programmers who are unfamiliar with the mainframe legacy systems can develop new OO programs.

Using an OO Language in an OO Architecture Model

Normally, if you implement an OO architecture, you probably also want to implement one or more programs written in an OO language. This makes OO benefits available on both the programming and the architecture level. Figure 3-3 demonstrates this type of system.

OO benefits can apply to programming and architecture

Note that the system still includes self-contained "programs" (represented by closed boxes), which create a level of indirection between the internal objects and the architecture-level objects. One reason why this might be necessary is that many of the existing runtime infrastructures include the concept of a program as a part of their basic underlying architecture. For example, in the CICS mainframe environment, the concept of "program" has traditionally been used to define the transaction. (A program corresponds one-to-one with a transaction.)

Such a system still observes traditional program boundaries

Similarly, stored procedures on a database server can be objectified and implemented inside an object architecture, but the call-and-return model by which they define database transactions still re-

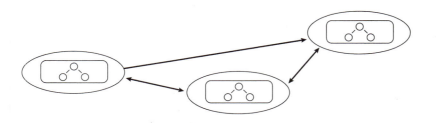

Figure 3-3 OO modules in an OO architecture

quires a concept of program boundaries. For example, a remote procedure call (RPC) normally needs to target a clearly defined program.

Some infrastructure services only apply to traditional programs

Using this approach, the program internals and the interprocess communication can be OO. However, we still do not have a totally OO system because certain essential services provided by the underlying system services can be applied to programs only in the traditional procedural sense. Development tools can help mask some, but not all, of the 3GL characteristics of such a system. Those characteristics are discussed in Chapter 9, which examines distributed development environments.

Objectifying an Entire System

An entire system can function as a sea of objects without program boundaries

If the right infrastructure support is present, the conventional program boundary can often disappear. The system then functions seamlessly as a series of object interactions, as shown in Figure 3-4. The great advantage is that objects and object interactions model real-world business processes accurately and easily. Of course, the disadvantage is that existing programs are difficult to incorporate into this kind of system. Therefore, this design is worth considering mainly for new development.

Figure 3-4 A totally objectified system

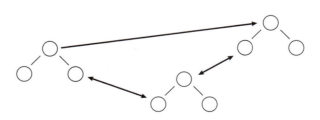

This approach combines OO modeling and an OO runtime infrastructure. The designer and developer work with a sea of objects rather than with objects living in programs or programs wrapped with object interfaces. Objects can send messages without having to be concerned about the containing programs of the receiving objects.

In this way, the entire enterprise communication network can be treated as a single computer that runs the business model as a network of objects. The communication network becomes part of the implementation details. Changes in the nature of the business system can be modeled by changes to individual objects and by redirecting messages, rather than by changing the system architecture. Chapter 13 details such an approach from a business engineering perspective.

The entire system is treated as a single computer

Working with a totally objectified system requires a different mindset than is currently found in most IS departments. This is as much, or more, a business issue as it is a software development issue.

Such a system requires a new mindset

Summary

When integrating objects into enterprise computing, the key question is what to objectify. Depending on the system and the degree to which objects are desired, there are four possible approaches.

- Objectifying the individual modules of a conventional system architecture is a manageable but limited first step.
- Objectifying the conventional architecture model lets programs act as objects that send and receive messages. Developers can wrapper legacy programs with OO interfaces so that the system views the programs as objects.

- Using an OO language within an objectified conventional architecture model brings OO benefits to both programming and architecture. Traditional program boundaries remain.
- Objectifying an entire system means that the system can function entirely as a series of object interactions. With this approach, the conventional program-based boundaries disappear.

4

Object-Oriented Clients

In a client/server system, the major functions performed by the client are user interaction and a certain amount of business logic (ranging from none to all). In this chapter, we use the term *client* to indicate the system component that sits between the human user and the rest of the system. For this reason, we focus on the user interaction aspects of the client. This relationship is shown in Figure 4-1.

The client sits between the human user and the rest of the system

A Historical View of Clients

The client side is where the client/server movement started. Looking at the evolution of clients can help us understand the roots of client/server computing and the reasons why object technology became dominant on the client side. A lot of the client evolution has to do with the steady increase in computing power available on the client side over the years. As client hardware became capable of doing more work, two things leveraged the increased power: better user interfaces and more business logic processing on the client side.

Clients have become more user friendly and perform more business logic

Text-based Clients

If we go back far enough, we find punch cards and toggle switches, but the text-based UI is the beginning of any system that fits the client/server perspective. In the beginning, clients ran on a text-based terminal with little processing power. As shown in Figure

Text-based clients contain little processing power

Figure 4-1 The client perspective

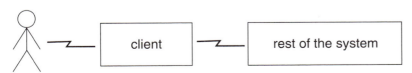

4-2, the text-based client typically contained very little. Sometimes "non-programmable terminal" or "dumb terminal" are used to distinguish these early clients from "programmable terminals" that have the processing power to run programs.

The text-based UI acts like a series of forms

In a text-based UI, each screen generally represents a form (similar to a printed form) that the user manipulates. When a user is finished with a screen, she uses the command line or function keys to advance to the next screen. The following are a few important characteristics of this kind of UI:

User interaction is command-line driven

- User interaction is essentially command-line driven. The system responds to the commands and parameters that the user types. Function keys can be seen as frequently used commands or keystroke sequences conveniently bundled for the user.

Keeping track of the UI mode is a burden

The interaction is **modal**—that is, the user moves through a sequence of screens, each representing an individual mode. For example, the second screen of an order entry application might represent a mode that presents a list of products for the user to choose from. This mode defines the context of the interaction. The interpretation of keystrokes—for example, the function keys—can change from mode to mode. Users can get unexpected results if they lose track of the current mode. Working with a modal application requires users to remember the answers to four questions:

Figure 4-2 Text-based client

1. Which mode am I in?
2. How do I get here?
3. What can I do here?
   (What operations or commands are allowed?)
4. How can I get out?

Keeping track of the mode is a cognitive burden that reduces user productivity and drives up training costs.

- The graphical resolution of the text-based UI limits the style of interaction. Multiple windows are uncommon because so little can be displayed if you split the already small screen among different windows. Some attempts have been made to add GUI features, such as overlapping windows and pull-down menus, to text-based user interfaces. Their success is limited by the screen resolution, as well as by the computing power of the server, which has to balance between processing the UI, running the business logic, and managing the data.

  The graphical resolution of the text-based UI limits the interaction

  (Actually, use of server resources is a general client/server architecture issue that affects GUIs, as well as text-based UIs. For example, X Windows, a graphical UI system, also requires the server to process the UI. Such processing competes with the logic and data processing for resources and limits the number of clients that a server can handle.)

Screen Scraper

Screen scrapers were popular at the beginning of client/server technology because they provided a way to create a GUI with little change to the overall system. A screen scraper intercepts terminal-bound screens, diverts them to a screen buffer, "scrapes off" the data, and renders it with a GUI. It also performs the same job in reverse, converting user input into a form that the host server expects.

A screen scraper renders terminal-bound data with a GUI

Figure 4-3 Screen scraping

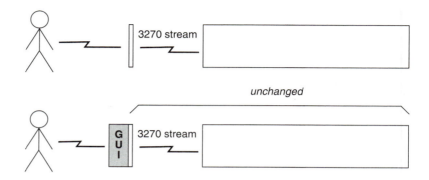

Screen scraping maintains existing presentation logic

Screen scraping maintains the existing presentation logic (the dialog structure and sequence) but gives the terminal-based interface a face-lift by adding the GUI rendering, as shown in Figure 4-3. The application on the host server runs unchanged, not realizing that it is talking to a workstation instead of a terminal. The improved display technology enables users to experience a better visual presentation, including better resolution and color. However, the interaction paradigm is essentially the same; thus, the application development issues are more or less the same as for the text-based paradigm.

Object Scrapers

Object scraping maps the data stream to objects

Object scraping, a derivative of screen scraping, has become increasingly popular. This technique tries to create objects out of the data displayed on the screen. In Figure 4-4, the right side of the picture remains the same as in Figure 4-3. The server still believes it is talking to a dumb terminal. The difference occurs on the client side: Instead of mapping the data stream from the server directly to the GUI, as in screen scraping, the object scraper maps the data stream to objects that represent server transactions. The client side code can use the objects to issue individual transactions or combine them to perform more complex processing.

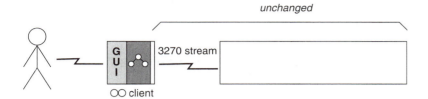

unchanged

Figure 4-4 Object scraping

For example, an existing legacy system supports two transactions. The "retrieve" transaction retrieves a record, and the "update" transaction modifies the record. With a text-based terminal interface, the user retrieves a record, updates it, retrieves another one, updates it, and so on. At a certain point, the business might decide to update this system with one that retrieves and updates records according to a set of business rules, calling for user intervention only when needed. Using the object scraping technique, the two transactions are mapped to objects. The business logic on the client side can now invoke these objects to get the job done.

Example: updating a business system with object scraping

Most people who use object scraping do it in conjunction with a GUI builder. The GUI generated by the builder invokes the objects generated by the object scraper. In the example above, instead of processing one record at a time, a GUI application can collect and list multiple records (thanks to the GUI's greater resolution and rendering abilities), allow the user to work on them at the same time, then update them all at the end. One example of this object-scraping technology is the IBM VisualAge IMS and CICS Connection.

Object scraping is often used with a GUI builder

Object scrapers can also be useful on the server side, for creating objects to be used by other server programs. For example, the business-rule processing code discussed above can be run on the server while leaving the user interface on the client. This can significantly improve the overall system performance because most record processing no longer requires network communications be-

Object scraping is not limited to the client side

tween the client and the server. We return to this subject later in the chapter and in the chapter on performance.

Graphical User Interface

The GUI client is fatter than the text-based one

The graphical user interface (GUI) revolution brought us windows, color, menu bars, scroll boxes, and pull-down and pop-up menus. Many kinds of information can now be displayed graphically—for example, pie charts and bar charts can be used to represent business data. GUI interfaces call for the use of a pointing device, such as a mouse. Multiple windows make it possible for a system to include multiple threads of dialog within a single client machine. Because the presentation processing (for example, the sequencing of dialogs) now executes on the client instead of the server, the GUI client is "fatter" than the text-based client, as shown in Figure 4-5.

The GUI paradigm is application-centric

The traditional GUI paradigm is application-centric. A GUI application usually consists of an icon, a primary window with a menu bar, and one or more secondary windows. The primary window represents the application, and the icon represents the shrunken window. The focus is on the task the application supports in the primary window instead of the objects being manipulated. Secondary windows and pop-up dialog boxes support ancillary tasks. Double-clicking on the icon is a signal to run the application. Menus provide a means of navigating within the application.

Figure 4-5 GUI vs. text-based client

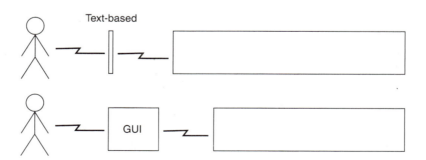

GUI applications alleviate many of the issues related to modal interfaces because users can keep track of where they are by referring to the icons and the title bars on the windows. It is also easier to navigate from one mode to another using icons and windows. Context-sensitive menus give explicit access to the operations that are allowed in a given mode. Some GUI applications may also provide direct manipulation, such as drag and drop, on an ad hoc basis.

GUIs are easier to navigate than text-based interfaces

OOUI

Object-oriented user interfaces (OOUIs) are a logical next step beyond GUIs. They first appeared on desktops supported by Macintosh, NextStep (appropriately enough) in the late '80s, and OS/2 in the early '90s, and were later adopted by the Windows operating systems. Today, OOUI is the pervasive user interface style on most clients. With the OOUI, direct manipulation becomes the predominant style of interaction.

OOUIs are the next step beyond GUIs

OOUIs simulate the way users interact with objects in real life. That is, they support an object-centric interaction style rather than the application-centric style of GUIs. The client interface simulates a desktop holding a collection of objects, which can be documents, folders, printers, customers, and so forth. The OOUI application is transparent to the user. Users interact directly with objects rather than with the applications that process the objects. Objects are created, communicated with, moved, and manipulated through drag-and-drop operations and pop-up menus. In this way, the OOUI provides a graphical model of a real-world situation.

They support an object-centric paradigm

In an OOUI, objects take the form of icons, and windows are views on the objects. Double-clicking on the icon is a way to request the system to "open a view." Each object also has a context-sensitive menu, which changes its contents according to the situation. Users can navigate within applications or across applications by directly manipulating objects. In this context, you could say that the desktop functions as one big menu.

OOUIs are not yet universally deployed

Though it is generally agreed that OOUIs are a superior form of GUI, they are not yet universally deployed in client/server systems. Even when clients are newly designed with the intention of following the OOUI paradigm, a lot of existing server-side code cannot be changed to fit the new paradigm. Some server-side business logic still requires a more traditional interaction style on the client side no matter what user interface technology we use. And in the end, it's the server processing that controls the way business is conducted.

Fat and Slim Clients

Clients display a wide range of functional richness

Remember that the PC is one of the driving forces behind the emergence of client/server computing. With the computing power that the PC brings to their desktops, people can download functions from centralized servers to clients. This creates a wide range of functional richness for the client in any client/server system. The client can be a bare-bones (thin) UI, such as a simple Web browser or X-Window client, as shown in Figure 4-6 (a); it can be a little heftier, with such functions as entry field verification and dialog logic (Figure 4-6 (b)); or it can be so fat that it includes every component of the application except the database (Figure 4-6 (c)). It can even include a local database to cache frequently used data.

Stand-alone client applications do not enter our discussion

In discussing fat and slim clients, we do not consider personal productivity applications such as word processors and spreadsheets. We assume that these applications run stand-alone on the client machine and therefore are not considered client/server. Efforts leveraging ActiveX and Java are underway to connect personal

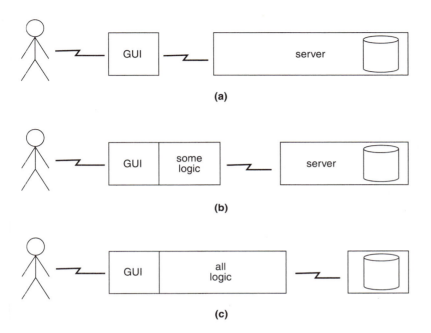

(a)

(b)

(c)

Figure 4-6 Fat and slim clients

productivity applications into the overall client/server environment. When these efforts bear fruit, their overall architecture can
easily fit into the structure discussed below.

The Rationale Behind Fat Clients

In addition to the advantages of using the client processing cycles,
there are good reasons to have at least something occur on the
client side. For example, what happens in an order-entry application if a customer tries to enter a delivery date that has already
passed, or a price that is way out of line, such as a negative number? Data verification is a must. There are certain benefits of doing
the verification on the client side, rather than the server side.

Some logic on the client side is healthy

- **Responsiveness** If the code that verifies the entry runs on
  the client side, it can provide user feedback much faster than if

the information is sent through the network for server verification.

- **Fine-grained feedback** As responsiveness improves, more immediate feedback becomes possible. Instead of waiting until the user finishes entering a screenful of data and then sending it to the server for verification, the client-side code can verify an entry field as soon as the user finishes typing it (or even as the user is typing). This fine-grained, immediate feedback makes the interface more user friendly.

- **More system scaleability** Client-side verification minimizes network traffic because fewer calls need to go to the server. The server and the network can use the saved bandwidth to serve more clients.

Can Clients Be Too Fat?

A very fat client may present its own problems

The rationale for fat clients certainly sounds good. However, as people try to offload more and more processing to the client, they discover that it's possible to go too far. If the client gets too fat, performance and other things can suffer. This often happens during an organization's second client/server project. If a first project demonstrates success in offloading UI functions from the mainframe, the tendency is to follow up by offloading more computation in the second project. This scenario has been common in OO client/server projects because until recently, object technology has only been available on the client side, as shown in Figure 4-7. For that reason, if a project wanted to maximize its leverage of object technology, its clients would get fatter and fatter.

Figure 4-7 A fat OO client

To see the problems of a fat client, consider a system that tracks customer sales. In such a system, closing an order might require complex computation that accesses data from different server-side databases (for example, the cost of production, competitor's pricing, customer order history, and customer credit standing). It is natural to store such information only on the server because of its size and the requirements for security and a single point of control. Not only must the computation access several databases, but it must access each one several times, as shown in Figure 4-8.

Client operations might require complex calculations and frequent server interaction

In this scenario, the client needs to make many calls across the network, and some of the calls may return large amounts of data. The networking middleware becomes a bottleneck and the system has difficulty scaling up to serve large numbers of users. For such operations, performing computations entirely on a server located next to the data can be a lot more efficient. Though the frequency of data access and the amount of information transferred do not change, local data access is a lot faster than access across the network.

Such operations can more easily occur on the server side

Also, on a typical server, a piece of commonly accessed data can remain in active memory. A smart server can take advantage of such a condition to totally avoid the follow-up disk access and, thus, greatly enhance performance. Such memory-based sharing is achievable only when processing occurs on the server side because the clients run on different machines that don't share common memory.

Servers can retain commonly accessed data in memory

Figure 4-8 Client-side computation using multiple databases

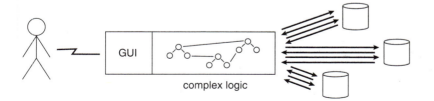

complex logic

Fat clients can make system management difficult

System management is also an issue for fat clients. As more code runs on the client side, updating the client/server system involves installing more changes to all the clients. If an application requires consistent behavior from all the clients, they generally require synchronized updates—all are completely updated or none are. This can be a daunting task compared with the traditional task of updating one server machine (or a few, at most). Thinner clients are also essential for the downloadable client paradigm supported by the Web to work well.

Such problems are typically referred to as the problems of a fat client. We discuss possible solutions to the these problems in the chapters on server objects and OO glue.

Objects in Client Development

Objects are useful in developing GUIs, OOUIs, and fat clients

Whether fat or skinny, clients increasingly make use of objects. This section looks at why object technology has become so dominant in client development and the contribution it makes in four areas: the complexity of client construction, direct manipulation techniques, the compound document paradigm, and the adoption of GUI builders. The discussion focuses on GUIs, OOUIs, and fat clients because these areas contain the majority of current client/server issues and are likely to continue to do so.

Complexity

Object technology can handle the complexity of GUI construction

As we saw in Chapter 2, object technology does a great job of controlling and managing complexity, such as the complexity of constructing a GUI. Because it maps user interface elements to corresponding software objects, object technology provides a way to deal with complexity.

In a text-based UI, the UI structure can be easily mapped to a procedural design, where procedures correspond to the UI screens and the screen sequence corresponds to the sequence of the procedure invocation. For example, the left side of Figure 4-9 shows an order entry application with three screens: a root screen that represents the system, a customer screen that gathers customer information for verification, and a Shopping Cart screen that captures the order for the server to process. The right side of the figure shows the program modules that correspond to the screens. The Order Entry module corresponds to the root screen; it invokes the "Verify customer" module that processes the Customer Info screen, and the "Capture order" module that processes the Shopping Cart screen. Each program module processes user input from the prior screen and generates the next screen. The programs can be implemented as transactions that run on the server.

In a text-based UI, procedures correspond to UI screens

There are several reasons why such tidy and clearly structured mapping does not work with today's GUIs and OOUIs and why object technology can provide a better solution.

This doesn't work with GUIs and OOUIs

Users Expect More Sophisticated Interfaces This adds to the programming complexity. For example, modern GUI programming offers a variety of possible user interface components: spin buttons, sliders, scroll bars, pop-up menus, radio buttons, combo boxes, and

Users expect more sophisticated interfaces

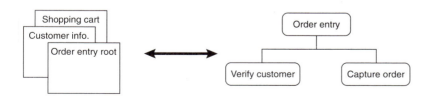

Figure 4-9 Procedure-based order entry application

so on. This enables a more powerful and useable interface to be constructed but adds to programming complexity.

Users also have higher expectations of the intelligence of the UI. For instance, in our order entry application, after the customer information is verified, users expect the interface to customize itself based on this information so that it provides only valid options.

The interfaces are no longer modal

Interfaces Are Not Modal Anymore Today's users can participate in multiple independent dialogs with the system. They can jump from one to another at any time, and they can also jump from one point to another within a dialog. For example, a user can interact with the order entry and payroll applications at the same time. While filling the order, the user may notice that he entered the wrong customer account number and decide to go back to the earlier window to fix it.

The client/server code is split between two machines

The Application Is No Longer a Single Piece The code for an application with a text-based UI generally resides in one piece on the server. The code for a client/server application with a GUI is split between two machines. As a result, the client-side front end must now deal with the connections to the server-side back end. Often the back end already exists before the client is developed, and developers might have to wrapper a back end that is not an easy fit for the GUI front end. Objects can wrapper the functionality of the legacy back end system, which enables the GUI to manipulate and integrate with the back end more easily, as illustrated in the object scraper example we discussed earlier.

GUIs and OOUIs are event driven

GUIs and OOUIs Are Usually Event-Driven Program flow is driven by user-generated UI events, such as mouse clicks and cursor moves, instead of following the preprogrammed dialog flow of a

procedural server program. The "main program" is often a sophisticated event dispatching mechanism residing in the UI system. New
user interfaces must strictly conform to the structure and rules of
this event loop.

Instead of having to understand fully such a complex event dispatching system and then write code to conform to it, interface
programmers are supplied with object-oriented UI frameworks that
embed most of the system's structure. The UI programmer's job is
to extend the framework with new objects that represent the
unique features of each application.

Direct Manipulation

Direct manipulation techniques found in OOUIs, such as drag and
drop, also add new programming challenges. For example, when
an icon is dragged over other icons and containers, the latter need
to provide visual feedback to the user about whether they can accept the dragged icon.

Direct manipulation techniques add new challenges

Such interfaces are user friendly but complex to develop. The UI
elements that participate in the screen interaction represent the
underlying application semantics. To determine the validity of a
certain UI operation, those underlying semantics need to be con-
sulted. As the user drags the icons across the screen, the program
must constantly consult a steadily changing group of semantic elements to provide feedback.

*UI elements repre-
sent underlying ap-
plication semantics*

Object technology enables programmers to encapsulate the screen
elements and the semantic elements as objects. The interacting elements can use generic messaging protocols without having to
know each other's implementation details. The controlling logic
that oversees the direct manipulation can also view the elements as
objects that understand certain control protocols. Such encapsula-

*Objects encapsulate
screen and semantic
elements*

tion of function enables GUI framework designers to provide good structure and order and still keep much of the complexity hidden.

The Compound Document Paradigm

Compound documents include different categories of content

The shift to the compound document paradigm is yet another reason why OO has become so common on the client side. The **compound document paradigm** allows the user to work with documents composed of many categories of content. For example, a document may contain text created by a word processor, spreadsheets created by a spreadsheet tool, and diagrams created by a drawing tool. Individual components of the document can themselves be compound documents.

Applications responsible for document components are invoked automatically

The user editing the compound document does not have to worry about which tools create and edit the different portions of the document. As the user navigates around the document, the applications responsible for the components of the document are invoked automatically. ActiveX (formerly OLE), OpenDoc, and JavaBeans are examples of commercial standards supporting the compound document paradigm.

Objects can represent compound document components and their relationships

Objects are ideal for representing the components of a compound document and the relationships among them. Objects can encapsulate a component's data and implementation details while surfacing the behaviors required to participate in the compound document paradigm. It is no wonder that all three of the compound document standards are object-oriented. Chapter 6 details these standards when it discusses local glues.

UI Builders

Current builder technology is predominantly OO

UI builders—tools that help developers construct user interfaces—are another reason that object technology has strong roots in the client side of the client/server system. As interfaces evolved from terminals to GUIs, UI builder technology evolved with them; present-day builder technology is predominantly object technology. To understand the reasons for this, let's look at how UI builders have changed over the years and how they address the underlying issues of user interface construction.

Text-based UI Builders Before the client/server wave, text-based UIs predominated. By the mid-'80s UI builder technology had converged on the concept of user interface management systems (UIMS). UIMSs were intended to follow the same paradigm as database management systems (DBMSs), which present a uniform programming interface to data management facilities by abstracting away the low-level details of physical I/O. In the same way, UIMSs aim to provide a uniform high-level programming interface to UI developers. Work on the UIMSs in the '80s evolved into a variety of user interface builders.

User interface management systems (UIMS) paralleled DBMs

A typical UI builder for a text-based interface allows the UI designer to specify character fields, with their screen location and length; limited visual properties of the fields, such as character color; and the actions associated with function keys. In addition, such builders can help the UI designer specify the next program (or portion of the dialog) to invoke when the user pushes the Enter key or certain function keys. They can also help to specify how to process commands issued from the command line at any point.

Text-based builders specify dialog sequence and command processing

The output of such a UI builder is often a file in a tag language format (analogous to HTML). This file serves as the input to generate an executable and a header file, as shown in Figure 4-10. The header file can be included in a server program so that the programmer can write code to access the information submitted by the terminal and prepare the data that go back to the terminal. The

They generally create a header file and an executable

**Figure 4-10 UI
builder output**

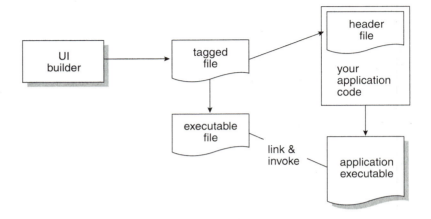

executable gets linked in with the code that the application programmer writes to perform the runtime services.

GUI builders specify more in terms of presentation and its relationship to logic

GUI Builders As the user interface evolved from the text-based UI to the GUI, the UI builders evolved with it. The increasing sophistication of the interface requires GUI builders to specify much more in terms of presentation and the relationship of presentation to application logic. The new presentation issues include the following.

- **GUI widgets** These include such items as buttons, text entry fields, list boxes, labels, and windows. GUI builders must specify the screen location and size of the widgets, along with visual properties such as font type and size, border, shadowing, foreground and background colors, icons, title bar color, title, and so on.

- **Visual feedback for user interaction** This involves changing the appearance of widgets or icons when users interact with them. For example, a button might change its appearance when it is clicked, or an icon might change when something is dragged on top of it.

- **Resize rules** These are perhaps the most complex of the presentation issues. In a GUI, interface components in a container have to resize and reposition themselves when the container size changes. The interface elements and the container often must negotiate the most appropriate arrangement. For example, a button with a text label can decrease its size and reduce the size of the label font when the containing window size is reduced. If the label font can't be reduced and still be readable, the button can keep its current size and let the container figure out how to position it.

  Containers can contain other containers, and resizing and repositioning affect all the UI elements involved. For example, scroll bars may have to be adjusted, added, or removed when a container resizes.

When we turn to the relationship of presentation to logic, the following issues are involved.

- **Mouse operations,** such as clicking, double-clicking, and drag-and-drop, must be associated with logical operations that depend on their context, as well as with changes in the GUI widgets they affect. Short-cut key sequences require similar associations.

- **Toolbar buttons** can be thought of as a more sophisticated version of function keys. Their associated operations often need to correspond to the current selection or cursor position. For example, a paste button for a word processor needs to paste the clipboard contents to the cursor location.

- **Context-sensitive operations** must be associated with the states of the screen objects they affect. This involves surfacing the available operations to the user through such devices as context-sensitive (pop-up) menus.

- **Dialog relationships** describe how threads of interaction relate to each other. The threads may exist independently or they may have a relationship that requires coordination. For example, users exiting an application can choose to commit or discard their work or cancel out of the exit dialog. Once the exit dialog box has been opened, the application prevents users from making any changes but permits them to go to other applications or invoke help.

- **Views and models** GUI elements often represent views of the "behind-the-screen" model, or business object, that the user wants to manipulate. The view and the model need to be connected to get the job done. As shown in Figure 4-11, a GUI can present multiple views for the same business model. The views can run in a single client program, different programs, or even on different machines.

The view-model connection provides three major functions

The view-model connection needs to provide three major functions. First, it needs to allow the views to query the model for information to render the desired GUI elements. Second, it needs to deliver user input back to the model. Third, it needs to notify the view when the model changes. Because a model can have multi-

Figure 4-11 Multiple GUI views of a single business model

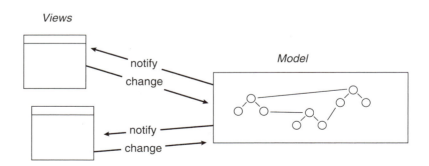

ple views, a change made by one view may need to be propagated to other views to keep them current.

OO Technology in UI Builders

Not only do objects make GUI programming easier, they also make it easier to develop GUI builders. As a result, almost all modern GUI builders present object-oriented interfaces to the user and are built with object technology. OO is an appropriate technology for GUI builders because of the following.

OO is the right technology for GUI builders

- Many GUI libraries are based on an OO framework already. The path of least effort for any provider of GUI builders is to make this OO paradigm already in the runtime library available to tool users instead of translating it into 3GL concepts.
- GUI builders are themselves graphical applications. They have all the OOUI bells and whistles, such as icons, pop-up menus, visual line-drawing capabilities, and dialog boxes. In fact, they tend to be more sophisticated and complex than typical GUI applications.
- Most GUI builders use direct manipulation techniques extensively, for example dragging and dropping widgets onto a container and resizing them. The object paradigm is natural for programming direct manipulation.

Summary

As the power of desktop computers has steadily increased, clients have become more user friendly and have performed more business. Clients have evolved roughly as follows, although all stages of client evolution are still in use in one form or another.

- **Text-based clients** contain little processing power.
- **Screen-scraping** adds more graphics to the user interfaces but little application logic.
- **Graphical user interfaces** add functional sophistication and relative ease of navigation.
- **Object-oriented user interfaces** are suited for direct user manipulation and the compound document paradigm.

Some logic on the client side is healthy. It can enable more-immediate feedback and help with system scaleability. Clients that contain a lot of functionality are referred to as "fat." Fat clients can be useful, but they also present certain limitations.

- They sometimes have to access server data too frequently.
- They can make it difficult to manage the system.
- They are often not suited for downloading from the World Wide Web.

The complexity of developing GUI applications led to the use of object technology for GUI construction. Similarly, the complexity of developing a tool to construct the GUI made object technology popular among the developers of GUI builders. As a result, object technology has firmly established itself on the client side of the client/server system.

5

Object-Oriented Servers

Server environments are different than client environments. Generally speaking, servers are multiuser computers that execute multiple programs concurrently. They use a large volume of CPU power, memory, and disk capacity, and they process a correspondingly large volume of data, often managing a database. They must also manage multiple transaction commit scopes and data security for multiple users.

Server environments are different than client environments

Until recently, objects have benefited only the client side. There does not seem to be any intrinsic or conceptual reason for this. Rather, it has been a result of timing, the availability of tools, and the conservative restraints that result from the mission-critical nature of server computing. The benefits that object technology has brought to client programming can apply equally well to the server side.

Benefits of object technology apply to server as well as client

Perhaps most important is the ability to manage complexity and change. The multiuser requirements and greatly magnified scale of the server side naturally lend themselves to complexity. In addition, today's business environment creates pressure for information systems flexible enough to cope with the rapid pace of change. Such flexibility is difficult to manage at the server level, as evidenced by pervasive IS backlogs. The encapsulation and reusability offered by objects can help manage complexity and system changes. They enable server programmers to insulate changes and minimize maintenance costs. The close mapping between the problem and solution domains allows building an implementation that maps directly to the business. This ensures that changes are made not only quickly but correctly.

Objects help manage system complexity and changes

Another reason why objects are needed on the server is that the fat-client model is reaching its limit. With server objects and their extension into distributed computing, OO program logic can reside on the server, as needed rather than on the client.

Types and Characteristics of Servers

Three major cate-gories of servers

Currently, technology providers are taking steps to implement objects on their servers. This chapter examines the move to object-oriented servers in terms of the three major categories of traditional servers.

- Transaction Servers: Servers that are built around a transaction processing (TP) monitor, often host-based
- Database Servers: The most pervasive servers in client/server computing, often relational, typically part of a fat-client configuration
- Native Servers: Servers that run directly on top of the operating system

No server type pro-vides all the function required by today's enterprise systems

Although all three server models offer unique advantages and drawbacks, none of them provides all the function required by today's enterprise systems. The marriage of objects and servers offers a unique opportunity to address some of the limitations faced by today's servers.

We look at servers from a user perspec-tive and server objec-tification from a technology provider perspective

We examine each server type in turn, looking at its traditional characteristics, its advantages and disadvantages, and the main scenarios it offers for introducing objects. In discussing the server's traditional characteristics, we take a user perspective; in the objec-tification scenarios, we take a technology provider's perspective. Finally, we look at the mid-tier application server, an approach that holds high promise for server objectification in the near term.

Note that the movement toward three-tier client/server applications pushes the vendors to address distributed computing issues in conjunction with adopting object technology. We briefly discuss the distributed computing issues most closely related to servers and leave the details to Chapter 6, which covers object-oriented glue.

Vendors introduce distributed computing as they adopt object technology

Transaction Servers

Transaction processing (TP) systems, such as those using CICS, IMS/TM, or TUXEDO, tend to be large and often span large geographical areas and heterogeneous computing environments. As they evolve, such systems fit naturally into the client/server model. The client typically invokes application logic as remote processes stored on the transaction server, often involved in accessing a database. The processes called by a single client request are treated as a single transaction.

Transaction processing systems can be large

Traditional transaction servers can be classified into two main categories: those that contain UI logic and those that do not. In UI-heavy TP systems, the server drives the client user interface. The client acts primarily as an I/O terminal, contributing little or no logic of its own to the transaction. Many existing mainframe systems are built around this model.

In UI-heavy TP servers, the host server drives the client user interface

In other TP systems, the client runs on a programmable workstation and contains the UI logic and implementation. The server is batch- or message-driven and avoids the overhead of user interface processing. Often, the server code is written in a third-generation language (3GL). Its main jobs are to run the business logic and ensure the integrity of the data. Figure 5-1 depicts a configuration in which a client sends requests to the server message queue and the server processes them. This is the most pervasive client/server TP configuration used.

With a UI client, the server runs business logic and ensures data integrity

**Figure 5-1 System
with transaction
processing monitor**

Because objects are already pervasive on the client side, the client is represented as an OO program. The server is a TP monitor running a procedural transaction program, connected to a database.

The TP Monitor

*TP monitors provide
transaction manage-
ment and resource
management*

At the heart of the transaction server is the transaction processing monitor (TP monitor), which can be thought of as the "operating system" for transaction processing. Although TP monitors vary widely in functionality and scope, they all support two important functions: transaction management and resource management. **Transaction management** guarantees the so-called ACID properties of transactions: atomicity, consistency, isolation, and durability (see sidebar). **Resource management** ensures efficient and proper use of system resources, such as communication, memory, disk space, and processes to support the transactions. The process management is especially important. It includes starting server processes (or threads), dispatching work to them, monitoring their execution, and balancing their workload.

*The TP monitor
schedules transac-
tions and coordinates
the commit, rollback,
and recovery*

Requests to execute transactions usually come through a message queue. The TP monitor schedules the transactions. In general, a program under the control of the TP monitor must access external resources through the TP monitor to ensure the transaction's ACID properties. (This is why we depict the TP monitor as a box.) The TP monitor needs to know what other resources the program has been interacting with to properly coordinate the commit, rollback, and recovery. Generally, the TP monitor makes use of a protocol known as a **two-phase commit** to accomplish this coordination.

The ACID Properties

Atomicity implies that every transaction is an indivisible unit of work. It may include many subactions, but if all subactions do not succeed, they must all fail. If any part of a transaction fails, the entire transaction is rolled back.

Consistency has a related meaning: After a transaction executes, it must leave the system in a stable state. If the transaction cannot be completed successfully, the system must be rolled back to its initial state.

Isolation means that a transaction's behavior is not affected by other transactions running concurrently. Any changes made by the transaction to the system's state must not be visible to other transactions until the transaction has been completed and committed.

Durability is also known as "persistence." Once a transaction has committed, the changes it makes to the system's state are permanent and should survive any system failure.

To understand why these properties are important, consider an ATM banking machine linked to a remote transaction server. When you make a withdrawal, the ATM gives you money and a receipt, updates your account, and makes an annotation in the bank's daily ledger. The transaction is atomic: If any of these events cannot happen, the transaction is rolled back so that none of them happens. The transaction is also consistent: The cash you withdraw must always match the accounting record created by the transaction. The transaction is isolated: Even if your spouse makes a deposit at another bank branch at precisely the same moment, the transactions are handled sequentially and are hidden from one another. Finally, the transaction is Durable: The bank record is now permanent and prevents you from withdrawing the same money twice.

Two-Phase Commits

The two-phase commit protocol is a widespread method for ensuring the ACID properties in transaction processing. The purpose of the two-phase commit is to synchronize updates to the various system resources involved in a transaction so that they all either succeed or fail. If they succeed they are committed; if they fail they are rolled back.

The protocol designates one of the system components involved in the transaction as the **transaction coordinator.** Other components involved in the transaction are **subordinate** components.

In the first phase, the transaction coordinator queries all the subordinates about whether they are ready to commit. If the subordinates have involved other resource managers as further subordinates in the transaction, they must in turn query these subordinates, and so on. Each subordinate must ensure that its own subordinates are ready to commit before sending its own ready-to-commit message to the transaction coordinator. If any of the resource managers does not agree that the transaction should be committed, the commit fails and the transaction coordinator orchestrates the transaction roll-back. When the transaction coordinator has received the go-ahead from all of its subordinates, it logs this information as a safeguard against system failure.

The second phase begins when every component involved in the transaction has signaled its readiness to commit. The transaction coordinator sends a commit command to its subordinates, who in turn propagate it down the line. As each component commits, it sends a confirmation to the component above it. A component can commit only when all its immediate subordinates have confirmed their commitment. Once the transaction coordinator has received all the confirmations, it signals to its client that the transaction is completed.

As the vendors of TP monitors propagate them to the workstation platforms (for instance, CICS/6000 and CICS/NT), the configuration shown in Figure 5-2 becomes more common, in which the transaction boundary is extended to include part of the logic executing on the workstation. The two TP monitors coordinate to provide the image of a single TP monitor spanning the network. Even though the work is split between two transaction servers, it is a single unit of work from the client perspective.

The transaction boundary can extend to more than one machine

Many of today's transaction servers are still UI-heavy, but as servers continue to evolve, the focus is on data, computation, and transaction processing. Increasingly, the GUI is off-loaded onto the client so that the server itself is "headless." By avoiding UI processing, the server can perform better on tasks that require server-side processing.

Increasingly, servers are headless

Advantages and Disadvantages

The advantages supplied by transaction servers include the following.

- They can support a large number of clients in pseudo-conversational style. (This implies that transactions need to be short-running and not hold locks on database records for a long time. This is good for server concurrency.)
- They can manage multiple resource managers.
- They make efficient use of system resources, such as memory, and are good at scheduling transaction execution.

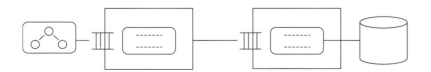

Figure 5-2 Transaction boundary extended to more than one machine

The corresponding disadvantages include the following:

- The conventional TP monitors, such as CICS and IMS/TM, often require an all-or-nothing execution of transaction programs. All statements in a program are part of a transaction that is committed or rolled back as a single unit. This implies that a program is the smallest unit that can be protected by the TP monitor (even though not every part of a program needs protection).
- The location in which a program runs determines whether it is transactional. A program is either transactional or nontransactional, depending on whether it is inside or outside the wall of the TP monitor.

Conversational and Pseudo-Conversational Communication

There are two main modes of communication between client and server: conversational and pseudo-conversational. With conversational communication, the client and the server establish a network connection through which they exchange messages. The connection is kept open for the duration of the communication.

Pseudo-conversational communication, on the other hand, does not maintain the connection. The connection is released after each request and reestablished when the next request comes in. System support enables the applications sitting above the communication layer to behave as if they are having conversational communication. Because pseudo-conversational communication releases the communication resources between messages, it can often use resources more efficiently. Servers such as CICS successfully use this kind of communication to support a large number of concurrent clients. Pseudo-conversational communication has a cost, however. The state of the application needs to be stored and restored between messages, and reestablishing the connection also consumes resources.

- Because the client is outside the TP monitor, the TP monitor, typically, does not protect it.

OO Transaction Servers

Two approaches are possible for introducing objects into transaction servers: objectified transaction servers and object TP monitors. The **objectified transaction server** approach introduces objects into the existing architecture of conventional TP monitors. The **object TP monitor** approach tries to design a new TP monitor to host objects.

Objectified Transaction Servers The objectified transaction server model usually entails a host-down approach, in which the TP monitors residing on host systems are objectified (by introducing OO APIs to access their services) and ported to the workstations and PCs. For example, IBM has made CICS available on platforms such as OS/2, AIX, HP-UX, Solaris, and NT. This approach uses a conservative but proven technology, with which IS organizations have two decades of experience.

Figure 5-3 shows a configuration in which the OO client communicates with an objectified transaction server on the middle tier, which in turn communicates with another objectified transaction server on the host, which is connected to a database. As the figure indicates, OO programs can run inside the protection of the TP monitor, but they are constrained by the boundaries of the transac-

Two approaches are objectified transaction servers and object TP monitors

Objectified transaction server: conservative but proven technology

Object benefits are constrained to transaction program boundaries

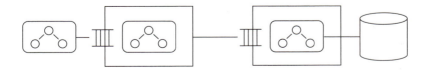

Figure 5-3 Configuration using objectified transaction servers

tion programs. This adds an additional distraction when mapping from an OO business model to an actual application design.

The paradigm is multiple transaction programs written in OO languages

Instead of thinking and developing in terms of a distributed object system spanning the three tiers, the developer/designer has to think in terms of multiple transaction programs written with OO programming languages. (Sounds 3GL-ish, doesn't it?) The benefit of object technology is limited to implementing individual transaction programs instead of covering the overall client/server scope.

The server transaction does not call back out to the client program

In such a traditional TP setting, in which the basic programming model is "call-return," the server transaction does not call back out to the client program. If the server computation needs access to only a small portion of the data on the client side, but that portion varies, depending on how the computation proceeds, the client code would still have to package all the possible information and pass it to the server at the call point. The client can not simply pass a reference to the collection of objects and let the server intelligently get the information it needs.

TP monitor services can be introduced into an existing object/component model

Object TP Monitors The second approach to OO transaction servers is the object TP monitor. Instead of taking an existing TP monitor architecture and fitting objects into it, object TP monitors take an existing object/component model and introduce TP monitor services into it. This technology is just emerging. At press time, technology vendors such as IBM/Transarc and Microsoft were working on bringing products to market. The Microsoft Transaction Server has just entered the market and the IBM CBSeries is in beta test.

COM and CORBA are standards used for emerging object TP monitors

As expected, Microsoft leverages its Common Object Model (COM) and ActiveX technology. This provides connectivity and defines interfaces and protocols for communication. Developers build and implement application components as ActiveX modules. In contrast, IBM and other vendors leverage the Object Management Group's Common Object Request Broker Architecture model (CORBA), and its Object Transaction Service (OTS) standard.

Both camps are trying to supply TP monitor benefits to their object models in an integrated fashion. These benefits include transaction management, resource management, security, performance, scaleability, availability, and reliability.

Transaction Server Considerations

In considering transaction servers, it is important to recognize that TP monitors tend to assume the role of the current operating systems. One important question is whether this is desirable for any system, considering the restrictions on the application programming models (for example, most TP monitors expect transactions to be short), and considering the overhead required by TP monitors in terms of configuration, resources, and maintenance.

TP monitors tend to assume the role of the current operating systems

Traditional TP monitors, such as CICS and IMS/TM, are based on a centralized model because they evolved from the mainframe environment, in which the host computer is the center of all computing resources. Workstation-based TP monitors, such as NCR's TopEnd, IBM/Transarc's Encina, BEA's TUXEDO, and the emerging object TP monitors, often explore a more decentralized transaction model, taking advantage of the multiple computing resources on the network. The major drawbacks of these TP monitors are their lack of scaleability, reliability, and most important, existing market share. This is especially true for the new object TP monitors. Lack of critical mass often makes it difficult for an organization to commit to a new technology in general, and to commit to a new TP monitor specifically, because adopting a TP monitor is a major decision that cannot be easily reversed.

Workstation-based TP monitors can mean a more decentralized transaction model

More work needs to be done on object technology in the TP environment

Also, even though TP monitor technology is well-established, object technology has only recently been introduced to the TP environment, and work remains to be done. For example, in order to complete the picture, client/server and server/server communication mechanisms need to be standardized, integrated with TP monitors, and objectified. These mechanisms might include transactional remote message sends or remote procedure calls (RPCs), and asynchronous message queuing.

Additional support is also necessary to make the program boundary of TP monitor systems less intrusive. This would enable a business application developer to focus on business transaction boundaries instead of the technical transaction boundaries forced on him by the underlying TP monitors.

Database Servers

Database servers execute SQL commands for accessing data

SQL database servers, such as those built by Oracle, Sybase, and IBM, currently form the technology base of the most pervasive client/server implementation. In this model, most of the application logic resides on the client, and the server manages SQL commands for accessing data.

Figure 5-4 shows the fat-client configuration that is the most common client/server configuration today. All objects and intelligence reside on the client side. SQL requests flow from the client to the database that resides on the server, which returns rows of data.

Figure 5-4 Fat client with database server

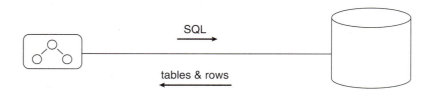

Database servers can provide some basic transaction-processing functions (such as commit/rollback changes to a table) and are sometimes referred to as "TP-Lite" servers (in contrast to the "TP-Heavy" servers that run TP monitors). TP-Lite servers provide features and utilities to help manage the database and may include advanced functions that go far beyond basic data management and retrieval.

Database servers can provide some transaction-processing functions

Database server architecture is good at handling transactions that involve a simple request from the client and a simple reply from the server. However, the model is less effective when the requests require a long reply (that is, shipping many table rows down to the client). With increasingly complex client/server interaction, the overall system can require more and more frequent requests and replies per client, and the model can begin to break down because of heavy network traffic.

Network traffic can be an issue

Stored Procedures

One way to reduce the increasing number of requests and replies is with **stored procedures.** These frequently used extensions to database management systems allow application logic on the server side of a client/server application, as shown in Figure 5-5. (The diagram is a conceptual picture. Although the stored procedure is drawn inside the database, it does not imply that the stored procedure actually has to run in the same address space or process that the database manager uses.) Most stored procedures are called by client programs, although the ones known as "triggers" are invoked automatically by a database event, such as an update to a particular field.[1] The database schedules the execution of the stored procedures.

Stored procedures encapsulate program logic in the database

---

[1]Normally, triggers are stored procedures, although they may take other forms.

Figure 5-5 3GL application logic in a stored procedure

Stored procedures can reduce network traffic

Stored procedures make it possible for a single remote request to invoke a series of SQL statements and thereby reduce network traffic. Client/server developers can use stored procedures to divide the logic between client and server at points where the traffic is light.

Stored procedures tend to be in proprietary languages

However, stored procedures have limitations. Because they tend to be written in proprietary languages, they also tend to be vendor-specific. For example, Sybase uses Transact-SQL and Oracle uses PL/SQL. As systems grow to include more than one type of database, the program logic provided by the stored procedures must be duplicated for each database, resulting in development and maintenance overhead. (The emerging SQL3 standard addresses this problem by introducing a standard stored procedure programming language.)

Stored procedures often do not provide full transaction protection

Stored procedures do not provide the levels of protection normally associated with TP monitors. Unit-of-work protection is often limited to the data controlled by the database. Any update to a resource other than the database itself, such as a VSAM file (a kind of record-based file commonly used on the mainframe), would not be protected as part of the transaction.

Stored procedures have other limitations

Stored procedures also tend to be data-oriented and have difficulty dealing with events or real-world models that are not concerned with data. Furthermore, stored procedures are not proactive—for example, it would be hard for stored procedures to implement an auction server to intelligently control the bidding flow among a group of clients.

Advantages and Disadvantages

The advantages supplied by database servers include the following.

- They are relatively easy to set up and manage because the database and most of the program logic (the stored procedures) are a single unit.
- Stored procedures and triggers enhance system performance.
- Most vendors provide integrated client/server development tools.

The corresponding disadvantages include the following.

- They only protect and control a single resource manager—namely, the database.
- Much of the program logic has to reside on the client.
- Stored procedures have such limitations as portability.

OO Database Servers

There are two approaches to OO database servers: object-oriented database management systems and objectified database servers. The **object-oriented database management system** (ODBMS) approach takes the OO concepts and introduces persistence to them. The **objectified database server** approach takes existing relational databases and fits object concepts into their existing architecture (that is, objectifies it) through stored procedures or through extending the databases to become so-called **object-relational database management systems** (O-R DBMSs).

There are two approaches to OO database servers

The fat-client model, often associated with database servers, suggests a client-up approach to objectification. The basic idea is to extend the benefit of rapid OO development to the server, following the lead of popular databases and such power tools as Power-

Database-centered solutions extend object benefits from client to server

Builder, Delphi, and VisualAge. This approach takes advantage of the mature object technology already available on client platforms. However, even when data access and stored procedures are objectified, they still face typical DBMS limitations in coordinating resource managers other than a single database and in the proprietary nature of stored procedures.

Figure 5-6 depicts the introduction of object technology to the data servers, primarily in the form of OO stored procedures. This configuration is in contrast to Figure 5-4 and Figure 5-5, which are typical configurations for the so-called first generation client/server applications.

ODBMSs often move an OO language's object model to the server

ODBMS ODBMSs often take a popular client-side OO language (such as C++, Java, or Smalltalk), add persistence to the language's object model, and move it to the server side. To support many client languages, adapters are provided to map the persistent object model to the client languages' object models. The closer the client language object model to the ODBMS's object model, the more seamless the data access can be. When the ODBMSs on the server side can execute behaviors defined on the persistent objects, the behaviors become a form of stored procedure. For example, the Gemstone ODBMS supports writing such stored procedures in OO languages.

Figure 5-6 Database system with OO stored procedures

OO Stored Procedures Following the OO stored-procedure approach, vendors, including IBM, are introducing nonproprietary programming languages, such as Java, C++, OO COBOL, and BASIC, for writing stored procedures for relational databases. OO stored procedures in nonproprietary languages address some of the limitations of database servers, but they do not remove limitations such as the inability to handle transactions across multiple programs in multiple resource managers. (See the sidebar on transaction protection.)

Non-proprietary OO stored-procedure languages overcome some limitations of database servers

Many relational database vendors are also moving toward the so-called object-relational databases. They begin by introducing new system-defined media or nontraditional data types beyond the base data types (such as "integer" and "string"). Then user-defined data types, such as "customer" and "account," are supported. In general, inheritance is allowed with these new data types. Note that the key word is *data,* which does not always imply that the *behavior* of the superclass is also inherited.

Object-relational databases (O-R DBMSs) extend relational databases with OO constructs

User-defined functions are added to allow operations to be performed on the data types. User-defined functions are associated with the data types to ensure type consistency. Additional support for abstract data types is possible—for example, to allow access to the data only through the pre-defined operations (functions) on the specific types. In spite of these new features, the SQL support is preserved. Users do not have to learn a brand new Data Definition Language (DDL) and Data Manipulation Language (DML), as in the case of an ODBMS. SQL is still the DDL and the DML, and it is extended to handle the new object constructs.

The new constructs preserve and extend the SQL support

The next step is to support full OO features, such as inherited behavior and polymorphism, in the database. If the RDB vendors achieve such functionality, the differences between an object-relational database and an object database management system

O-R DBMs could support full OO features to be more similar to ODBMSs

(ODBMS) will be far fewer than they are today. However, they will still differ on what they use as their data definition and manipulation languages. ODBMSs will still support derivatives of object-oriented languages while the object-relational databases will stick with the SQL extension. As the Object Database Management Group works with the SQL standard committee to include standard data definition and manipulation languages in the SQL3 standard, a common standard language could emerge for ODBMSs and relational databases.

RDBs and ODBMSs are still optimized for different tasks

Even if such standards come into being, one key distinction still won't go away. ODBMSs have been optimized to perform well on complicated fine-grained data that is usually found in the CAD/CAM arenas. In contrast, relational databases are optimized for the structured and less complex data most often found in the business processing world. This optimization runs deep into the architecture and can not be changed easily. (See Chapter 7, on object persistence, for more details.) This implies that performance characteristics will set the ODBMS and object-relational databases apart for many years to come.

Native Servers

Native servers run directly on top of the operating system

Native servers run directly on top of the operating system and often put logic in front of the database. For example, many remote procedure call (RPC) servers are native servers. Some native servers also invoke transactions to accomplish specific services, functioning as a client to a transaction server. Figure 5-7 shows one example of a native server (depicted by the shadowed box) that attaches to a database and to a transaction server.

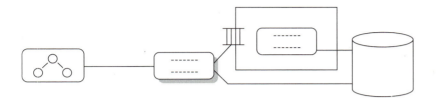

Figure 5-7 Native server fronting TP monitor and database

Because native server programs do not run under the control of a TP monitor, they usually interact with only one resource manager (generally a database) at a time. It is difficult to write application code for native servers that coordinate multiple resource manager updates. Unlike programs in database servers and transaction servers, which usually run for a short duration, a native server program can run for a long time. For example, a printer server program is a native server that might well run all the time.

Native server programs usually interact with a single resource manager

---

Transaction Protection with a Database Server

Transactions are different in the context of a database server than they are in a transaction server. This concept is critical but often misunderstood. The assumption that transactions are all the same no matter what server type they occur in can lead to a dangerous loss of integrity in some situations.

In the diagram below, a client is trying to update two different databases (for example, DB2 and Oracle) as a single unit of work. If the database commands include keywords like *begin* and *commit*, they can lead the user to believe that the client code is under the protection of a transaction when actually it is not. (In most cases a database begin/commit only works for a single database.) If the client program crashes between the commits of the two updates or aborts instead of committing, the two databases are likely to be in inconsistent states.

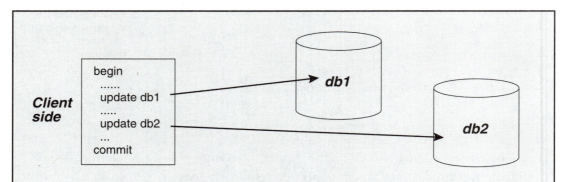

Some data server vendors (both OO and non-OO) offer ways to execute logic (that is, stored procedures) under the control of the database, as shown below. In order to solve this problem, it is tempting to bring application logic into one of the databases and expect transaction protection. In reality, unless the two database vendors have an agreement to synchronize their transactions, the same problems exist. When the code crashes or aborts, the update to db2 is not rolled back. Note that some database products, such as Oracle7's Open Gateway, can now manage two-phase commit across heterogeneous XA-compliant databases. However, restrictions exist—for example, the gateway does not allow multiple stored procedures in different databases to participate in a single transaction. Because the Open Gateway approach requires writing stored procedures, it also inherits the typical pros and cons of stored procedures.

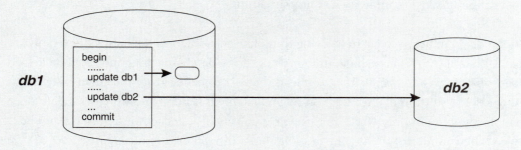

One way to get the necessary transaction protection is to run the code under the protection of a TP monitor, as shown. When the code runs into errors or aborts, the TP monitor takes care of rolling back the participating databases and thus preserves the integrity.

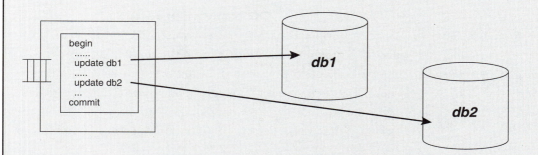

The key to understanding this situation is to remember the two roles in a transaction processing environment: transaction manager and resource manager. A resource manager is any piece of software that manages shared resources—for example, a DBMS, a persistent queue, or VSAM. A transaction manager coordinates multiple resource managers and allows multiple programs to participate in a single transaction. Without the presence of a transaction manager, updates to multiple resource managers are not coordinated.

Advantages and Disadvantages

The advantages supplied by native servers include the following.

- They can be long-running, compared with a typical program running under a TP monitor or on a database server.
- They can be proactive in scheduling client actions (in contrast to stored procedures, which are passive).
- Their architecture allows an easier and more natural mapping from OO design because they attach fewer semantics (such as transaction scoping) to the program boundaries.

The corresponding disadvantages include the following.

- Transactional support for native servers is not yet mature.
- Commercial tool support is not yet as fully mature as it is for database servers and transaction servers.

OO Native Servers

The first step is to introduce an OO language to the native server

The near-term approach to objectifying native servers is to introduce OO programming languages on the server platforms, as shown in Figure 5-8. Communication between objects on the client and the native server can be made more seamless and less 3GL-ish because the native operating system prescribes fewer restrictions than those associated with a transaction or a stored procedure.

OO native servers are capable of transaction support without a TP monitor

Transaction support is a key feature required before native servers can become full-function enterprise servers, capable of handling the mission-critical applications that require transactional protection. OO native servers, particularly in the model presented by the OTS architecture (see Figure 5-9), hold the promise of transaction support without the presence of a TP monitor (which provides resource management in addition to transaction management).

This calls for a distributed object approach supporting transactional behavior

Adding transaction support to the native server model involves a distributed object approach that supports transactional behavior in a distributed, heterogeneous environment. Distributed objects can encapsulate transaction semantics in their messaging and, in this way, provide the benefit of commit/rollback capabilities. (We discuss how that works in the next chapter.) Note that although

Figure 5-8 OO languages on the native server platforms

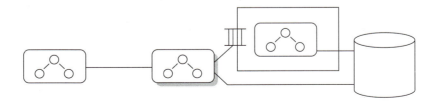

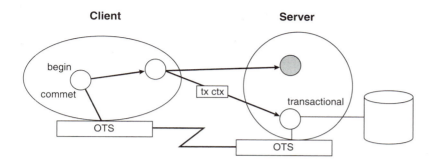

Figure 5-9 OMG's object transaction service

transaction protection is provided, there are no TP monitor boundaries to cross. This means that, in contrast to the objectified transaction server, mapping from an OO business model to an application design is more direct.

As shown in Figure 5-9, the OMG's Object Transaction Service (OTS) follows the distributed object approach by defining and governing transactions in terms of **transactional objects.** OTS allows the creation of applications that satisfy the full range of transactional requirements, particularly the ACID qualities, without requiring a TP monitor and the centralized programming model that some TP monitors require. We discuss how OTS works and explain Figure 5-9 in detail in the next chapter. Because a single transaction can call applications and resources that are either object-oriented or procedural, object-oriented server technology can be gradually phased into existing systems. However, this technology is still maturing and does not have the advantages of proven technology offered by the more evolutionary solutions already discussed.

The Object Transaction Service supports distributed OO transactions

Pathways to OO Servers

In spite of the potential advantages, the move to OO server implementations is taking time. One reason is the natural conservatism toward making changes in servers because they are so often mission-critical. The complexity of the servers plus their high

Server objectification takes time because servers are mission-critical

performance and reliability requirements contribute to the reluctance of IS managers to move quickly into new server technologies.

Another reason is a common story in the industry: critical mass

Another reason is a common story in the industry: critical mass. An organization cannot afford to maintain an entire proprietary OO programming language or server environment just for its own use, and tool developers are hesitant to develop the needed tools until there is a proven market for them. However, as tool providers converge on architectural and language standards, cost and risk factors decline. Later in this section, we examine how these factors fall into place for server objects.

Servers follow certain paths for OO adoption

Figure 5-10 summarizes the discussion of OO servers from the technology provider's perspective and shows the paths of OO adoption for different servers. It is no surprise that the commercial products from the vendors are following these paths. For example, O-R DBMSs are coming from the traditional relational database vendors and object TP monitors are coming from the TP monitor vendors.

Though two OO server technologies have different origins and migration paths, they may be similar

Even though the OO server technologies have different origins and migration paths, they are not very different, in the end. For example, the CORBA-based object TP monitor is not that different from the objectified native server with distributed transactional objects because of the common ORB and OTS technology they share. The key difference between them is the existence of a TP monitor and the heavyweight services that come with it. With the TP monitor services, the object TP monitor is likely to be able to scale up to many users and support mission-critical applications better. However, the object TP monitor is also likely to be large and complex and, therefore, is not a good candidate to run on client machines. The objectified native server with distributed object and OTS sup-

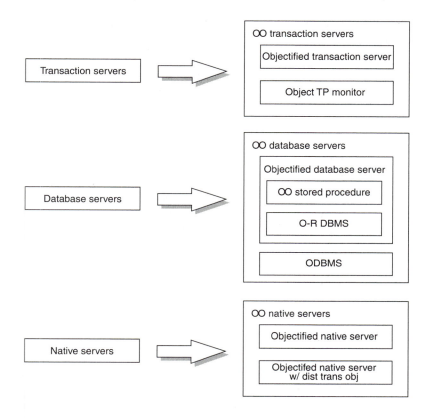

Figure 5-10 Pathways to server objectification

port is lightweight enough to run comfortably on the client side and thus extend the transaction boundary to the clients. Instead of staying distinct, we expect the two technologies will blend into one and provide a comprehensive solution.

OO servers can leverage the existing technology base to accelerate the pace of their development toward maturity. For example, Transarc and Iona recently delivered an objectified native server with distributed transactional objects (an OTS solution). Essentially, Transarc contributes the transaction manager from its existing Encina technology to integrate with the Iona ORB.

OO servers can leverage existing technology to accelerate their development

Server objectification is a dynamic, ongoing process, for which our analysis simply represents a single point in time. We expect OO server technology and products to continue to evolve, with mergers and convergence of existing technology and products, and the emergence of new ones.

Critical Mass

OO server technology is reaching critical mass

When an emerging technology reaches critical mass, it becomes a relatively permanent part of the information industry. Its major implementations are relatively stable and it has adequate vendor and tool support for organizations to adopt it with confidence. For any technology to reach critical mass, certain key factors must be in place. These factors are now falling into place for OO server technology, specifically in the areas of standards, customers, applications, languages, and tools.

Common standards for OO servers are increasingly accepted

Standards As with any new technology, common standards are required for OO server technology to gain widespread acceptance; such standards are increasingly evident. The CORBA standard has gained acceptance and has come to provide the basis for the OTS distributed object architecture. In addition, two distributed transaction standards with OO implications are widely recognized: the X/Open Distributed Transaction Processing (DTP) model and the ISO OSI-TP standard. Standardization of programming languages is equally essential. In recent years, the industry has begun to converge on Java, C++, Smalltalk, and OO COBOL standards.

Standards can help to ensure that objects developed using different vendors' tools are mutually compatible. As software vendors develop OO server components that conform to these standards, customer confidence will continue to grow and customers will increasingly adopt this new technology.

Customers and Applications Because current client/server applications are pushing the limits set by existing server models, customers are ready to use the new technology as soon as it is sufficiently mature. With architectural and language standards gaining widespread acceptance, the next challenge is to bring the standards to life in a mature application model and in a mature runtime environment robust enough to handle large-scale, mission-critical applications.

Customers and applications are emerging

Languages and Tools For many IS organizations, it is desirable to apply a single paradigm and, therefore, a single programming language and object model across client and server. The benefits of a single paradigm have led vendors like IBM to populate the popular workstation OO languages, such as Smalltalk, Java, and C++, on the server. The single paradigm can provide tremendous maintenance advantage, not only from a training perspective but also in terms of flexibility: Program objects can be distributed across the components of a system and more easily relocated as needed. The single paradigm also makes client/server communication and integration easier. Tools can provide a high level of abstraction to the application developer because common assumptions can be made about both client and server.

So are end-to-end programming paradigms spanning client and server

Although the single-paradigm model provides the highest level of abstraction and tool support, in reality, most IS organizations have to deal with heterogeneous systems. We look at the implications of this in the next chapter.

Most IS organizations deal with heterogeneous systems

As OO server tools evolve, they are likely to be hybrid workstation-host tools. This makes it possible to develop applications with highly interactive tools that run on the workstation, then test and tune those applications against the real data on the

Development tools are likely to be hybrid workstation-host tools

server. Host-only development tools are less desirable because host CPU cycles are relatively expensive, and crashing the host during development can have widespread effects. The trend in OO server development will likely be to provide as much workstation simulation/emulation as possible while integrating the development environment with a host-based final test/tune tool set.

The Beachhead: Mid-Tier Application Object Server

In the near term, the mid-tier application object server offers opportunity and growth

Object server technology can be applied to many situations. In the near term, the mid-tier application object server is likely to be among the situations that provide the most opportunity and growth. As shown in Figure 5-11, the mid-tier server is a logical notion. It is a portion of the system that sits between the client and the back end. The client can be a conventional OO client; a Web browser; a more specialized client, such as an ATM machine; or even a 3270 terminal. The back end can be a TP monitor; a legacy or new database; a native OO program; or other program, such as a SAP application.

This portion of the system serves application objects to the clients

This middle portion of the system is called an application object server because of the task it performs. It serves application objects (white circles), such as accounts and customers, to the clients. The application objects may also have persistent states or behaviors managed by the back-end systems. These are wrappered as objects (gray circles) and managed by the application object server too.

This server introduces objects without great impact on the existing systems

Such an object server presents a way to introduce object server technology and its benefits (such as flexibility and complexity control) without a great impact on the existing systems. Existing clients can continue to communicate directly with the back-end systems while the object server is serving the new clients and business requirements. As the object server's capabilities grow, existing clients can begin to use it.

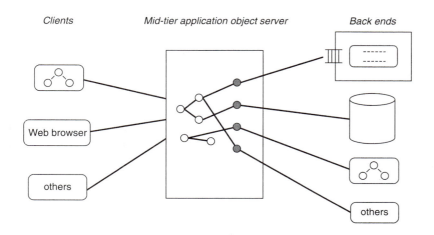

Clients   Mid-tier application object server   Back ends

Figure 5-11 Mid-tier application object server

To be successful, such a server must satisfy certain requirements beyond serving the clients and accessing the back end. First, it must support transaction coordination among the participating programs and resource managers. It also needs to provide features such as security and directory service, and it needs to be scaleable and reliable. System management needs to be an integral part of the server. Finally, the server must support application frameworks, libraries, and development tools.

No existing product satisfies all the requirements today, though many of the pieces already exist. As application object servers appear on the scene, the robustness and completeness of their functionality is only one point that will differentiate them. More important, they will be differentiated by the degree to which they can seamlessly integrate all their functions.

The mid-tier application object server needs to address a number of requirements

Summary

Although server objectification has lagged behind the clients, vendors are now taking steps to objectify their servers. The three basic types of servers require different pathways to objectification.

1. Transaction servers provide transaction management and resource management, often for large enterprise systems. Objectified transaction servers leverage conservative but proven technology, in which objects are constrained to the boundaries of the TP monitor. Workstation-based object TP monitors are emerging but lack a proven track record.

2. Database servers execute commands (for instance, SQL) for accessing data and can use stored procedures to encapsulate logic in the database. Database-centered solutions extend the benefits of objects from the client to the server. Some OO databases support the use of OO stored procedures, and object-relational databases extend relational databases with OO constructs.

3. Native servers run on top of the operating system. With architecture models such as OTS, objectified native servers offer the promise of transaction support in conjunction with distributed objects.

The move toward OO servers is approaching critical mass in terms of technology, languages, and standards. In the near-term, the mid-tier application object server holds promise. It offers a pathway to server objectification with minimal impact on the existing system.

6

Object-Oriented Glue

As long as a system is partitioned, either across the network or across process boundaries on the same machine, it needs a glue to tie its components together. The glue is the software that makes communications possible—in other words, the "/" in "client/server." Our notion of glue applies to the logical client/server model. That is, the glue ties together system components whether they are client/server, client/client, or server/server.

The glue ties together the objects in the system

Of course, all client/server systems need glue, whether they are object-oriented or not. The difference is that as we introduce objects on both sides of the client/server picture, communications can occur in a greater variety of ways. Communications can be based on the traditional procedural call model or the object messaging model or some combination of the two. The exact nature of the glue depends on the degree of OO integration in the enterprise system and the level of abstraction at which communications occur.

OO systems use a wider variety of glue than traditional systems

We prefer the term *glue* to the more common term *middleware*. Middleware can be ambiguous because of the broad spectrum of software that it covers. It sometimes refers generically to any software that happens to sit in the middle of a client/server system, regardless of its function. For example, networking software, such as TCP/IP, can be considered middleware, and so can such things as database access services that support SQL and run on top of the networking software. Some people consider databases and TP monitors to be middlewares because they sit between the operating system and the applications.

We refer to "glue" rather than the potentially ambiguous "middleware"

Glue means plumbing, programming model, and supporting tools

In contrast, we want to use "glue" in such a way that we can more precisely fit it into our logical client/server model. To us, glue refers to three aspects of that model.

- The low-level plumbing (such as the networking software)
- A programming model visible to the developer of the client/server application
- The tools supporting the programming model

Plumbing and programming model can best be considered separately

The plumbing and the programming model often tend to be clumped together. We prefer to consider them separately because the industry tendency is to make the plumbing invisible and differentiate products based on the programming model.

The rest of this chapter proceeds from the ground up. After a brief look at the plumbing, we'll turn to the programming model, which has a more direct impact on OO client/server architecture. We'll proceed from there to look at the different kinds of glues, as determined by the nature of the components being connected. The third element of glue, the programming tools, are a subject for Chapter 9, on end-to-end OO distributed development.

The Plumbing

Plumbing is low level and often not a concern for developers

First things first. In order to get to the programming model for the glue, we need to take a quick look at the plumbing. What we are calling the plumbing is also known as the transport mechanism. It consists of the actual networking or interprocess communication services that ship information across the process and/or machine boundaries. Examples are TCP/IP (Transmission Control Protocol/Internet Protocol) and SNA (Systems Network Architecture). As we've already mentioned, the tendency in the industry is to hide the plumbing as much as possible. Most tools strive to provide a programming model that runs equally well on top of different transport protocols.

This tendency to hide the transport layer comes about because most IS organizations have existing networking infrastructures. It is in the tool vendors' interest to support these existing infrastructures rather than try to impose a networking infrastructure based on the tools' requirements. Most IS organization would find another vendor who supports their infrastructure instead of changing the infrastructure just because of the tools.

Vendors hide the plumbing in order to support existing IS networking

Programming Models

Programming models sit on top of the plumbing. They are what application developers work with. The model forces the developers to implement the client/server communication in a certain programming style. For example, in a **remote procedure call** (RPC) model, the code would be structured in call-return style similar to typical 3GL programming. In a **message queuing** model, the code would write queues and send messages to queues in an asynchronous fashion. In the **peer-to-peer** model, the two communicating components would act as peers to each other, and either one could originate the sending of information.

Programming models are high level and very visible to developers

It is worth noting that multiple plumbing structures can support the same programming model. For example, as shown in Figure 6-1 (a), the message queuing model can run on both TCP/IP and Advanced Program-to-Program communications (APPC). Multiple programming models can also be supported by a single plumbing structure. For example, in Figure 6-1 (b), TCP/IP carries both RPC and message queuing.

Multiple plumbings can support the same programming model

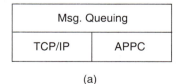

(a)

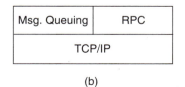

(b)

Figure 6-1 Relationship of plumbing to programming model

One programming model can be extended to simulate the effects of another

Developers can make a programming model simulate the effects of another model by adding a layer on top of it. For example, some applications have been known to stack synchronous messaging on top of an asynchronous message queuing system (or vice versa). This happens because most applications of any complexity follow more than one programming model. For example, many business processes require both synchronous and asynchronous processing. In the planning stage, an IS organization would usually pick the model that supports the majority of a planned application's tasks most naturally and efficiently. They then extend the model to support other needs.

Programming Models for Object-Oriented Glue

The object model provides a definition for the objects connected by the glue

The programming model for OO glue must define what the run-time will be connecting—in other words, what the objects are and what mechanisms they will use to communicate with one another. This is fulfilled by the particular glue's object model. In this sense, the object model (at least the part of it that applies to the glue) is a subset of the programming model. Rather than focus on the many details and issues of object models, our purpose is to look at some of the key issues they address, including

- How to specify an object interface
- Whether to separate the object interface from the object implementation
- How the component interface is published so that it is accessible to the user of an object
- How inheritance is handled
- How to send messages to an object
- How failures are exposed

Object model is related to approach

The relationship between the object model and the programming model depends partly on the approach to objectifying the enterprise system. As we saw in Chapter 3, you can objectify

- Individual components within a standard program structure
- The communications mechanisms between standard program components
- The communications mechanisms between objectified program components
- The entire system, so that component boundaries no longer exist

The first approach implies that each component conforms to one of the object models provided by the various OO languages, such as C++ and Smalltalk. The video store example in Chapter 2 illustrates a simplified version of a language-based object model.

OO programming languages can provide object models for components

As shown in Figure 6-2, in this approach, even though the internals of some components are objectified, the communications mechanisms observe a conventional architectural structure. This means that the glue is based on a conventional programming model, and the object model does not apply to it. (Note that in this approach, various components can easily conform to different object models.)

Components with internal object models still communicate conventionally

The second approach treats the components themselves as objects and requires an object model to glue them together, as shown in Figure 6-3. Such a model is provided by specifications like DCOM and CORBA. This kind of object model can be simpler than the language-based models because it needs to specify only the inter-

When components act as objects, the glue requires an object model

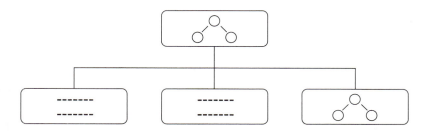

Figure 6-2 Objectifying within a conventional architecture

**Figure 6-3 Objectify-
ing the architecture**

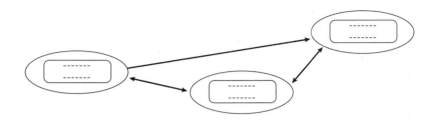

faces of objects, and not their internals. Both DCOM and CORBA are intended to be language-neutral. Although each provides its own interface definition language, these are much simpler than full-fledged OO programming languages.

*Systems can have
OO components and
OO glue with a tra-
ditional program
structure*

The third approach may appear to yield a totally objectified system—a set of client/server components written in OO programming languages that communicate with one another by means of COM, CORBA, or some other OO glue, as shown in Figure 6-4. However, it's important to note that although the programs consist entirely of objects and the glue conforms to an object model, the architecture is still not seamlessly OO all the way. It still specifies clearly defined program components communicating with one another.

*In this type of system, the two object
models are still distinct*

In terms of object models, the important thing to note about this third approach is that the component object models and the glue model are distinct from one another. The glue model is concerned with only the interfaces of the system components, and the language-based models are concerned with only the internals of

Figure 6-4 OO modules in an OO architecture

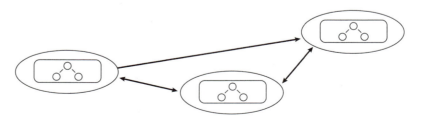

those components. It is possible that such a system can be based on several object models—one for the glue and different ones for the independent client/server components, depending on the OO languages used to create them. It is also possible to use two or more glues, each based on a different object model, and then deal with the interoperability issues among the glue object models. An example of this is the COM/CORBA *Internetworking* from OMG. However, with such an approach, the components will never be able to fully collaborate across the object environment even if they are all implemented in a single OO language because of the dissimilar glue object models. For example, if a C++ object supports a DCOM feature not expressible by CORBA, a CORBA C++ client object could not invoke the feature.

In the fourth approach, program boundaries disappear and the system functions seamlessly as a series of object interactions. A single object model accounts for both internals and communications. From a programmer's perspective, there is only a single object model to learn and use. The program boundaries typical of 3GLs disappear. Though practical concerns (such as performance and network-failure handling) may still force the programmer to recognize process and machine boundaries, the conceptual object model itself imposes few boundaries. The common-language approach discussed below often allows the vendors to come close to this Nirvana.

When program boundaries vanish, a single object model accounts for internals and communications

Communications Levels

Another factor that influences the programming model is the **communications level** between the system components. This depends in large part on the degree of similarity between the components that are communicating. Similarity is measured by what the two communicating components have in common. There are three general possibilities—they can share the same buffer for-

The right communications level depends on the similarity between two components

mat, the same communication middleware, or the same programming language. Figure 6-5 shows three possible approaches. The greater the degree of similarity, the more services can be provided by the underlying system and the fewer services have to be programmed into the individual application components. This can yield three important benefits.

- A higher level of abstraction for the programming model
- More sophisticated tool support
- A more seamless runtime operation

Similar components can communicate at a high level of abstraction

By "a higher level of abstraction," we mean that the developer can be more concerned with implementing the actual business rules that govern the application under development and less concerned with the nuts and bolts of implementation, which the system can take care of.

This leads to better tool support

This abstraction leads to more sophisticated tool support, which means the development tool suite doesn't have to provide a lot of low-level tools and can instead focus on high-level issues. For example, the tools can debug the business logic instead of the calls to the networking software.

Figure 6-5 The three communications levels

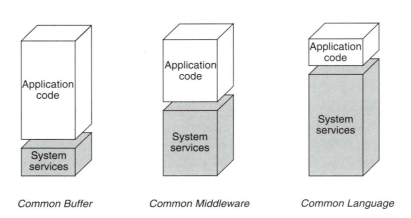

Common Buffer   Common Middleware   Common Language

By "a more seamless runtime operation," we mean that less translation is required between the communicating partners. Not only is the performance better, but also the entire client/server system acts more like a single integrated component rather than like multiple pieces.

They can also achieve more seamless runtime operation

But, of course, there's no such thing as a free lunch. Gains in level of abstraction, tool support, and seamlessness often come at the cost of a less heterogeneous system. Because the gains and losses come as trade-offs, client/server developers should carefully consider which communications level to use.

Gains in abstraction level and seamlessness affect system heterogeneity

- The common buffer approach is used when the programs communicating are dissimilar.
- The common language approach is used when the programs are highly similar.
- The common middleware approach covers the territory in between.

In the common buffer approach, the client and server agree privately on a buffer format and the communications middleware ships the buffers back and forth between them. The application code has to take care of low-level duties, such as data marshaling and data conversion between the client/server platforms. Although the abstraction level is low, this is the most heterogeneous approach. For instance, by using common buffers, a Visual C++ client can interact with a mainframe server program written in Assembler. The languages or vendor products used to implement the client and the server are not restricted.

Using a common buffer is the most heterogeneous approach

In the common middleware approach, the client and server are connected by a middleware service, such as an object request broker (for example, Orbix, ParcPlace Distributed Smalltalk, and DCE RPC). Here the abstraction level is higher, which enables more tool

Common middleware enables more tool support and higher productivity

support and higher productivity. Data conversion and marshaling are done by the middleware, and interaction across languages is possible. However, there is less heterogeneity than with the common buffer model. For example, consider a Visual C++ client that interacts with a legacy server program for which the source code is not available. In this case, it is more feasible to use the common buffer approach. It would be rather difficult to generate middleware stubs for legacy code without source and then link-edit the legacy code with the stubs.

A common language provides the highest level of abstraction

The common language approach takes advantage of both client and server being implemented in the same language. Example systems are Java RMI, IBM VisualAge Smalltalk Distributed and 4GL, and Forte. The goal is to provide high local/remote transparency (not just at the syntax level, but also at the semantics level) that masks the existence of underlying middleware as much as possible.

Using a common language enables programs to be created in a single address space and then partitioned into pieces to run on different machines without source code changes. Because the client and server follow the same protocols, additional services are available (for example, distributed garbage collection) that are infeasible with common buffers or common middleware. The common language approach achieves the highest levels of abstraction and productivity, at the expense of some heterogeneity.

These models will coexist

It's not likely, or even desirable, that any of the models mentioned above could so dominate the industry that the others become unnecessary. In addition to pushing the boundaries of each communications level, vendors need to ensure that the models coexist and are complementary.

Different Kinds of Glue

A number of different glues are in common use. These depend partly on the function of the components being linked. From a usage perspective, we can think of glue as falling into two major categories.

Glues fall into the categories of local and distributed

1. Local (desktop-oriented) glue
2. Distributed (client/server and server/server) glue

Local glue often links desktop components on the same machine. Distributed glue links the clients accessed by end users to the components that provide services, as well as components that typically request services of one another without a direct relationship to a client. These two categories of glue, similar in many ways, also show a number of significant differences.

Local Glues

We define local glue as the software runtime, programming model, and supporting tools that integrate objects on the same machine. The primary objective of such glue is to present the computer user with an integrated view of desktop components from different sources. The majority of its use is in desktop environments. However, nondesktop usage, such as gluing local components on a server, is also permitted by some local glues, such as JavaBeans. This is not yet a common practice, but its very existence is the reason why we did not name this section "Desktop Glues."

Local glues normally integrate client objects on a desktop

This section indicates the key features common to local glues rather than all the details of individual glues. Local glues are supported by such technologies as COM/OLE, OpenDoc, and Java-Beans/InfoBus. Although we draw our examples from the existing technology, we do not attempt to provide comprehensive coverage

We look at local glue in general, rather than the details of specific models

of it because it is constantly changing. We want to provide a framework for understanding local glue in general rather than an understanding of any specific implementation of it.[1]

For readers who want to dig deeper into implementation details, many excellent publications are available on the latest incarnations of the desktop technologies. *The Essential Client/Server Survival Guide,* 2nd edition, goes into great detail on them. (See *References and Further Reading.*)

What Does Local Glue Do?

On a componentized desktop, components can act as logical clients or logical servers

With the increasing complexity of desktop systems and the desire of users for increasingly rich function on the desktop, there is a tendency to componentize desktop function into different modules. Going back to our logical model of client/server systems (Chapter 1), we recall that any component that requests services is considered to be acting as a client, and any component that provides these services is acting as a server. Thus, the componentized desktop can be considered a small-scale client/server system, with all components running on the same machine.

On the ideal desktop, different vendors' components inter-operate seamlessly

A single desktop system can consist of modules supplied by different vendors, operating in different ways. The goal of the componentized desktop—and of the local glues—is seamlessness. In the

---

[1] A case in point is the rapid evolution of Microsoft's OLE technology. Originally used to designate Object Linking and Embedding technology, the term became identified with the OLE controls that grew out of that technology. Eventually, the controls were renamed ActiveX controls, and the term *OLE* was returned to its original usage of designating a technology. If we discussed OLE in detail, we could easily create confusion over what usage of the term we really intend. Therefore, we discuss the technology only to illustrate our concepts. We use the term *OLE* to refer to the general technology, not to the OLE (now ActiveX) controls.

ideal world, the user can move seamlessly back and forth between very different applications as though they were all parts of a single integrated application.

The benefits extend to the vendors, as well. By componentizing the functions provided by their applications, they stand a better chance of sharing common components among various applications—their own applications and those of other vendors that are enabled for the same type of glue. For example, a text editor, a spreadsheet, and charting tools could all share the same spelling checker. From the vendors' standpoint, this can reduce the size of the overall executables they provide, as well as the effort required to produce them.

Shared components can reduce the overall size of executables

Object technology is well established in desktop applications, as we saw in Chapter 3. Therefore, it should be no surprise that object-oriented local glues are currently the most pervasive type of OO glue. Historically, OLE and OpenDoc originated from the need to provide desktop integration—in other words, the need for local glue. However, they have now gone on to provide functions beyond this need. This has occurred because the vendors have leveraged the recognized names of these specifications to introduce more powerful, although related, functions. However, the core of such specifications is still their capability for desktop integration, and this is where they excel.

Though local glues extend beyond the desktop, their initial goal was desktop integration

As the vendors work to extend the local glues across networks into a broader client/server space, they are also working to provide interoperability among the different specifications. It would provide many advantages to users in terms of getting different vendors' components to work together. However, at the same time as this interoperability is evolving, there is no sign of any camp giving up its own specification and endorsing one of the others.

Vendors promote their own specifications while looking at interoperability

Desktop Object Models

Technologies that specify local glue also specify an object model

OLE, OpenDoc, and JavaBeans all provide a different object model that defines what it is they are integrating. Some key concerns shared by these object models are discussed below.

Specify an object interface Most local glues separate the interface from its implementation by using some version of an OO interface definition language to specify the interface. OLE uses ODL (Object Definition Language), OpenDoc uses CORBA IDL (Interface Definition Language), and JavaBeans uses a restricted form of the Java language.

Publish and communicate the interface specification OLE stores the information in Type Libraries and requires that an interface querying mechanism, the "IUNKNOWN" interface, be supported by all OLE objects. OpenDoc uses the interface repository defined by CORBA. JavaBeans supports an "Introspection" mechanism, which makes it possible to determine, at runtime or with a development tool, which properties, events, and methods Java-Beans supports.

Handle inheritance Both OpenDoc and JavaBeans support multiple inheritance of interfaces through subclassing. OLE, on the other hand, supports a mechanism called "aggregation," which means providing a component that encapsulates the services of other objects. When a request is sent to the component, it delegates the execution responsibility to the objects it encapsulates. Inheritance is achieved through a web of pointers to objects that aggregate different interfaces.

Event handling Event handling is the mechanism by which components (objects) "raise" or "broadcast" events that happen to them in order to notify other components that have an interest in those events. Notified components typically perform some function in response to the notification. Generally, there are two kinds of events. System events, such as "window close" or "resize," are defined by the glue itself. Component-defined events, such as "spell checker finished," are at a higher level that generally has to do with the services provided by the component.

Compound Document Service

Some form of compound document service is essential to the operation of local glue. This is the service that enables different documents (such as text, graphical data, and images) to be integrated as one on the desktop. In addition to event handling, key considerations of the compound document service include containment relationships and layout.

This service integrates documents created by different applications

Containment relationships specify what documents contain other documents and how they are contained. A contained document can be embedded or linked. Embedding means that the contained component's data is actually stored within the containing compound document. Linking means that the contained document is stored in its own file, to which the containing document contains a reference. The containment relationship also defines what functions the contained and containing documents must support.

It specifies the containment relationship of documents

Layout deals with the question of how to share the screen real estate among the documents. This includes services for handling appropriate behavior when the component is activated or the container is resized. Some layout mechanisms can also include such details as menu bar merging.

It also specifies how screen real estate is shared

Persistence and Data Format

Local glue often supports some means of object persistence

Persistence is the mechanism for storing the state of components in a nonvolatile place. This is such an important topic for all varieties of OO enterprise systems that the next chapter is entirely devoted to it. For the time being, though, we can briefly summarize its implications for local glue. The component state is stored in the context of the container and in relationship to other components. OLE supports a "compound file" architecture that essentially supports a file system inside a file so that multiple document types can be stored and managed in a single file. OpenDoc and JavaBeans have similar functionality.

It also defines a unified data transfer mechanism

Data format is a related issue. For different documents to participate in drag-and-drop, clipboard, and linking, the glue must define a unified data transfer mechanism, which defines data formats and APIs to support movement of data.

Scripting

Scripting is the means of dynamically binding components at runtime

Scripting is the way in which the glue dynamically binds the components together at runtime. Scripting has to be dynamic because desktop components are provided by different vendors at different times, are brought to the users' desktops in different sequences, and form different combinations based on the individual user's needs. It would be impossible to compile all the possible usage combinations during glue system development, when most of the relevant information is not available.

The glue must provide a scripting service

The scripting service provided by the glue defines what a scriptable object must provide at runtime, including a list of objects it contains and operations it supports. OpenDoc provides an open scripting architecture, which is an extension of the Macintosh's Apple Events. OLE defines OLE Automation objects and corresponding mechanisms to invoke their methods from a scripting language such as BASIC. JavaBeans uses Java as the scripting language.

Distributed Glues

Distributed glues can connect clients with servers and servers with servers. Logically, we have been considering the requesting program as the client and the program providing services as the server, and in this sense, server/server connections are essentially client/server connections. Therefore, we do not distinguish between server/server and client/server glues in our discussion. We'll start by examining the contrast between distributed and local glues. From there, we'll take a look at the messaging models that the glues implement. Then we'll turn to the different object server types discussed in Chapter 5 and see how they can be glued to clients, as well as to one another.

Distributed glues connect clients with servers and servers with servers

Distributed Glues versus Local Glues

There is a key difference between the local glues and the distributed glues discussed in this section. The former focuses on the interactions among components on a single computer; the latter focuses on the interactions among components over a network. In addition to the need to consider the significantly slower speeds of a network, the developer and distributed computing infrastructure also need to provide appropriate recovery and resynchronization mechanisms to protect against failure of software, hardware, or network. The discussion of distributed computing in Chapter 1 goes into more detail about the challenges of managing system communications across a network.

Distributed glues manage interaction over a network

As we saw in the previous section, some vendors have begun to extend their desktop integration specifications to the network. However, this means that they are attempting to extend a single-machine desktop component model to encompass all the requirements demanded by complex heterogeneous networked

Extending a desktop model to encompass network require-ments is difficult

computing environments. Such a strategy is fraught with problems and trade-offs.

Desktop and distrib-
uted glues can have
mismatched func-
tionality

For example, there can be a mismatch of functionality. In an embedded distributed system with no user interface, the rich screen space negotiation protocol supported by a desktop oriented glue is completely useless and introduces unnecessary overhead.

Services associated with the glue can also have different requirements. For example, directory service is typically used to access the associated attributes of objects. A *person* object, for example, can have a number of attributes, such as the person's surname, telephone numbers, electronic mail address, postal address, computer account, and authentication information (that is, his password or X.509 certificate). A distributed directory service adds many concerns, such as security, availability, and update propagation, that a local directory on a single machine often does not worry about.

Vendors address
desktop and network
concerns in the same
object model

Consequently, vendors are trying to separate the concerns specific to desktop glue from concerns specific to distributed glue while ensuring their interoperability by sharing the same object model. In the case of OLE and DCOM, the model is COM. In the case of OpenDoc and ORB, it is the CORBA object model.

Variations of the
same local glue can
also follow this ap-
proach

Even variations of the same local glue follow such an approach. For example, while ActiveX and OLE are both based on COM, they provide different services to developers. COM provides the low-level object-binding mechanism that enables objects to communicate with each other. OLE runs on top of COM to provide high-level application services, such as linking and embedding, to enable users to create compound documents. ActiveX, on the other hand, provides a substantially slimmed down infrastructure to enable controls to be embedded in Web sites and respond interactively to events. While OLE is optimized for end-user usability and integration of desktop applications, ActiveX is optimized for size and speed.

Messaging Models

One of the most important features of distributed glue is that it must be responsible for transmitting messages between objects in different address spaces. For the purposes of our discussion, OO glues can be divided into three categories, based on the type of messaging they support.

Distributed glue can provide three types of messaging

- One-way messaging
- Two-way messaging
- Queued messaging

One-Way Messaging The one-way messaging model resembles a 3GL subroutine call and is most often seen when a legacy system is involved in the communication. As shown in Figure 6-6, the calling program on the left hand side invokes the program on the right hand side, which does some processing and then returns control to the program on the left. There is no message invocation from right to left during the execution of the called program. The called program terminates when it returns to the calling program. All parameters are passed by value (i.e., copying the values of the parameters); there is no use passing any object references to the

One-way messaging resembles a 3GL subroutine call

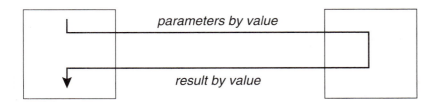

Figure 6-6 One-way messaging

Figure 6-7 One-way messaging with proxy object

called program if it isn't going to invoke methods on those references.

Tools on the calling side can provide proxy objects

Tools on the calling side can provide proxy objects, which make the crossing of program boundary syntactically transparent, as shown in Figure 6-7. However, the caller of the proxy needs to prepare all parameters by value and can not expect a reference from the called program (because the called program terminates at the point of returning). This forces application developers to be aware of the program boundary whether or not such awareness is necessary. If the components of such an application require repartitioning, alterations in the code are likely to be required.

This model includes most database server glues and conventional transaction server glues

The one-way messaging model includes most database server glues, such as ODBC and stored procedure invocation, and conventional transaction server glues, such as CICS ECI. It's easy to understand why these glues do not require any callback—the called side traditionally doesn't include an object model, and so the computation can't involve objects on the calling side by sending messages to them.

Two-way messaging corresponds better to the typical OO messaging pattern

Two-Way Messaging Figure 6-8 shows the process involved in two-way messaging. Two-way messaging corresponds better to the typical OO messaging pattern. Consider a group of objects collaborating with each other. If they are partitioned into client and server address spaces, it's quite common to have the thread of execution go back and forth between the two spaces. Because the thread of execution is nothing more than the sequence of messages, this means that there is two-way messaging between the client and the server spaces. It's even possible that during a thread of execution, an object may receive messages from the very objects it sent messages to. For example, a sending object might pass a reference to itself, and the receiving object might invoke methods on the sending object in order to access the required parameters. This is a common technique used to avoid sending a large object over the network when only a few of its attributes are needed.

Figure 6-8 shows a single logical thread of execution through the client and server spaces. (Physically, this thread may be implemented with multiple operating system threads on each side.) However, there is no reason why the logical thread of execution couldn't fork additional logical threads. This can result in multiple logical threads of execution weaving between the client and the server spaces.

The two-way model is not restricted to a single logical thread

With the two-way model, proxy objects are created on both sides, as shown in Figure 6-9. (In this light, it's interesting to note that one-way messaging is actually a more limited subset of two-way messaging.) The interaction among objects in a single address space and objects across different address spaces can be more transparent

With the two-way model, proxy objects are created on both sides

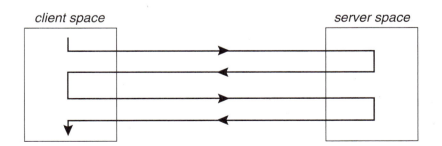

client space   server space

Figure 6-8 Two-way messaging

Figure 6-9 Two-way messaging with proxy objects

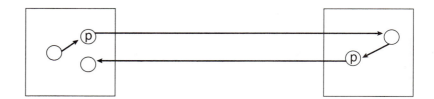

with the support of appropriate tools. Native server glues, object TP monitor glues, and some peer-to-peer TP monitor server glues (such as APPC for CICS) make use of this model.

Queued messaging generally handles unstructured or semi-structured data

Queued Messaging Asynchronous messaging systems have store-and-forward capabilities and generally handle unstructured or semi-structured record-oriented data. Most popular commercial implementations of asynchronous messaging support the notion of message queue. Data can be forwarded immediately or stored for later delivery, as necessary.

Queued messaging often supports transaction capabilities

Asynchronous messaging systems often provide some form of data integrity/transaction capability. A queue can be thought of as a resource manager. It can implement simple single-phase commit to an associated disk so that the get/put operations to a queue represent a single unit of work. A queue can also support external coordination protocols, such as XA, and let an external transaction coordinator, such as a TP monitor, coordinate its commit. When a TP monitor is involved, sending a message to a queue can be part of a transaction that exhibits the full ACID properties.

It works for inter-enterprise and intermittent communications

IBM's MQ Series, Microsoft's Message Queue Server (MSMQ), and DEC's DECMessageQ are just a few of the messaging products available in the market. These systems are good for interenterprise connectivity and intermittent communications. Application developers can set up queues at the program boundaries for communication as shown in Figure 6-10. Both one-way and two-way messaging can be supported. Alhough message queuing middlewares usually can connect many types of client and server, some of them, such as MQ Series and Falcon, have a strong association with transaction servers. We will discuss such association at the end of the section on OO transaction server glues, later in this chapter.

Extending Existing Systems

Often, client/server systems use a mixture of one-way and two-way messaging models mostly because so many systems are built by extending existing systems. In Chapter 3, we discussed integrating OO and enterprise computing by objectifying different aspects of the system. Nirvana—the ultimate system—would treat the entire enterprise network as a single computer. In such a system, objects would collaborate with each other without any program boundary and two-way messaging would be pervasive.

Ultimately, the entire enterprise network could work as a single computer

However, such an enterprise system could only be built from scratch, and in the real world, people can seldom build large OO enterprise systems from scratch. Adding objects to an enterprise system normally means extending the existing 3GL system. Figure 6-11 shows a sample approach. The existing 3GL system is represented by the transaction on the right, which includes both a procedural and an OO component. The extension to the existing system is represented by the distributed objects on the left. When an OO transaction is added as an interface to the 3GL transaction,

Objectifying normally means extending the existing system

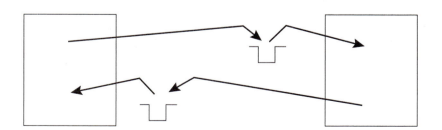

Figure 6-10 Asynchronous (queued) messaging

Figure 6-11 Extending an existing system with objects

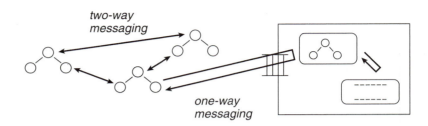

the rest of the system can view the 3GL transaction as a single object. Objects elsewhere in the system can access the services of the 3GL transaction through the OO transaction.

Such systems usually combine one-way and two-way messaging

Such systems are likely to display a mixture of one-way and two-way messaging. On the left side, which represents new OO development, communication can use two-way messaging. As we cross the legacy system boundary, the one-way messaging model becomes pervasive. Because the legacy portion of the system can't recognize OO concepts, it can't send messages back to the OO side of the system, even if it is wrapped with an OO interface. The OO client still sees a one-way model when interacting with it.

OO Database Server Glues

OO database server glue connects the client with an OO database server

The first of the OO distributed glues we'll look at is the glue that connects OO database servers to clients. The database server glue (OO or not) is usually provided by the database or a portable layer that sits on top of the database communication mechanism. Two examples of such portable layers are open database connectivity (ODBC) and Java database connectivity (JDBC). OO database server glue is similar to the non-OO database server glue, except, of course, that it connects the client with the OO database server. (Remember, ODBMS, O-R DBMS, or an RDB with OO stored-procedure support are all OO database servers.)

Typical database glue consists of APIs that provide the following services to connect the client to the database server.

Database glue provides several services

- Data manipulation, such as SQL, or an OO programming language serving as the data manipulation language (DML)
- A TP-Lite model that controls commit and rollback and gives the user a way to declare units of work
- A way to invoke logic (stored procedures) in the database

With OO stored procedures, the most common model is the one-way, call-return model that allows the client to call the server logic like a remote procedure call. This is the model of the RDBMS stored-procedure mechanism that OO stored procedures evolved from. In this model, the call is usually short (not in minutes or hours), the beginning of the call signals the beginning of the transaction, and the return of the call commits the transaction. There is often no need to declare explicitly such transactions in the application code.

OO stored procedures commonly follow the one-way, call-return model

ODBMSs, such as GemStone, support two-way messaging between the object client and server. This model, less frequently seen, can be thought of as a long-running stored procedure. A client establishes a session with a dedicated service program on the server that executes the server objects. This service program interacts with the client until the client disconnects. The number of instantiations of the service program (in different processes or threads) is the same as the number of active client transactions because the processes/threads are used to implement transaction boundaries. These could be multiple messages back and forth between a client and a server during a single unit of work. If both the client and the server support the same OO programming language, common language support can be provided. Such is the case with the GemStone Smalltalk implementation.

Two-way messaging is supported by some ODBMSs

The long-running, multiple-message model is useful in some OO applications

The long-running, multiple-message model can be beneficial in certain OO applications. For example, a client might need to interact with a complex server business model (such as an insurance company). The server can instantiate the business model in memory (including objects representing policy holder, policy terms, beneficiaries, properties, past claim history, and so forth) and then allow multiple messages before tearing the model down and storing it back to disk. The alternative would be to use a pseudo-conversation model that involves storing and restoring the object model between invocations.

Database locks affect whether to keep the object model instantiated

If locking is not a big concern, keeping the object model instantiated can improve performance. On the other hand, holding locks on the object model for each client can impede server concurrency and hurt the system throughput. This is one of the reasons why most ODBMSs support the optimistic locking mechanism, which allows concurrent updates on the same object model. At commit time, a resolution process determines whether there are conflicts among updates and how to resolve the conflicts. If the updates do not create any conflict (for example, if they affect different unrelated objects), they can all be committed without extra processing. If the updates do create conflicts, additional processing is required to "resolve" the conflicts. The term *optimistic* comes from the approach's optimistic hope that such a condition is true most of the time.

Other server types can use this model

The potential benefits and limitations of the long-running, multiple-message model are not exclusively associated with the database server. Most server types that we discussed can leverage this model and enhance their performance.

O-R DBMS glues are likely to be extensions to existing RDB glues

Just as O-R DBMSs are extensions of traditional RDBMSs, the glues for the O-R DBMSs are likely to be extensions to existing relational database server glues. The O-R DBMS is newer than ODBMS and is still evolving. Therefore, anything we say about it here is subject to change as the technology continues to unfold.

In typical O-R DBMS glue, the SQL programming model is extended with additional syntax to accommodate object method invocations in a conventional SQL statement. Methods defined on a class (or functions defined on an abstract data type, depending on the terminology) are invoked as the entire SQL statement is being executed. Because the database server executes the methods, the execution happens on the server side. The messaging model is a one-way SQL call from the client to the server. Multiple calls from a client can participate in a single unit of work, just as in a traditional SQL call.

Typical O-R DBMS glue extends the SQL programming model

Because the database defines its own object model, which is different from any object models supported by the client-side programming languages, the highest level of communication achievable is the common middleware level.

O-R DBMS glue communicates at the common middleware level or below

OO Transaction Server Glues

This section discusses the glues for two types of OO transaction servers: the objectified transaction servers and the new object TP monitor. OO transaction glues provide a wide variety of services.

OO transaction glues provide a variety of services

- They define the transaction scope.
- They find and invoke the transaction objects on the network.
- They provide information needed by the security system.
- They propagate the transaction context and support commit coordination.

Defining the Transaction Scope Transaction scopes can be declared implicitly or explicitly. Explicit declaration provides more control and flexibility for developers while implicit declaration is simpler to

Transaction scopes can be declared implicitly or explicitly

program. Objectified transaction servers, such as CICS, often implicitly associate the transaction scope with the program that the client invokes in the TP monitor.

The Microsoft Transaction Server supports implicit declaration

The Microsoft Transaction Server, an object TP monitor, also supports implicit declaration from a programmer's perspective. Transactions are implemented by setting a property of an application component (COM object). If the component is marked "transactional," the transaction server creates a transaction around its processing. Invoking a transactional component starts the transaction; returning from it ends the transaction. Systems such as OTS, Encina, and TUXEDO achieve the same results by explicitly specifying begin and commit statements.

The glue must find and invoke the transaction objects

Finding and Invoking the Transaction Objects on the Network The glue must provide a way for the client to locate the transaction server and then tell the server which transaction program it wants to interact with. This can often involve a directory service, such as the CORBA naming service for OTS or the Windows Registry for Microsoft Transaction Server. After the program is activated by the server, the target object inside the program is located and sent a message to start the execution. To locate the transaction objects, CICS uses the server's system ID and the transaction name. Encina uses a transactional RPC (remote procedure call) handle.

Providing Information Needed by the Security System This often includes authenticating the user, checking the access rights, and sometimes encrypting the transferred data. For a more detailed discussion of object security, see Chapter 12.

The glue must propagate the transaction context and support commit coordination

Propagating the Transaction Context and Supporting Commit Coordination Along the chain of invocations, the glue must propagate the transaction context so that receivers of the messages know they are participating in a transaction and can act accordingly. At commit/rollback time, the glue also carries the negotiation traffic between the transaction manager and the resource managers. The OTS sidebar gives more details on how this works. It is important to recognize that OTS is being used as an illustration of the general architecture. We use OTS because it has an established standard at this time. Other OO glues, such as DCOM, provide similar functionality.

A key distinction between the transaction server and the database server is that the transaction server allows multiple distributed transaction programs to participate in a single unit of work. With such capability, the transactional glues not only connect client and server, but also connect multiple programs or objects running on the servers.

Some transactional glues connect server programs as well as client and server

Transaction servers, such as CICS, make a distinction between the two types of glue: the glue that connects the nontransactional world (clients) to the transactional world (servers), shown by (a) in Figure 6-12; and the glue that connects the transaction programs inside the transactional world, shown by (b). The following discussion refers to Glue (a) as client/server glue and to Glue (b) as server/server glue.

Transaction servers distinguish between non-transactional and transactional glues

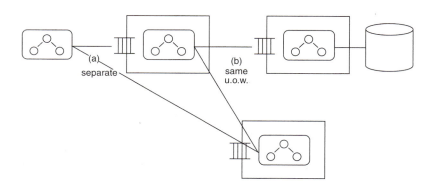

Figure 6-12 Transaction server glues

How OTS Works

As an illustration of OO transaction server glue, let's take a conceptual look at how an implementation of the OTS could work. The OTS sits on top of the ORB and adds transaction semantics to the ORB (a nontransactional, two-way messaging glue). The figure shows how this would work in a simple configuration. Object A on the client side begins the transaction scope by issuing a message to the OTS service that glues client to server. OTS creates a "transaction context;" we can think of this as an identifier that uniquely identifies the transaction. Object A invokes methods on Object B, which in turn sends a message across the network to Object C. Because Object B has now been included in the transaction, the transaction context created by the OTS is passed along with the message so that Object C knows it will be providing services as part of the transaction. Although Object C typically doesn't have "recoverable states" (data that is affected by committing or rolling back a transaction), it can, as part of the transaction, interact with a database that does have recoverable states.

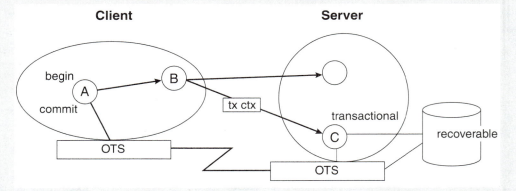

By passing the transaction context to the database, Object C enables the database to connect to the server-side OTS and register that it's doing work for the transaction. When Object A is ready to commit the transaction, the OTS services across the network negotiate with each other using a two-phase commit protocol to ensure that all the resource managers involved (in this case, databases) are committed or rolled back together.

Conceptually, the OTS may sound straightforward, but under the covers, a lot of work occurs to ensure that nothing goes wrong in any possible circumstances. For example, logs are created so that in the event of a crash, the recovery procedure can return the entire system to a consistent state. This is the key value a distributed transaction object service can provide. Without the presence of this function in the glue, much more application code would have to be written in order to account for all kinds of error detection and recovery states. When the transaction coordination and recovery functions are provided by the underlying system, application developers can focus on the real functions required of the application.

In the case of CICS, the key difference between the two types of glue is the server/server glue's capability to coordinate multiple transaction programs and resource managers. The presence of a transaction coordinator on the server side makes the difference. The server program located between (a) and (b) in Figure 6-12 can use the glue to invoke other transaction programs while still maintaining a single unit of work.

Server/server glue can coordinate multiple transaction programs

In contrast, if the client program tries to invoke two transaction programs, as shown in Figure 6-12 (a), there will be two unrelated transaction scopes (units of work) instead of one. Even though the client programmer may have transaction commands (such as "begin" and "commit") to work with, in reality, a transaction never begins on the client. When a client makes a transactional call, the transaction begins when the server component is invoked. From such a client's perspective, a TP monitor is just like a resource manager (for example, a database manager) when it comes to transaction boundary control. Invoking two transaction programs in two transaction servers will not be coordinated, just as invoking two

Clients and client/server glue often do not coordinate transactions

databases is not coordinated as discussed in the sidebar on page 134.

CICS uses a variety of glues

Since CICS was designed as a centralized server and later evolved to support client/server configurations, it's not surprising that CICS has separate client/server and server/server glues. The External Call Interface (ECI) is provided as the primary glue that enables clients to access the transactional world. Once inside, CICS supports Distributed Program Link (a RPC-like mechanism) as the primary glue for communication among transactions. (Note that there are many other CICS-supported mechanisms, such as APPC, but they are not as widely used.)

Modern TP systems often use a single glue model

Modern workstation-based TP systems tend to be designed with distributed processing in mind. They often use a single glue programming model to achieve both kinds of connection. For example, Encina uses transactional remote procedure calls (TRPC), TUXEDO uses TxRPC (TUXEDO RPC), and OTS uses ORB messaging.

A system supporting client-side transaction coordination can use a single glue

There are two ways for a system that includes distributed transactions to use a single glue. The first is to make the client and server sides alike in functionality by having the transaction system support client-side coordination. This is the approach taken by OTS and Encina. If client and server can both perform the same task with regard to transaction coordination, then a single glue programming model can be used for both client/server and server/server interactions.

A system can use a single glue if it does not let application code combine transactions

The second way to allow a distributed transactional system to use a single glue is to avoid expressions in the programming model that would allow the code to combine different transactions. Avoiding expressions that combine transactions eliminates the issue, so once again, the client and server look the same and a single glue programming model can be used. For example, although the Microsoft Transaction Server (MTS) is similar to CICS in not supporting client-side transaction coordination, it can use a single glue (DCOM) because transaction declaration is done by setting a property of an application component instead of coding.

Because the MTS associates transaction control only with the server transaction object, a client must end a transaction on the same server object it began on. Therefore, a client can never create a single transaction that goes to two different servers. Note that database vendors commonly use this same technique. From a client perspective, the scope of a transaction to a database is associated with the connection to the database. There is no way for a client to combine two SQL statements into a single transaction unless they are all going to the database through the same connection.

Database vendors commonly associate transactions with a server component

In general, client-side support for transaction coordination requires more infrastructure on the client side but enables more transaction-related logic to reside on the clients. However, the trade-off is that, with more infrastructure and more logic on the clients, system configuration and management become more complex.

Client-side transaction coordination has advantages and drawbacks

Message queuing glues are often provided in association with transaction servers. CICS, Microsoft Transaction Server, Encina, and TUXEDO all provide asynchronous queuing mechanisms that can be used between servers, as well as between clients and servers.

Message queuing is often associated with transaction servers

From a transaction manager's perspective, a persistent message queue can be considered a resource manager that participates in a transaction. Because the queue is persistent, writing to such a queue is similar to updating a database, and the queue can also

Message queues can be persistent resource managers

participate in the two-phase commit protocol just like a database. If the application is asynchronous in nature, using message queuing glues can enhance the overall system responsiveness and performance.

A transaction can conclude after it writes to a persistent queue

As an example of asynchronous messaging glue, Figure 6-13 shows a transaction that updates a record in the payroll database and initiates a check to an employee by writing to a persistent queue between the transaction program and the check processing system. The transaction concludes successfully when the write to the queue returns, and the server is free to process the next request. Without an asynchronous glue, the transaction would have to wait until the check processing system actually cut the check before it could conclude.

This works only with asynchronous applications

Note that asynchronous message queuing works only if the application allows asynchronous processing. For example, in an ATM withdrawal transaction, queuing the update to the bank database would not work because the delay could allow a second withdrawal to be processed before the first withdrawal was asynchronously updated. This could enable a user to withdraw money from an account that already had insufficient funds.

Figure 6-13 Asynchronous messaging glue

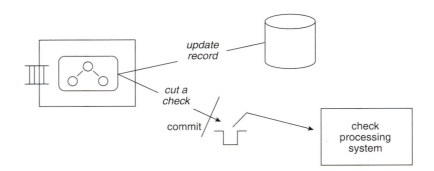

OO Native Server Glues

This section discusses the glues that connect clients to objectified native servers, with or without distributed transactions. Objectified native server glue supports the partition of logic by connecting objects running across the network. In such a system, the glue usually provides a mechanism to activate the server when a message is sent to a server that is not up and running. Once connected to the client, the server-side glue service resolves the destination object for the message.

Objectified native server glue connects objects running on native operating systems

Different types of native server glues provide different levels of support. For example, ORBs provide common middleware-level support. Common language-level glue support is available from Java RMI, Forte, and IBM Smalltalk Distributed. All of these glues support two-way messaging—because the native server tends to communicate with the client for longer periods of time than database and transaction servers, one-way messaging is usually insufficient.

Different native server glues provide different levels of support

Though message queuing glues are commonly mentioned in conjunction with transaction servers, most of them can be used independently. When application semantics are asynchronous, message queuing glues can be used on objectified native servers.

Message queuing glues can be used on objectified native servers

It's common for providers of native server glue to also provide transaction support as an extension to the native messaging system. By adding transaction semantics to the object-to-object messaging, this glue strives to preserve the OO model as much as possible while gently introducing the benefits of transaction processing. Instead of adding object technology to the existing transaction infrastructure, as in the objectified transaction server, this approach adds transactions to the existing OO messaging system.

Native server glue can also provide transaction support

The resulting system often feels more like a sea of transactional objects (Figure 3-4) than a series of objectified 3GL transactions (Figure 3-3).

We call the server in such a system an objectified native server with distributed transactions, as discussed in the OO Native Servers section of Chapter 5. Examples are OTS (discussed in the sidebar on page 134) and Forte's Transactional Object-Oriented Language (TOOL) support.

Transaction and Object

Transaction nesting and concurrency control are related to OO glue

Transaction nesting and concurrency control are not glue issues per se; they are related to issues of transaction support in the glue. Both issues have a direct effect on transaction coordination. In a distributed environment, the glue service is essential for supporting transaction coordination across the network. That's why we have chosen to wait until now to discuss these two issues.

Nested Transactions In some transactional environments, it is possible to nest transactions inside one another. These nested transactions allow a subtransaction to be trapped and retried using an alternative method, without causing the main transaction to fail. In this way, they allow more granular transactions.

Transaction nesting can be very useful when objects support transactions

When objects meet transactions, people find another reason that nested transactions are attractive. It has to do with the modularity of objects. As shown in Figure 6-14, an OO enterprise system can have many objects distributed across the network, invoking each other's methods to get the job done. Objects A, B, and C can be supplied by different vendors and developed at different times and places. If an explicit transaction declaration method is used and no nesting is allowed, a developer of a reusable object (for instance,

Object C) could not use any transactions in his code. Otherwise, if anybody (for instance, Object A) who uses his object also declares transactions, nesting would occur because now we have a begin/commit pair (in Object C) nested in another begin/commit pair (in Object A). Because nesting is not supported, this could constitute an error.

Note that just avoiding transactions in one's own objects may not be enough. This becomes clear when you consider Figure 6-14. Though Object B does not contain any transactions, Object A can not safely use them, because Object C, which was not developed by the provider of Object B, may contain transactions. Unless every object provider guarantees that no transaction is used in the implementation of the objects, the user of the system cannot be sure that no nesting will occur. In addition to the fact that such disclosure runs counter to the encapsulation of objects, it would be extremely difficult to enforce. Allowing transaction nesting eliminates any such requirement and thus becomes attractive, especially in an OO client/server system.

Transaction nesting removes the need to disclose whether objects contain transactions

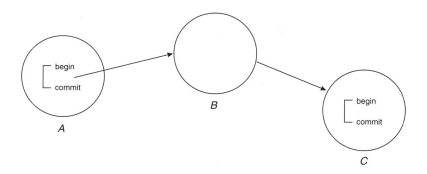

Figure 6-14 Transactions nested within objects

In practice, flat transactions are more common than nested ones

In practice, nested transactions have not been widely used. For a long time, Encina was the only system that supported them, until various OTS implementations began to reach the market. The complexity of the nested model often presents problems for developers. Also, the vendors have yet to demonstrate a high-performance production application system that uses a lot of nested transactions. Until that day arrives, flat transactions are the proven high-performance solution. As long as the transaction declaration method is implicit, nesting cannot be expressed and flat transactions must be made to work with objects. This is the approach taken by the Microsoft Transaction Server.

In a distributed environment, objects often run concurrently

Concurrency Control In a distributed environment, objects often run concurrently and each can potentially have multiple threads of control running through it. If concurrent execution were not allowed, we would essentially be serializing the execution of all computers on the network, which eliminates the performance gains of running multiple computers concurrently.

OO concurrency control management protects clients from interfering with each other

OO concurrency control management seeks to protect resource objects that can be accessed by multiple concurrent clients so that the clients won't interfere with each other. For this purpose, locks are placed in front of the shared objects. To access a shared object, a client must first obtain the right kind of lock. The Object Management Group (OMG) defines this kind of concurrency control with its Object Concurrency Service (OCS), which supports both transactional and nontransactional modes of operation.

OO lock management requires special attention with transactions

Although OO lock management can exist whether or not transactions are involved, it requires special attention in systems in which OO transactions are present. Figure 6-15 shows a nested transaction case in which Transaction 1 invokes two subordinate transactions. Transaction 2 obtains a write lock and updates a record in

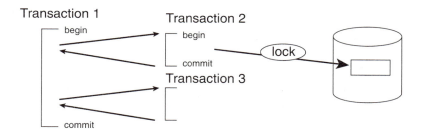

Figure 6-15 Locking with nested transactions

the database. In ordinary situations, the lock would be released when Transaction 2 commits. However, in this nested transaction, the lock cannot be released because the parent, Transaction 1, can issue a rollback, which would change the unlocked record back to its original value. If the lock is released prematurely, when such a rollback occurs, the incorrect transient value may be used by another process. The concurrency mechanism provided by the system to manage the locks needs to work hand in hand with the transaction manager to preserve the correct behavior.

Glue and Application Development

Real-world application development requires programmers to understand the factors that go into OO glue and also understand that the different types of glue do not exclude one another. Because applications need to interface with multiple systems, and because systems often contain different types of servers, application developers must often use multiple glues. After our discussion of object persistence in the next chapter and the Internet/Web in Chapter 8, we will be prepared to look at OO enterprise development, in Chapter 9. That chapter will fit what we've learned about OO clients, servers, and glue into the development process and show how development tools help to create end-to-end OO client/server applications.

Application developers must often use multiple glues

Summary

OO glue ties the objects in the system together. OO glues can require their own object models, which can be distinct from the object models used by the components they connect. Three glue communications levels are possible, depending on the degree of similarity between the communicating components.

- Common buffer
- Common middleware
- Common language

OO client/server glue can be local or distributed. The local glues integrate client objects on a desktop. The distributed glues connect clients with servers or servers with servers.

Distributed glues can support a variety of messaging models—one way, two way, or queued. Distributed OO glues can be classified according to the types of servers they connect to.

- OO database server glues connect the client with OO database servers and are likely to be extensions to existing database server glues.
- OO transaction server glues must find and invoke the transaction objects, propagate the transaction context, and support commit coordination.
- Objectified native server glues connect objects running on native operating systems across a network and can sometimes provide transaction support.

Various issues, such as nested transactions and concurrency control, affect the OO glues.

7

Object Persistence and Sharing

Any interesting application is likely to exhibit persistence. Persistence provides long-term or permanent memory to ensure that the effects of an executing program last beyond the end of the program execution. Persistence is related to information sharing between applications, but the two are not necessarily coupled together. Some stand-alone programs have persistent effects but don't share information with other programs. Likewise, programs can share information without the information being persistent. (For example, two programs can establish a common middleware link and talk between themselves without involving a service that enables persistence.) However, most forms of sharing do involve persistence, for the following reasons.

Most forms of information sharing involve persistence

- Most interesting programs involved in sharing are designed to have persistent effects.
- Programs that need to share information may not all be running at the same time. There is a need to store information somewhere so that sharing does not require all parties to be running at the same time.
- Sharing often requires services that enable participating programs to maintain the integrity of the data they are sharing, to prevent them from becoming confused. For example, locking prevents two programs from writing to the same record at the same time.
- Databases conveniently group the necessary sharing services with persistence support. By using a database, you automatically get both services.

OO technology changes some persistence issues

Object-oriented technology does not eliminate the need for persistence and sharing, but it does change some of the issues involved. That's why we devote this chapter to the issues of how to make objects persistent and how to share them.

Object Persistence Concepts

The main objective is to move objects in and out of a data store

The primary objective of object persistence is to bring the objects in and out of a data store for persistence and sharing purposes. The data store can be as simple as a file or as sophisticated as a set of multiple databases. Both conventional databases (relational and hierarchical) and object-oriented databases (ODBMSs) are possible.

Object schema, data schema, and mapping are the three key elements

The three fundamental elements of object persistence are shown in Figure 7-1.

- Object schema
- Data schema
- The mapping between the two sets of schema

Object schema define object structure on the application side

Object schema define the structure of the objects on the application side. For example, a *Customer* object can contain an *Address* object and a *PhoneNumber* object. The object schema defines which

Figure 7-1 Fundamental elements of object persistence

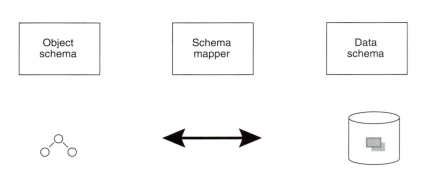

elements of the structure need to be made persistent and shared. In an object-oriented development environment, the object schema can be specified with programming language tools that directly define the object classes, or with a language-independent tool that can define data objects for multiple languages. Object schema can also originate in the analysis and design phase of application development. Object relationships can be captured and then refined to obtain object schema.

Data schema define the structure of the data stored in the data store. Different data stores have different data schema definition facilities. For example, a relational database would use the SQL data definition language (DDL) to capture the data schema. The *Customer* and *PhoneNumber* information might be stored in one relational table and the *Address* information might be stored in another. In contrast, an ODBMS might use an object oriented DDL (often a derivative of an OO programming language) to specify the data schema. The OO DDL specifies objects instead of tables.

Data schema define the structure of stored data

Schema mapping is the magic that makes it all work. In OO programming, objects are often represented in the data store differently than they are represented in the application. Therefore, it is essential to have an object persistence mapping mechanism to transfer the objects between the two representations. The concept is simple: Take the instances of objects described by the object schema and map them in and out of the data records described by the data schema. Figure 7-2 shows an example using a relational database as the data store. Object messages cause the mapping mechanism to issue SQL statements to the relational database. The database returns table rows to the mapping mechanism and it maps the rows to objects for the application.

Schema mapping brings them together

Figure 7-2 Schema mapping with a relational store

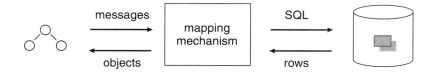

messages

objects

mapping mechanism

SQL

rows

Four basic elements need to be mapped

Four basic elements need to be mapped.

- Object identity: Persistent object identifiers must be created and managed so that they can be used to locate data in the data store.
- Object attributes: The persistent attributes (instance variables) of an object need to be mapped to and from the records in the data store.
- Object relationship: Persistent objects can have references pointing to each other. They represent relationships with associated cardinality and semantics (such as containment, in which the deletion of a container object means the deletion of contained objects). Such relationships need to be preserved in the mapping.
- Inheritance: The object inheritance hierarchy needs to be mapped to the corresponding data schema in the data store

Schema mapping may sound simple, but implementation is difficult

However simple the concept, actual implementations tend to be complex and difficult. Granted, the mapping portion can be made easier with an ODBMS, because both object schema and data schema describe objects and both can be highly similar. Unfortunately, such an ideal situation seldom exists. First, most databases in use are not ODBMSs. In fact, IMS, a hierarchical database, still stores the majority of the world's operating data. Relational databases come in second and ODBMSs are far behind.

Mapping simplicity requires the use of a single OO language

Even with an ODBMS, mapping simplicity can be achieved only if you restrict both application programming and DDL/DML to a single language (thus a single object schema). As soon as the ODBMS starts supporting clients written in more than one OO programming language, mapping between different object schemas is required.

Real-world ODBMS cases that use a single object schema actually do achieve a performance edge because simple mapping requires less computation and less management. However, most enterprise applications do not have this luxury. Therefore, we will focus our discussion on implementations you are more likely to run into, and we will return to ODBMSs toward the end of the chapter.

Simple mapping is not often possible

Transparency

The transparency of the persistence mechanism determines how much the application code needs to explicitly control the object persistence. The more transparent the mechanism, the less code the application programmer needs to write to deal with persistence.

A transparent persistence mechanism means less code to write

An issue related to transparency is the issue of single-level stores vs. two-level stores. A user of a single-level store does not have to be aware of whether the object is in memory or disk. In contrast, the two-level store separates memory from persistent storage.

Single-level data stores are more transparent

In a single-level storage system, the memory and the persistent storage are treated as one big persistent virtual store (thus the "single" level). IBM's OS/400 and some ODBMSs support such a model. Though they often let you use transaction boundaries to flush a memory cache to the data store, most of the object storage management is transparent to the programmer. A developer would create persistent objects just as he would other objects. In this model, objects generally obtain persistence in one of the following ways.

In a single-level store, memory and persistent storage form one virtual store

- By declaration in the class definition, which can include inheriting from a persistent superclass or some other way to mark the class definition
- By being referenced by some persistent collection
- By sending the object a message to mark it persistent

Once the object is marked persistent, storage and retrieval to and from the data store is done transparently.

In a two-level store, objects are explicitly staged from a data store into memory

In the two-level store, with memory separated from persistent storage, the object must be explicitly staged from a database (or file) into memory, and vice versa. For example, most OO programs using a relational database fall into this category. Here the developer needs to explicitly issue commands to send the objects into the data store and bring them back out from time to time, which is why it's less transparent.

Transparency is not unique to ODBMSs

Though many ODBMSs support a high level of transparency, it is not a property unique to ODBMSs. An ODBMS can be thought of as an application implemented on top of a file system, which uses the services from the file system to support persistence. It is certainly possible for a mapping tool on top of a file system or a relational database to support the single-level storage model by doing the work that an ODBMS does.

What's Already There

The difficulty of object persistence and sharing is related to the existing system

The difficulty of object persistence and sharing is largely controlled by what exists in the system already. From an architectural standpoint, there are four possible cases, which we present in order of increasing difficulty.

1. New object, new data
2. Old object, new data

3. New object, old data
4. Old object, old data

New Object, New Data This is the situation in which you develop a new system from scratch. It is the easiest case. There is no existing data or existing OO applications. Most OO tools support this scenario. Automatic generation of the data schema based on the object schema is quite common. Unfortunately, not many projects have the luxury of starting from scratch.

"New object, new data" is the simpest

Old Object, New Data This situation can occur when an existing application needs to access a different back-end data store (for example, when changing from a file system to a relational database). For example, a company that bought another company would probably want its existing applications (representing the existing business practices) to operate on the data of the acquired company.

"Old object, new data" is more involved

The old object, new data situation can also occur when adding some persistence to the objects of an existing application. This situation is relatively rare because persistence and sharing affect the fundamental architecture of any application, and it is not easy to "transform" an existing application to add persistence. Most often, serious re-architecting is required. By the time everything is said and done, the whole activity would resemble the new object, new data scenario above. From a historical standpoint, data has been around far longer than OO technology and OO applications. This further decreases the likelihood of having to add persistence to old objects.

New Object, Old Data This is the predominant case, in which an organization starts to introduce objects into the information system. Most businesses have a wealth of existing data. The new OO appli-

"New object, old data" is pervasive and often complex

cations need to fit in and work with the existing data. Several factors can affect the difficulty of this situation.

Changing data schema is difficult for legacy data

- The more freedom to adjust the existing data schema, the easier it is to handle this case. Unfortunately, most legacy data is closely associated with one or more legacy applications. Changing the data schema often requires changing those applications, as well. Thus the degree of freedom is limited.

Simple, organized data schema simplify object mapping

- The simpler and more organized the existing data schema, the easier to find the right mapping to the objects. For example, a relational database with normalized tables and few indices is easier to map than one with a lot of denormalized tables and indices.

Data abuse makes mapping harder

- The less the data has been "abused," the easier it is to do the mapping. For example, in an abused IMS database, the interpretation of a segment might depend on certain records in it. If the third byte is an *S*, the following nine bytes are interpreted as a social security number. If it's a *D*, the following seven bytes are a driver's license number and the two bytes following that are the abbreviation for a state.

  The problem with using the data this way is that the data schema is not captured in one place. The programs that use the database in the above example also implicitly define part of the data schema. This makes it difficult for a tool to provide assistance. It's hard enough for a tool to deal with complex legacy schema when it's well-defined and completely captured. It's almost impossible to create a tool that can reverse-engineer the implicit schema definition by analyzing applications that abuse the data.

Complexity increases when legacy data can be updated by multiple applications

- From a sharing perspective, the complexity increases when legacy data is accessed by multiple applications. Read-only data requires less coordination than read/write data shared among new OO applications and existing 3GL applications.

When the data can be updated by existing applications, care must be taken to make sure that transaction semantics are preserved when OO programs are added to the system.

- The number of different databases is also a factor. It's easiest if the persistent mapping code needs to deal with only one database. Then the persistence concerns are similar to those involved in developing a fat client for a single database. However, if multiple databases are involved and the persistence mechanism needs to update more than one of them at a time, maintaining data integrity becomes complex.

The number of different databases is also a factor

Old Object, Old Data Every scenario described so far turns into this scenario after the first release of the application. Understandably, things get even more difficult in this case. Now, instead of having the freedom to adjust the object schema or the data schema, programmers are tied to the existing schemas of the legacy OO applications. As always, it's easier when both the object schema and the data schema are explicitly captured and kept in single places. However, because of the complexity involved, no tool on the market does an adequate job of automatically generating the mapping involved in this scenario. Most tools require extensive human intervention to arrive at a reasonable mapping.

"Old object, old data" is the most difficult

Basic Tool Support

For the four object persistence and sharing cases discussed, the basic idea behind tool support is rather simple. Tools should assist in capturing and managing the object schema and data schema and in generating the mapping code. However, some of the conditions we discussed can make the tool issues more complex and interesting. The tools are also affected by the constant quest for better per-

Tool support is needed for all three fundamental areas of object persistence

formance. We can start by looking at the relationship of tool support to two of the elements of object persistence shown in Figure 7-1: the object schema and the data schema. Then we can consider the additional tool support topics of upper CASE linkage and record mapping services.

Additional tool-related issues, such as transaction models and performance, affect the entire persistence scheme. These are discussed in later sections.

Tools and Object Schema

This section discusses some of the characteristics of the left-hand side of Figure 7-1, the object and object schema side, that can affect the tool support. We'll focus on the issues of type information handling and garbage collection.

Object types and data types must correspond

Object Types Persistence and sharing mechanisms need to map the object types to and from the data types supported by the data store without losing information. When we look at the left side of Figure 7-1, we see the object schema, which in our discussion, is implemented with an OO language. In general, OO languages support two categories of data typing: dynamic and static.

OO languages can support static or dynamic data typing

Languages such as C++ are statically typed. In this case, the type information of the application object schema is captured in the program declaration. This reduces the need for tools to supplement the type information. On the other hand, languages such as Smalltalk are dynamically typed. That is, the type information of the object may not be known until runtime. At development time, the program may not fully specify the type of a persistent object. Often, additional tools are required to let the developer specify the static typing information necessary to support the mapping.

Garbage Collection Many of the more dynamic languages, such as Java and Smalltalk, support automatic memory management. The memory management system performs garbage collection. When an object is no longer referenced by any other object in the system, garbage collection reclaims the space it occupies. This poses some interesting issues.

Dynamic languages support garbage collection

First, the garbage collector moves objects around. Therefore, application developers must take care to "lock" an object at a fixed memory location if a reference to it is passed to the outside for persistence processing and there is a chance that garbage collection can happen during that processing. Because the locked objects are beyond the scope of the garbage collector, it is also the developer's responsibility to free the locked objects to prevent memory from overflowing with obsolete objects.

The garbage collector moves objects around

Note that this is a generic problem. It can occur in any situation involving an out-bound call that passes a memory pointer to an object. When that happens, it becomes necessary to handle the complications arising from garbage collection.

Memory pointers passed to the outside need to be protected

Garbage collection must be integrated at the language and persistence levels. For example, in Figure 7-3, the object in the lower right of the box representing the application is being garbage collected. What should happen to the record in the data store that corresponds to the object? Should it also be removed? If the application on the left-hand side is the only one that was referencing the record, it may be desirable to remove the record.

Garbage collection must be integrated at the language and persistence levels

However, detecting who is referencing a data record can be a sizeable task. Essentially, we are asking the persistence mapping mechanism to extend garbage collection semantics to a data store that may not support the same storage management policy. Because

Detecting references to a data record can be nontrivial

Figure 7-3 Garbage collection and persistence

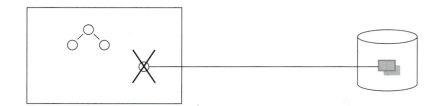

this is difficult, most tools take the easy way out and ask the user to explicitly free the records.

Explicitly freeing the records introduces new problems

However, this solution introduces a new set of problems. First, the persistence mechanism is less transparent because additional code must be added around the objects that cross over the persistence boundary. Also, without support from the underlying system, it's easy to cause referential integrity problems. For example, a program can delete a record that it's no longer using without knowing whether other programs are still using it.

These issues in automatic memory management help to explain why active research and development is still going on in this area.

Tools and the Data Schema

Persistent data stores take many forms

Persistent data stores can take many forms.

- File systems: flat files, record-oriented files, such as VSAM, and so forth.
- Conventional databases: relational databases or hierarchical databases like IMS.
- OO databases: GemStone, Versant, ODI, and so forth.
- Programs: Application code that sits between the persistence mechanism and the database. This includes transaction programs that run under the control of a TP monitor.

This section discusses the general considerations of persistent data stores and their relationship to the required persistence mapping mechanisms. "Databases," on page 177, compares the pros and cons of the types of databases available for objects.

File Systems These offer the simplest form of persistence. The objects are mapped into a file. Most of the time there is little sharing because file systems are usually not very good at handling sharing. This form of persistence is good for simple operations that do not involve concurrent access from multiple users. It's also useful for storing large objects, such as multimedia data, where the performance advantages of the raw file system are useful for real-time playback.

File systems offer the simplest form of persistence

Conventional Databases When objects are mapped to a conventional store, such as a relational database or IMS, the object identifiers often contain key information for search and retrieval of the data that constitutes the object. The simplest relationship, shown in Figure 7-4 (a), is when a single object maps to a single data entry in the database. In this case, a data entry can be a row in a relational table or a segment in IMS. The attributes (instance variables) of an object map to the fields in the data entry.

Conventional databases enable search and retrieval of objects

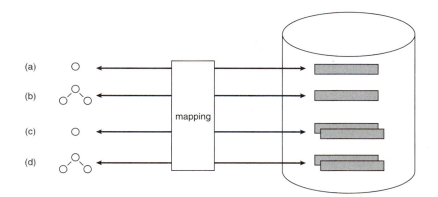

Figure 7-4 Objects mapped to a conventional database

Figure 7-5 A persistent object mapped to two database tables

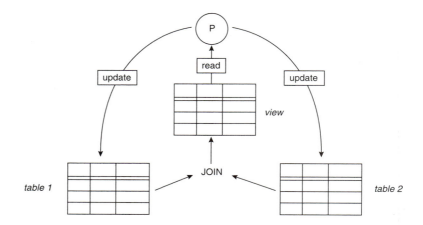

Figure 7-5 A persistent object mapped to two database tables

Multiple objects can map to a single data entry, or vice-versa

Things get more complicated when multiple objects map to a single data entry (b) or a single object is stored in multiple data entries (c). For example, in a relational database, when a persistent object, Object P, is mapped to a view of two base tables (Figure 7-5), the read and write operations may have to take different paths. The read operations can work directly with the view, which is obtained by performing a JOIN between the two base tables. However, most commercial relational databases do not support update operations on views. Therefore, the mapping code would have to map the updates on the persistent object to update operations directly on the base tables. This scenario is one of the simplest cases. For example, if table 1 is not a base table but another view on other tables, complexity can increase very quickly.

Multiple object mapping to multiple data entries is even harder

Figure 7-4 (d) shows multiple objects that map to multiple data entries. This scenario compounds the issues of the scenarios we have discussed so far. It is the most complicated case and can be difficult to specify and maintain.

Mapping objects to an ODBMS can be straightforward

Object-Oriented Databases Mapping objects to an ODBMS can be straightforward if what the ODBMS stores is similar to what is defined by the OO language, as shown by Figure 7-6. Because of the

Figure 7-6 Mapping objects to an ODBMS

mapping

low impedance mismatch between the database and the application program, the mapping can be thin and high-performance. Such mapping support is often provided by ODBMS vendors as part of the database.

Often when an ODBMS is used, the objects required by an application are not stored exclusively in the ODBMS. ODBMSs are relatively new and currently cannot handle amounts of data as large as that handled by relational and hierarchical databases. For example, Figure 7-7 shows some objects stored in an ODBMS and others in a conventional database. The mapping layer takes care of storing and retrieving objects to the right places.

Applications often do not store objects exclusively in ODBMSs

Mapping services that can do multiple data stores are available from third party vendors other than the database vendor. A naive mapping service might map to the lowest common denominator of

Mapping services for these situations give varied performance

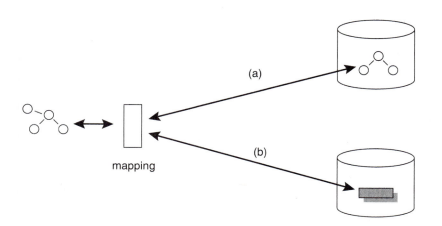

Figure 7-7 Mapping objects to an ODBMS and conventional database

(a)

(b)

mapping

(a) and (b) and force the high-speed route (a) to go through a lot of unnecessary code. This would diminish the performance advantage of storing objects in an ODBMS. A more sophisticated tool could take advantage of the ODBMS by using thinner and more direct mapping to obtain optimal performance. Care must be taken to evaluate mapping service tools. The best way is to build some benchmarks and test cases, and to try it out yourself.

The legacy gateway approach puts the ODBMS on the middle tier

Figure 7-8 shows a **legacy gateway,** a third data mapping option commonly supported by ODBMS. In this scenario, the path between the application object and the ODBMS is still the same as shown in Figure 7-7 (a), although the path to the legacy data is through the ODBMS legacy data gateway. In this case, the ODBMS is often positioned on the second tier of a three-tier configuration and provides data caching and replication for the third-tier data stores. The application sees only the ODBMS and the persistent objects stored in the ODBMS.

The legacy gateway works best when data does not require real-time update

In general, such a configuration works well when the legacy data is read-only or does not require real-time update. Transferring the legacy data down to the middle tier and then to the client requires one more layer of processing than if the client directly accesses the legacy data. The legacy gateway approach produces better perfor-

Figure 7-8 ODBMS with legacy gateway

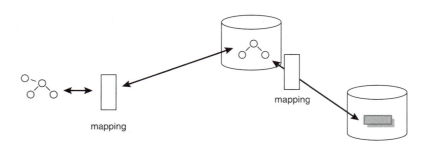

mapping

mapping

mance only when data can be transferred and mapped to objects once and then used multiple times or by multiple clients.

Writing updates back to the legacy database has similar perfor- mance characteristics. If real-time update is required for the legacy database on the third tier, the operation will require updating the middle-tier ODBMS, committing the changes, and propagating the changes to the legacy data store. In contrast, a client directly con- nected to the legacy data store can avoid the processing on the middle tier. Still, a legacy gateway can be efficient when updates can be batched (thus not requiring every update to be propagated to the legacy data store right away). By batching the updates, the client can update the middle-tier database more efficiently than going straight to the legacy data store.

Using a legacy gate- way involves an extra layer of pro- cessing

Note that using an ODBMS to stage legacy data also requires a fair amount of management effort. Maintaining two databases and keeping them synchronized is never an easy task. If the scale of the application is such that multiple ODBMSs on the mid-tier are re- quired, the cache synchronization issues among the mid-tier ODBMSs and the legacy data store can make application design and management even more complex.

Using an ODBMS to stage legacy data in- creases the manage- ment effort

Programs The target of the persistent mapping mechanism can also be a 3GL program that sits between the objects and the data store, as shown in Figure 7-9. Often, these programs are legacy transac- tions running on the host system that can be invoked through some communication middleware. This is a common approach be- cause many corporations do not like to have clients that can access data directly. They would rather have the client programs go through a layer of code (often implemented as transactions) that controls access and executes logic to enforce certain business rules. The code can be simple or can perform a lot of computation.

The target of the per- sistent mapping mechanism can be a 3GL program

Figure 7-9 3GL Program as target for persistent mapping

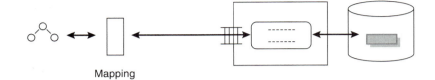

Mapping

The mechanism maps between intermediate program and application objects

In these cases, the communication often occurs at the common buffer level and the persistent mapping mechanism takes care of mapping between the data stream supplied by the program and the persistent objects in the application. Note that there is also some mapping between the intermediate program and the data store. Though the program is written in 3GL, it avoids most of the issues discussed in the section on conventional databases above.

Each data mapping target presents different tool challenges

Challenges of Mapping Each type of target for data mapping presents different challenges for the persistence mapping tools. Even within the same general category, different data stores can present different characteristics to the programmers who actually have to implement the mapping support. For example, to map to an IMS database, one would have to

- Select the glue that enables access to IMS
- Map the object navigation to the IMS querying mechanism, which requires the use of the IMS segment search arguments (SSAs)
- Once the segment is located, map the data fields to the object attributes

All of these can be different from what is required to map to a relational database. Therefore, it's important to carefully weigh the claims of any vendor that offers object persistence and sharing tools. Even if a vendor claims to have a flexible architecture, that doesn't mean you can make the vendor's product work with the data store that you actually want.

Upper CASE Linkage

As described earlier, the object schema is a fundamental element of object persistence. Accurately capturing the object schema is an essential first step to persistence. One way to achieve this is for the developer or development team to manually enter the schema. Another way is to reverse engineer the object schema from the existing objects in the application code. These two ways are both time- and labor-intensive. If the project uses upper CASE (for instance, analysis and design) tools, deriving the schema using the information captured by the tools can be a better way.

Upper CASE tools offer a way to capture the object schema

When the application calls for new objects and new data, upper CASE tools can provide input to both the lower CASE programming tools and the persistence mapping tools to generate a lot of the application automatically. Because many persistence decisions, such as performance tuning, can be related to the intended use of the objects, the analysis and design information can streamline the job of producing quality persistent objects.

With new objects and new data, upper CASE tools are especially useful

However, even in the case of new objects and new data, code generation based on an upper CASE tool can still present challenges. If the flow of input is only one way—from the analysis and design tools to the persistence mapping tools—the developers should not augment or alter the persistent mapping code after it has been generated. Otherwise, the persistence schemes can easily fall out of sync with the analysis and design.

Analysis and design must stay in sync with persistence schemes

When objects and data are not altogether new, even greater hurdles stand in the way of using upper CASE tools to capture the object schema. Unfortunately, the real world is full of existing objects

Despite the hurdles of using upper CASE tools, they can still help

and data. Unless the legacy data and objects are created with the same tool and they have been kept in sync with the design-level information, the upper CASE approach could still require a lot of effort. However, this is no reason for being discouraged. If you don't have the luxury of integrating upper CASE tools with the persistence mechanism, you can still try to exploit portions of this approach. For example, single-directional generation is better than no generation. However, when bi-directional linkage exists, both forward from the upper CASE tools to the persistence mapping tools and backward from persistence to CASE, it can yield rewards in productivity and ease of maintenance.

Record Mapping Services

Vendors supply record mapping between objects and the buffer in and out of the store

One of the services that every vendor supports is record mapping between objects and the data in the data store. The primary concern of such a service is to map the data types between the two sides—for example, mapping a database string to a string object representing a customer name. After the records in the database have been mapped to the record-level objects, they can be used to compose application-level objects (such as a customer object), as shown in Figure 7-10. Often, tools will use existing record definition to generate the mapping. Some common examples of this are relational database data catalogs; legacy screen definition, such as BMS and MFS; and COBOL copy books. Parsers that can parse the files containing the information or tools that can access the information source are used to retrieve, analyze, and supply the input to the mapping mechanism. Some IS shops store the data schema in a data dictionary that is independent of the databases and programming languages they use. Such a data dictionary can be a good place to obtain the record-level typing and structure information.

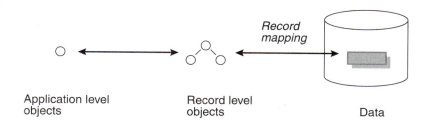

Figure 7-10 Record mapping between objects and data store

Record mapping

Application level objects

Record level objects

Data

Transaction Models

In order to coordinate multiple data accesses, the object persistence and sharing mechanism often needs to surface the notion of trans-actions to the user. When this is the case, the issues affect object schema, data schema, and mapping mechanism alike. We will look at several approaches. The simplest approach is surfacing the data store's transaction model. Some tools prefer to present their own transaction model: others use transaction models from transaction managers.

The persistence mechanism often needs to surface the notion of transac-tions

Surfacing the Data Store's Transaction Model The simplest case is to surface the data store's transaction model to the user in a format that makes sense from a client perspective. Figure 7-11 shows this case. A begin transaction on the client side maps to a begin trans-action on the data store (usually through the handle obtained when the connection is established with the data store) and a com-

It's simplest to sur-face the data store's transaction model

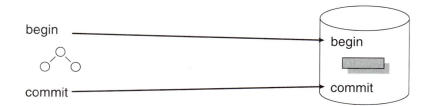

Figure 7-11 Surfacing the data store's transaction model

begin

commit

begin

commit

mit on the client side maps to a commit on the handle. In this case, the persistence mapping tool does not provide any additional transaction semantics beyond what the data store already provides. It just faithfully presents what's there.

This approach yieds simplicity and fidelity

The advantages of this approach are its simplicity and fidelity (that is, what the database supports is what you get). It is easily to support and is relatively lightweight. Its fidelity is high because it does not attempt to do any mapping on top of the data store's transaction model. The disadvantage of this approach is that if the application accesses two or more back-end stores with different transaction models, the application programmers have to be aware of and deal with the differences.

Some tools present their own transaction model

Tool-Provided Transaction Models Some tools attempt to provide their own transaction model. This model can be syntactically or semantically different from the one supported by the data store. If the tool is just providing some syntactic sugar with no real functional difference, this does not affect the simple case described above. However, if the tool introduces semantic differences, the user must be aware of them before using the tool.

Without understanding how the tools handle transactions, it is easy to write the wrong code

For example, some tools permit syntax for nested transactions on the client side, which most data stores do not support. In this case, the tool must either implement full support for nested transactions in the mapping code or support some, but not all, of the functionality and impose restrictions on nesting that takes place in the application code. The latter is often the case. Without a full understanding of the tool-based restrictions, it is easy to write code that executes differently from what is intended. This also means that whoever maintains the application code must understand not only the code itself but also the interpretation of nesting and the restrictions introduced by the tool.

Concurrency Control Other issues raised when a data mapping tool provides a transaction model involve concurrency control. Does the tool allow multiple concurrent transactions? If so, what kind of isolation policy does it have? Remember that the ACID properties of the transaction must be maintained.[1]

Concurrency control is a related issue

Figure 7-12 shows a case in which the application program forks into two execution threads and each thread creates a transaction using the transaction syntax supported by the mapping tool. The transactions proceed to exercise the persistent objects and eventually cause changes to the data store.

Each application thread can create a separate transaction

Questions arise about the relationship of the two object transactions. If they are independent of each other, then two commit scopes must be created on the data store side to support the semantics. Isolation also has to be enforced on the object side to prevent the transactions from interfering with each other. Because they run in the same address space, the system cannot enforce isolation (as with many TP monitors). Therefore, a certain level of programming discipline is often required.

The issue is whether these transactions are independent

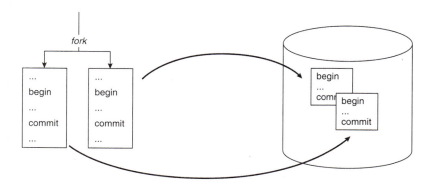

Figure 7-12 An application with two concurrent transactions

---
[1] For a discussion of the ACID properties, see page 79.

If not, their relationship can be ambiguous

If the two object transactions are not completely independent, their relationship must be specified. Can they form any nesting relationship? Do they have two different commit scopes or just one? If there is only one commit scope, which commit on the object side triggers the commit on the data store side?

Most tools with their own transaction model permit only one transaction at a time

Because concurrency issues are not easily resolved, most tools that provide their own transaction model take the easy way out and restrict the user to one transaction at a time. That is, they serialize all the transactions in a program on the object side. This is hard to enforce because it's often difficult to determine whether two transactions are going to overlap until execution time. This kind of serialization is also more restrictive than most other relational database access support. It's quite common for a fat-client program to read data from one relational database, process it, and write the output to another relational database. Moreover, such serialization can limit concurrency and reduce system performance, especially if the objects are to be executed on a server.

Multiple resource managers—data stores—require coordination

Coordinating Multiple Resource Managers This is another issue for tool-provided transaction models. In this case, data stores are the resource managers. Although persistence mapping tools often allow you to access more than one data store, most of these tools cannot support the necessary transaction coordination among the data stores to guarantee data integrity. This is because two-phase commit protocol support and the necessary recovery service is far too much for a persistence mapping tool to provide. Note that using an ODBMS gateway does not make this problem go away because ODBMSs are resource managers, too, and do not coordinate external resources. As mentioned in Chapter 5, when we talked about OO transaction servers, the transaction manager is usually what supports two-phase commit. It's not normally a task that databases are up to.

Because most data-mapping tool vendors are not in the business of providing transaction managers, many of them have opted to support only single-phase commit even when they permit an application to update multiple resource managers. Data integrity can be lost when something goes wrong between the updates, like a program crash.

Most data-mapping tool vendors support only single-phase commit

Another option for coordinating multiple resource managers is to have the data mapping code try to administer the two-phase commit and implement the necessary recovery service. However, doing this essentially duplicates most of the services of a transaction manager. Implementing this in a robust and high performance way is difficult for a persistence mapping tool vendor who is not specialized in transaction management. Also, if the mapping code provides some transaction manager functionality, it will be difficult later on to run any application code that uses such functionality under the control of the transaction manager; in that case, it would be unclear who would provide the coordination service.

Complications arise when the mapping code provides some transaction manager functionality

Having a concept of a transaction that is independent of the data store is not a bad idea. Not providing the support to back it up is where the trouble lies. In a real-world application, objects can be stored in multiple data stores with different transaction models. Rather than requiring the user to understand all the transaction model differences, it is desirable to provide an object-level transaction model that works with all the data stores. Without such support, the transparency would weaken and the objects and the data stores would be unnecessarily coupled.

Transactions independent of the data store need to be supported

Providing this object-level transaction model is in line with the desire to present persistent objects independent of the data stores they are retrieved from. Most users of persistent objects do not

An object-level transaction model supports object independence

want to have to understand where an object is stored and change the way the object is treated based on where it is stored.

Transaction Managers

A transaction man-ager can be used to support transactions in persistent objects

In the face of the problems raised by fitting object persistence into transaction models, one easy way out is to use the services of a transaction manager. Such transaction managers as Microsoft Transaction Server, CICS, Encina, TUXEDO, and OTS can provide the necessary transaction service for persistent objects. Running the code under the control of a transaction manager solves many of the transaction problems raised already. Figure 7-13 shows an example of objects and mapping code running under the protection of a TP monitor. Instead of taking on the responsibilities of a transaction manager, the mapping tool generates code to leverage the transaction manager in the TP monitor.

With proper integra-tion, the transaction manager can be transparent

If the integration between the object environment, the persistence mapping tool, and the transaction manager is done properly, the user of the persistence mapping tool does not have to be aware that the code runs under the control of a transaction manager. The IBM VisualAge 4GL product provides an existence proof. There are several things the persistence mapping tool needs to do to take ad-

Figure 7-13 Objects and mapping code inside a TP monitor

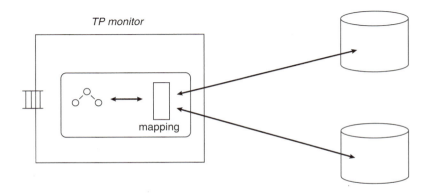

vantage of the transaction manager services. The most important ones fall under the categories of transaction handling, XA support, and resource manager lock management.

Transaction Handling Instead of inventing a new transaction model, the persistence mapping tool simply adopts the transaction model supported by the transaction manager. Instead of issuing its own commit or rollback directly to the data store resource managers, the mapping code asks the transaction manager to do it. Because the data stores are handled through the transaction manager, the transaction manager now knows how to coordinate access to them.

A tool can adopt the transaction manager's transaction model

The persistence mapping tool must not require the application to issue explicit connection statements to a resource manager such as a database. Explicit connections are not needed because most TP monitors take over the management of the connections to optimize performance. A common optimization is to allocate a pool of connections at start-up time so that the application code does not have to pay the connection cost at runtime. It can actually be harmful for an application to issue explicit connection requests to the database when running under the control of a TP monitor. Not only can performance suffer, but more important, the transaction manager is not given the chance to shake hands with the database to establish the necessary context for transaction coordination.

The tool must not require explicit database connection statements

In Encina and OTS, in which nested transactions are permitted, the transaction manager also takes care of mapping the nested transaction operations to operations on resource managers that don't support nesting.

Nested transaction issues can also be handed

XA Support XA is an industry-standard transaction coordination protocol. When resource managers follow this protocol, the transaction manager can coordinate the transactions that involve them. CICS, Encina, and OTS are all capable of using XA, and most data-

XA enables transaction managers to coordinate the resource managers

bases support it. Because XA runtime calls occur between the transaction manager and the resource managers, the persistence code using the transaction manager does not need to do anything. However, some system configuration work is needed so that the data stores are registered as XA resources to the transaction manager.

The persistence tool must observe the transaction manager's locking policy

Resource Managers Lock Management on/or after Commit The persistence mapping tool must also follow the locking policy of the transaction manager. In CICS, for example, because a CICS program can issue commits (EXEC CICS SYNCHPOINT) along the path of its execution, the persistence mapping code must recognize that locks are released at such commit points and ensure that further actions on the persistent objects will trigger reacquisition of the locks if the transaction has not been terminated.

Performance

Performance is a major factor in object persistence

Our discussion of persistence mapping hasn't touched the issue of performance yet, but that doesn't mean it's not important. In fact, in many situations, performance can be the most important factor in determining whether the persistence mapping tool can be used. Good optimization requires insight into the three elements of persistence mapping (data schema, object schema, and the mapping) and the actual usage pattern for the persistent information by the application. Performance issues can often add complexity to an already complex situation. We will discuss some of the common optimizations below. They range from a local level to a global level.

Pre-fetching brings in all referenced objects when a persistent object is invoked

Pre-Fetching Because the OO application and the persistent data store do not run in the same address space (and often, not even on the same machine), going back and forth between them decreases performance. When a persistent object is invoked by the application, the mapping mechanism can bring in all persistent objects referenced by the initial persistent object, in expectation of a future need for them. This technique, called pre-fetching, is an effective way to reduce the potential network traffic between the application and the data store, as shown in Figure 7-14 (c).

Lazy Fetching On the other hand, in some situations only one or two objects are accessed and actually used out of a network of many. In this case, there is no need to bring the whole object network (which can be very big, such as a list of customers) into the application's address space. The mapping mechanism can then bring in the single object being accessed (Figure 7-14 (a)). If a certain object referenced by the initial object is later needed, the persistence mechanism fetches the object (for instance, a customer) from the data store at that time. This is called **lazy fetching** and it guarantees that the object application does not retrieve objects unnecessarily.

Lazy fetching brings in objects only as needed

In order to achieve good performance, it is important to strike a balance between too much network traffic and too many cached objects. This is illustrated by Figure 7-14 (b), where part, but not all, of the object network is brought in and cached to enhance per-

Striking a balance requires user input and tool flexibility

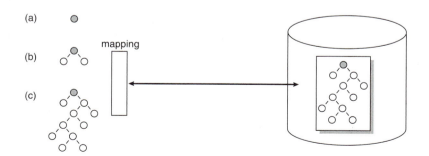

Figure 7-14 Fetching the objects

formance. Such a balance point is determined by the application's actual usage pattern of the persistent objects and cannot be easily inferred without user input. Therefore, a persistent object tool with good performance optimization must be flexible enough to allow user input on caching and lazy evaluation.

The page server opti-mization scheme combines pre-fetch-ing and lazy fetching

Some ODBMSs, such as ObjectStore, implement a low-level opti-mization scheme, called **page server,** that uses a combination of pre-fetching and lazy fetching. As shown in Figure 7-15, the data-base stores the objects in pages corresponding to the operating sys-tem's swapper pages. When Object 1 is first accessed, the entire Page A is shipped over and the mapping mechanism "swizzles" the pointers in the page to become native pointers on the client ma-chine. In this way, the other objects on the page are pre-fetched at the same time. When the client accesses Object 2, it simply follows the "swizzled" memory pointer. When the client follows the pointer from Object 2 to Object 3, an operating system page fault occurs because Page B is not there. The mapping code catches the page fault and retrieves Page B from the database. After swizzling the pointers in Page B and attaching it underneath Page A, the client can now follow a memory pointer to Object 3. In a sense, Object 3 is lazy fetched.

Figure 7-15 A page server ODBMS

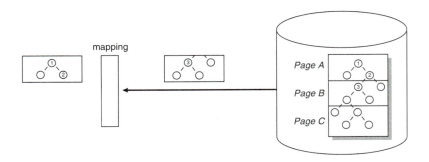

The page server approach has its trade-offs. For example, it can provide high performance when objects are accessed by following pointers (instead of by issuing queries). However, because it stores objects in memory format, the objects are hard to share across different programming languages, which often don't use the same memory layout for their objects. Also, using pages as the unit of fetch makes it more difficult to implement efficient locking at the level of individual objects.

The page server approach has associated drawbacks

As discussed in the section on data servers in Chapter 5, moving the persistence-related code closer to the data can often greatly improve the performance of the entire system. Some operations, such as searching through a large collection of objects, are best done on the server side so that the network won't be overwhelmed. The techniques that make this possible include query push-down, stored procedures, and transaction programs.

Placement of the persistence-related code can affect performance

Query Push-Down You can use this technique if the operation on the persistent objects can be mapped to the query language supported by the database (for instance, SQL). Instead of moving all the objects in the collection to the application address space and then querying the collection, a tool can translate the search operation into the query language and hand it to the database. The database does the search and returns the data, which in turn are mapped to the resulting objects.

With query push-down, objects are located by the database and then mapped

Stored Procedures This is another way of executing logic closer to the data. Depending on the expressiveness of the stored procedure language, persistent object methods can be implemented in stored procedures and can be executed very close to the data. Some ODBMSs, such as GemStone, have OO languages as their stored procedure language, which makes the task relatively straightforward.

Stored procedures can implement persistent object methods close to the data

So can the transaction monitor server and distributed OO transactions

Transaction Programs These can also be used to bring the persistence-related code closer to the data. For example, the entire configuration of Figure 7-13 (TP monitor, persistent objects, persistent mapping mechanism, and databases) can be made to run on a single machine. A distributed OO transaction mechanism, such as OTS, can also be used to put some of the objects closer to the data.

Performance monitoring and analysis are critical

These optimization techniques—pre-fetching, lazy fetching, query push-down, stored procedures, and transaction programs—can be used alone or in various combinations. No matter what techniques are used, performance monitoring and analysis are critical in determining object placement. Therefore, a sophisticated persistent object tool should support hooks in the generated mapping code to monitor and collect data for performance tuning.

Reasonable Expectations

Even with good tools, the hard work is left to the developers

The current state-of-the-art persistence mapping tools are best suited to straightforward, simple, repetitive tasks. Most persistent data mapping tools do well with new data and objects but have difficulty integrating the variety of pre-existing objects and data. This means that for most cases in the real world, persistent data mapping tools can only automate the mechanical part of the job, such as parsing existing schema and record mapping. Most of the difficult tasks are left to the developers, such as optimizing the object schema and data schema and mapping to obtain high performance. This is why many vendors offer consulting services together with their persistence mapping tools. As more human knowledge and experience are incorporated into the tools, we hope the reliance on heavy human intervention will gradually decline.

Databases

Databases are a prominent feature of any large-scale enterprise application. Therefore, they are also a feature of any discussion of object persistence. Relational databases have dominated the data management scene since their appearance 15 years ago. They manage a tremendous and growing amount of business data. One key advantage of the relational technology is the table-based relational model, which is easy to understand and has a strong theoretical foundation. Another advantage is the use of SQL, which is standardized across the industry and provides a declarative and integrated database language.

RDBs offer the advantages of SQL and the table-based relational model

In contrast, object-oriented database management systems are a new and emerging technology. They do a good job of managing complex data that can not be easily expressed in a relational scheme. For certain types of applications, they provide a significant performance advantage. ODBMS vendors still support their proprietary DDLs and DMLs as the primary mechanism to interact with the databases. However, with the work of the Object Database Management Group, standards for ODBMSs are beginning to emerge.

ODBMSs do a good job of managing complex data

Relational versus OO Databases

A commonly asked question is, "Because I am developing an object-oriented enterprise application, does that mean that I have to use an ODBMS?" The answer is a definitive "No." Most existing data is not stored in ODBMSs, and as we have seen, there are many other mechanisms to support object persistence and sharing. A better question is, "When and where should I use an ODBMS?" To answer it, we need to look into the pros and cons of ODBMSs compared with relational databases.

OO enterprise applications can use both relational and OO databases

Despite early claims, ODBMSs have not dominated the market

When ODBMSs first appeared, their vendors touted performance statistics showing order-of-magnitude improvement over the relational technology. However, after many years, ODBMSs are barely moving out of the niche CAD/CAM market into commercial data processing. If the common wisdom in the database business says that performance is the most critical factor, why haven't ODBMSs dominated the market?

Figure 7-16 Generating a list of suppliers from a conventional database

CUSTOMER/PART

CUSTOMER	PART
customer 1	part 1
customer 1	part 2
customer 2	part 3
......	......

SUPPLIER/PART

SUPPLIER	PART
supplier 1	part 1
supplier 1	part 2
supplier 2	part 2
......	......

SELECT

JOIN

CUSTOMER	PART	SUPPLIER
customer 1	part 1	supplier 1
customer 1	part 2	supplier 1
customer 1	part 2	supplier 2

PROJECT

SUPPLIER
supplier 1
supplier 2

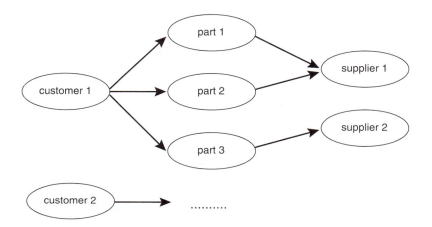

Figure 7-17 Generating a list of suppliers from an ODBMS

There are several important reasons. In addition to the difficulties of migrating existing data from one technology to another and the limits on the maximum amount of data that ODBMS implementations can currently handle, there is also the understanding that high performance does not come free. Often, ODBMSs trade flexibility for performance.

The high performance of ODBMSs is not free

The example in Figure 7-16 shows a simple customer/part/supplier database containing two relational tables. Let's say we wanted to generate a list of suppliers of *customer1* (a common request that the customer service department might make). The way to do this is to select *customer1* out of the CUSTOMER/PART table, do a join of the resulting table and the SUPPLIER/PART table, and then do a project of the supplier column. This gives us the list of the suppliers.

Example: generating a list of suppliers

Now let's look at a typical ODBMS design for storing the same set of information. In Figure 7-17, customer objects contain references to the part objects they use. The part objects contain references to the supplier objects that supply them. To generate the list of suppliers for *customer1*, all that's necessary is to follow the parts object

To find the suppliers, the ODBMS is clearly more efficient

references out of the *customer1* object, follow the supplier object references for these parts, and put them in a collection of all the resulting supplier objects. For this task, the ODBMS is clearly more efficient than the relational database.

The ODBMS is good at "clustering" related structures

In contrast, the relational join and project operations require more processing and intermediate tables, which make them several times slower. The ODBMS can also **cluster** better. Clustering is a technique that allows the database designer to place related structures (such as customers and the parts they use) closer to each other in disk storage. This dramatically reduces retrieval time for the related data because all data could be read with one, instead of several, disk reads. With a relational database, related rows are spread out over multiple tables (in our simple example, two), so it is much harder to devise a clustering scheme that would bring related rows physically together in a variety of circumstances.

For queries not considered in the original design, the ODBMS is often slower

For our specific query, the ODBMS is clearly the performance winner. However, let's try asking a different question: "What does *supplier1* supply?" This is a typical question that the inventory department might ask. With the relational database, one would do a select from the SUPPLIER/PART table and then do a project to get a list of the parts from *supplier1*. In our ODBMS design, however, there is no back pointer from the suppliers to the parts they supply. To answer the question, one would have to traverse the entire object structure, starting with the customers, to find out what parts point to *supplier1*, then collect all the parts. In this case, the ODBMS can be slower than the relational database because the query was not considered in the original schema design.

There is a trade-off between performance and flexibility

These examples illustrate the trade-off between flexibility and performance. The key reason that the ODBMS is faster in the first example is because the database schema is designed to facilitate the search from customers to parts to suppliers. In effect, the pointers among objects in the ODBMS capture the result of the join in the relational database. Because the join does not have to happen dynamically at runtime, better performance is obtained. On the relational side, the information is stored in a normalized format that is flexible but requires more operations, such as joins, to obtain the query result.

However, when an unanticipated question is asked, such as in our second example, the ODBMS does not have the luxury of having the pre-computed equivalent of the join already stored in pointers. Therefore, it performs a lot more slowly than in the first example while the relational database performs as well as it performed in the first case.

The ODBMS does not always capture the pre-computed equivalents of joins

It's important to look into database performance issues with the flexibility factor in mind. If the data is well understood and has a stable access pattern, then taking advantage of ODBMS performance optimization can be a good choice. If the access patterns for the data cannot be predicted ahead of time, a relational database might be best. These factors are closely related to the nature of the business—for example, a business merger can change the way data is used. Relational databases provide better facilities to deal with change. Because of the years of research on optimizing SQL, relational databases give good, but not stunning, performance.

The more flexibility required, the better the RDB performs

There are ways to create indices to an ODBMS so that non-mainline operations don't necessarily have to be slower. However, indices (in ODBMS and in RDB) raise their own set of issues. The more indices an object participates in, the harder it is to create, delete, and move (because all the indices have to be updated, as well). This can make the objects in the system less flexible and less adaptive to change.

Indices enhance performance but raise their own issues

Object-Relational Databases

It's clear that the ODBMSs and relational databases are good for different purposes. The natural question to ask is why we can't have the best of both: the formalism, optimization, and flexibility of relational databases plus the object types, encapsulation, complex data structure, and performance of the ODBMS.

O-R DBMSs extend the RDB with additional OO features

That's exactly where the relational database industry is heading, as discussed in Chapter 5. It is trying to extend the relational database model with additional OO features so that relational databases can do a lot of what the ODBMSs can do. Often these take the form of object-relational DBMSs (O-R DBMSs). No wonder these new databases are sometimes referred to as "extended relational databases."

The SQL3 standard covers the new work on O-R DBMSs

Much of this new technology is covered by the development of SQL3 standard, the next-generation SQL. Its intent is to combine the formal and powerful query mechanism of SQL technology with object features, such as encapsulation, inheritance, and methods. ODBMS vendors are also participating in the SQL3 work, and attempts to incorporate the ODMG standard into SQL3 are underway.

Introducing objects adds to the complexity of the relational model

A challenge to the O-R DBMS movement is the complexity of introducing object notions into an already complex relational technology. Some additional complexity is unavoidable. However, the more elegant and simple the resulting model, the more accessible the O-R DBMS will be to everyday IT developers.

What Kind of Database Do I Choose?

Select databases that support your business needs

We believe the SQL3 movement is a crucial development to watch. Still, the key issue is to select databases that best support your business needs and fit well with existing and future systems. Remember that object-oriented databases are by no means a requirement for objectifying a system. Objects can be stored in many types of database. Our recommendation is to analyze the needs of the system as a whole, then pick the database that best suits those needs, without regard to whether it is a relational database or an ODBMS.

Summary

With object persistence and sharing, the primary objective is to bring objects in and out of a data store. The three fundamental elements are

- Object schema
- Data schema
- Schema mapping

The difficulty of object persistence and sharing is related to the question of what objects and data already exist in the system.

A complete object persistence solution requires tool support for capturing and managing object schema and data schema and for generating the mapping between the schemas.

The persistence mechanism often needs to make transaction support available. There are three basic approaches.

- The simplest case is to surface the data store's transaction model.
- The mapping code can provide some transaction manager functionality, but this leads to complications.
- Using a transaction manager enables the persistence mapping tool to adopt the transaction manager's transaction model.

Performance is a key issue for persistence mapping. Techniques such as pre-fetching, lazy fetching, query push-down, stored procedures, and transaction programs can enhance mapping performance.

Three database options are available for storing objects.

- Relational databases offer the advantages of SQL and the table-based relational model.
- ODBMSs do a good job of managing complex data. Their high performance can come at the cost of flexibility.
- Object relational databases extend the relational database model with additional OO features.

8

Objects Across the Internet

In this chapter, we examine the topic of OO enterprise computing on the Internet. As most people are aware, the Internet is growing exponentially—most particularly, a "killer application" of the Internet known as the World Wide Web. This chapter discusses the impact of the World Wide Web, looks at client/server architecture as related to the Web and the Internet, and then examines the role object technology plays in the evolution of the Web.

The Internet is growing exponentially

We choose to define Internet in a general sense. The Internet is a network of networks, based on a common communications protocol, TCP/IP (Transmission Control Protocol/Internet Protocol). Note that TCP/IP is not the only protocol used on the Internet. There are other protocols at lower levels, such as the User Datagram Protocol (UDP), and at high levels, such as the Hypertext Transfer Protocol (HTTP). For example, media broadcast applications, such as audio and video streaming, often take advantage of UDP for better performance.

The Internet is a network of networks based on a common protocol, TCP/IP

The Impact of the World Wide Web

The Web is not synonymous with the Internet—rather, it is a means of accessing information over the Internet. However, the Web is such a major part of the Internet that to some users, the terms have come to mean the same thing. The correct relationship between the two is that the Web is a networking application supporting a protocol (HTTP) that runs on top of the Internet. There are other applications that also run on top of the Internet but are not part of the Web—for example, X Windows, E-mail, PointCast, and secured fund transfer protocols.

The World Wide Web is not the same as the Internet

The World Wide Web

Many methods of accessing data have evolved over the 30-odd year history of the Internet, but the World Wide Web has come to predominate. The World Wide Web dates from 1990, when Tim Berners-Lee, a computer scientist at the Center for Nuclear Research (CERN) in Switzerland, developed the two technologies that form the foundation of the Web: **HTML** and **URLs.**

HTML (Hypertext Markup Language) is a simple tagging language now universally used for presentation of text and graphics in Web browsers. It allows for a consistent way of authoring and rendering documents across the various hardware and software environments of the Internet. Its most powerful feature is its hypertext ability to link words, phrases, and graphics to information in other documents at remote locations throughout the world.

The ability to link is made possible by Berners-Lee's other technological contribution: Uniform Resource Locators (URLs—also known as "Unified Resource Locators"). The URL provides access to any document located on any Internet host in the world by combining the access protocol and the Internet domain name (representing the IP address) with the directory and file name of the HTML document requested—for example,

http://www.yahoo.com/index.html

The *http* indicates the hypertext transfer protocol required for accessing the object of the search in a Web browser. It is an RPC-like protocol for accessing resources that are pointed to by URLs. HTTP is a stateless RPC. For each call, it establishes a client/server connection, transmits and receives parameters and a return file, and breaks the connection. Other protocols can also be used within URLs.

The Web grew slowly in its early years; in 1993, only 40 Web sites existed. In that year, a team at the National Center for Supercomputing Applications at the University of Illinois, in Urbana-Champaign (Marc Andreessen was a member) created Mosaic, the first GUI for the World Wide Web. Distributed free, Mosaic prompted a boom in Web usage. Andreessen eventually went to work for a new company called Netscape, and the Mosaic browser evolved into Netscape, the commercial-grade Web browser that paved the way for the Web as we know it.

Businesses increasingly rely on the Web to make information available, and the Web is becoming an important commercial force, as well.

At press time, the number of Web servers doubles every 55 days, and a new Web site (commonly known as a "home page") is added every five seconds. This rapid growth combines with an inherent effect of the Web, known as **disintermediation,** to suggest that the World Wide Web is paving the way for fundamental changes in how we use and view computers.

The Web brings fundamental change in how we use and view computers

To understand disintermediation, we need to return to our definition of the Internet, which stresses that communications are based on a common network protocol. One of the most important effects of using TCP/IP as a common protocol is that networking applications, such as Web browsers, have a standard and common platform to live on. They are equally effective whether information sources are within an organization or outside that organization. This means the Internet makes possible a new world in which there is little difference between the fundamental architecture, development, and deployment of applications for internal corporate use and for the world at large.

The Internet makes information and services available internally and externally alike

The architectural difference between internal and external networks diminishes

From a developer's perspective, the enterprise network and the external Internet are connected and can be treated as a single network, as shown in Figure 8-1. Access to the network is controlled by business rules and security considerations. Often, nothing but the corporate security firewall stands between access and manipulation of data on corporate servers by corporate employees and the access and manipulation of that same data by external customers and partners (such as a parts provider). Moreover, internal and external users may use the same application (for instance, the Web browser) to perform their tasks.

Disintermediation brings service and information directly to external users

Disintermediation means that customers can go directly to a source of service and information, bypassing the middlemen. For example, if they want the latest information on a college, they can go immediately to the Web home page for that college and have access to a range of data, such as faculty, courses offered, and admission criteria. This is in contrast to the situation just a few years ago,

Figure 8-1 Convergence of enterprise network and Internet

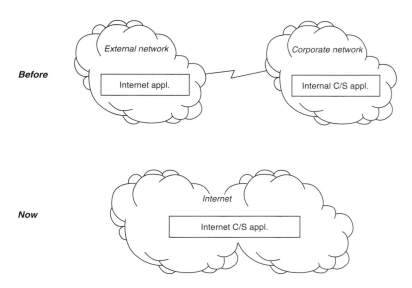

188

when the best source of information about a subject might be an **aggregator** of information, such as an online service or a reference book.

Disintermediation also means that customers can order products directly from manufacturers, with order applications accessible from the same company home page that provides the product information. Furthermore, information from the customer order can be directly used to update corporate databases.

Customers can order directly from manufacturer

Although the Web and its capacity for disintermediation can make applications and data widely available, they also raise major issues of data security and management complexity.

An Architectural View of the Web

In this section, we discuss the Web from an OO client/server architectural perspective. We prefer to view the Internet as just another client/server platform, with most of the same architecture models and issues. Our discussion of object technology and client/server components applies as well to the Web because, viewed as a client/server application, it's likely to follow the patterns that we have been discussing. The Web is being extended to participate in several forms of client/server computing, and issues, such as rapid change and complexity, which have been driving traditional enterprise computing toward object technology, are driving the Web and Internet computing in the same direction.

The Web is an example of OO client/server architecture

Early Web Architecture

The first-generation Web model is shown in Figure 8-2. The client side consists of a Web browser, such as Netscape or Mosaic. This browser requests contents from the Web server using the HTTP protocol. The Web server uses the URL provided by the client to ei-

The first-generation Web model

**Figure 8-2 First-
generation Web
model**

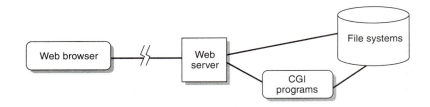

ther find the requested Web page in the file system or invoke a CGI (Common Gateway Interface) program that does some computation to construct the page that the client has requested. The Web server uses environment variables to send parameters to the CGI program.

*CGI programs run
on top of the operating system*

CGI Programs The CGI standard was devised for interfacing external applications with Web servers. A CGI program is just another program that runs on top of the operating system. The CGI program can be written in any language, for example C or Perl. It can access external resource managers, such as files and databases. It can also communicate with other programs (transactional or not) using any of the communication middlewares (such as RPC, object messages, and CICS ECI). The two main drawbacks of using CGI are low performance (a new process has to be created for every request) and platform dependence.

*The use of early Web
browsers is similar
to the use of a 3270
terminal*

A Web browser in such a configuration is little more than a fancy display monitor, such as a 3270 terminal. All the contents are prepared on the server side, and there is little intelligence on the client side. The partition point for this first-generation Web model is shown in Figure 8-3. And as we discussed in Chapter 1, when the partitioning is defined by a protocol (HTML, in this case), it is generally not flexible.

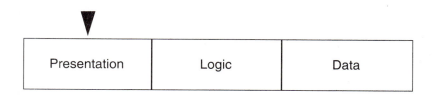

Figure 8-3 Partition point for the first-generation Web model

Doing Business on the Web As the Web increased in popularity, people began to realize that they could use it to do more than display pre-built (static) HTML pages. When organizations began doing business on the Web, they began to have more sophisticated requirements. Before more advanced mechanisms (discussed later in this chapter) were available, they fulfilled these requirements by writing CGI programs. For example, a Web-based company might want to take orders from customers over the Web. This would require, in addition to a set of static pages, a CGI program to perform the necessary processing logic.

Organizations doing business on the Web have more sophisticated requirements

Another requirement for Web business is persistence. This was achieved by writing CGI programs that store information in a persistent data store (either flat files or a database). This manner of achieving persistence is not much different than the way a typical client/server application does it.

CGI programs can help achieve persistence

Companies started to find it useful to give customers access to their existing IS functions through the Web, which often meant providing access to enterprise transactions and data. IS organizations started writing CGI programs to access databases and invoke the existing business transaction programs. The resulting Web servers execute logic on top of the operating system and without transaction protection; they are essentially native servers, as shown in Figure 8-4 (Compare to Figure 5-7).

Web servers can provide access to enterprise transactions and data

**Figure 8-4 Web
server functioning
as a native server**

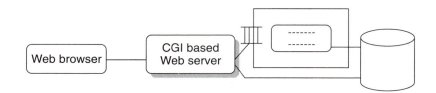

*Session state man-
agement needs to be
handled*

For many enterprise applications, multiple pages (that is, screens in
3270 terminology) are needed to complete a job. The client and the
server are actually having a conversation. The pages are required to
come in a certain order and the information presented or collected
in a page often is affected by the user interaction with the prior
pages. However, today's HTTP protocol is stateless. That is, the
server forgets everything after it hands over a reply to the client.

*Traditional tech-
niques can help with
session state man-
agement*

Such infrastructure is not sufficient to support state-oriented
client/server conversations. Fortunately, because the Web browser
is similar to a 3270 terminal in many ways, some of the proven
techniques used in programming traditional mainframe applications apply. For mainframe programmers, session state management is a familiar topic. In pseudo-conversational communication,
the transient states of a session also need to be stored and restored
between screens. There are two general approaches.

- Use hidden fields to store the information from the previous
  screens in the next screen. The user will not see the hidden information because the client does not render the hidden fields.
  When the user returns from the screen, the hidden information is carried back to the server to provide session state information. This essentially uses the client to remember the
  transient states.
- Use hidden fields to store a token representing the session.

The server keeps the state information related to the session on the server side and uses the token as a key to find it between screens. This uses the server to store the transient states while asking the client to help remember the key.

One can also imagine mixing the two approaches for performance or security purposes. The techniques used on the mainframe can be adapted to the Web. If we replace *screen* with *page* in the above description, the same approaches can be used to address the Web session state management problem. In fact, they are. Session tokens and actual data can be encoded in the pages and the URLs.

The techniques can be mixed for performance or security

Unlike a dumb terminal, a Web browser running on a PC can retain information in its local storage. A Web client can allow servers to store and retrieve information in **cookies** that reside in files on the client machine. Such a mechanism is useful in many applications. For example, shopping applications can store information about user-selected items; for-fee services can send back registration information and free the customers from retyping such information on the next connection; and sites can store individual user preferences on the client and retrieve those preferences every time the user visits the site.

Web servers can store and retrieve information on clients

The Web Client/Server Partition

If we look at the evolution of Web architecture, we find that it follows the same lines of reasoning as the evolution of client/server application architecture, with objects coming to play roles in much the same way and for the same reasons. The similarity is not coincidental but rather rooted in the issues that both architectures address. We will look at the architecture model from two perspectives: where the client/server partition occurs and how the server itself is evolving.

Web architecture follows the evolution path of client/server architecture

The evolution of Web partitioning resembles evolution in enterprise computing

The evolution of client/server partitioning on the Web has been similar to earlier evolution in general enterprise computing. As we saw in the last section, the initial static Web browsers are similar to the 3270 "dumb" terminals of the early client/server days, handling nothing except a portion of the presentation. From that point, the Web partitioning models have evolved and diversified to include logic and data on the browser (client) side too. We will take a look at the progression from static browsers through plug-ins, applets, and ActiveX components to data replication and Web-casting, pausing on the way to consider the popular language, Java.

Plug-ins provide additional processing on the client side

Plug-ins Plug-ins are software executables that run on the Netscape browser (the client side) and interpret the data received from the server. They are called plug-ins because they can be plugged into the browser. Plug-ins can come packaged with the Web browser or be downloaded from servers over the network. They are most commonly used in extending the browser to process multimedia data like video and audio.

For example, a graphics plug-in can render complex 3-D pictures on the client

Plug-ins can greatly enhance Web application performance. One example is a graphics plug-in that can render complex 3-D chemical structures. Without the plug-in, the server would have to do all the work of rendering the picture onto a display format, such as GIF, and then transfer the entire image across the network to the client for display to the user. With the plug-in, the server can simply transfer the data that describes the chemical structure and let the plug-in do the rendering. The data often can be many times smaller than the fully rendered image, and using the plug-in can greatly reduce the amount of data that needs to be sent over the network. In the 3-D chemical structure example, the plug-in can also support local manipulation of the structure, such as rotation and zoom with cursor movements. Such manipulation can be costly and slow if the server is to do all the work.

With plug-ins, more of the presentation logic is moved from the server to the client and the partition point is moved further to the right, as shown in Figure 8-5. Because plug-ins can contain general programs, the partition point can come further to the right, in the logic portion of the continuum.

Plug-ins move logic to the client

Note that in general, each plug-in provides a fixed partition point, which is determined by the protocol. A protocol defines the information that flows across the wire and how to interpret it. For example, in the 3-D chemical structure example, the protocol could define that the server ships the wire-frame data and the shading method of a 3-D chemical structure to the client and the plug-in does the computation and rendering.

Plug-in architecture normally provides a fixed partition point

Applets The next step in Web evolution involves downloading executable code (so-called applets) from the server and executing them on the client. Java is an object-oriented language designed to help develop applets. In Figure 8-6, the applet model moves the partitioning point further to the right and gives the application designer/developer the flexibility to determine where to split the application.

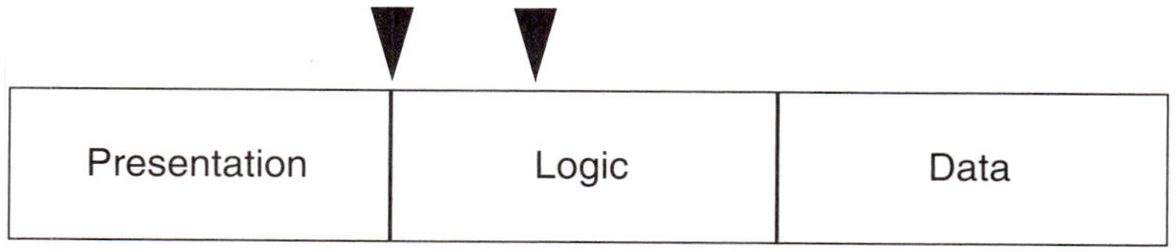

Applet download adds flexibility and dynamics in partitioning

Figure 8-5 Partition point for Web system using plug-in

Presentation	Logic	Data

Figure 8-6 Partition point for Web systems using applets

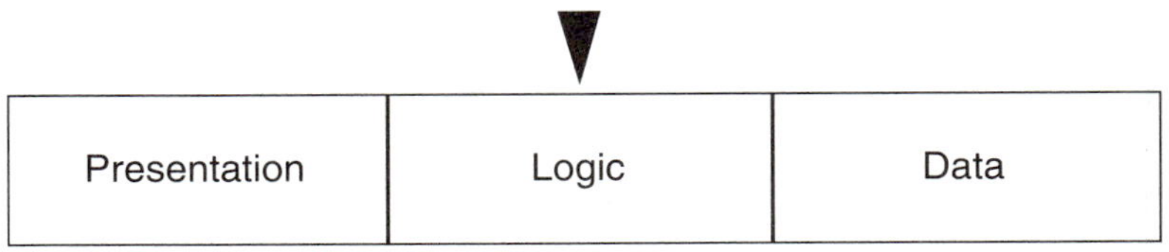

Presentation	Logic	Data

Applets lead to more dynamic client/server partitioning

Because applets are designed to be downloaded at runtime, the partition of the client/server application is more dynamic than with plug-ins. For example, a Web server may supply different applets depending on the speed of the connection between it and its clients. If a client has a low speed connection, an applet that does a lot of processing on the client side can be used in order to minimize the network crossing. If the client has a high-speed connection but low CPU power, an applet can be used that relies on the server to do most of the computation-intensive work.

Applets require several services

The concept of the applet is not new. It's essentially a way to ship and execute code at runtime. Many of the mobile agent systems (for instance, General Magic's Telescript) implement similar concepts. For applets to work, several services must be present.

Distribution mechanism and execution context

- Distribution mechanism and execution context: An applet must have a destination to go to and a distribution mechanism to get it there. In this case, the Web browser is the destination and HTTP and the Internet are the distribution mechanism. There is also a need for an execution environment that receives the applet, loads it, lets it execute, then unloads it and releases the system resources. The Web browser and the Java virtual machine provide this execution context.

Portability

- Portability: The applet needs to be able to execute on a variety of platforms. This requires a portable executable format, which is provided by the Java bytecodes. There also need to be con-

sistent underlying platform services (such as a GUI, communications, and threads) for the portable executables to run on,
which are surfaced through the standard Java class libraries.

- Safety: The receiver of an applet must have confidence that
  the execution of this piece of code will not do harm to the receiver's system. Various measures are required to address this.
  For example, a server authentication mechanism is needed to
  ensure that the applet is from the right server. Secured transport is needed to ensure that no one tampers with the applet
  when it's being transmitted. A security check may be performed on the receiving side to analyze the applet before allowing it to execute. A restrictive execution environment can
  be provided to limit an applet's capabilities (for example, pre-
  venting local file access).

Safety

It's worth noting that although the download model has been associated with Java by many people, the model has very little to do
with language-specific features. It has more to do with how the
language is implemented (for instance, using an interpreter and
safety check of bytecodes) and the context in which it is introduced
(for instance, the Web). Any language with an interpreter and a
portable executable format can be a candidate for downloading.
For example, many people have pointed out that Smalltalk can
also work well. It is because the applet download concept was first
implemented with Java that people make the association.

*Downloadable ap-
plet support has
more to do with
language implemen-
tation than the lan-
guage itself*

The Java Language Java is a language with many features friendly
to the programmers (for instance, garbage collection, no pointers).
We expect it will enjoy significant growth in two directions.

*Java will grow in
two directions*

As a Web language, Java will continue to be strong in the applet
development arena. As with other OO programming languages,

As a Web language

people will want to use Java on the Web server side, as well. Some people call the Java programs running on the Web server **servlets.** Like applets, servlets are often tightly integrated with the Web server environment to support unique Web requirements, such as server-side safety and performance.

As a general purpose OO programming language

As a general purpose OO programming language, Java can be used to create all the components in an enterprise system. For example, a Java client that has nothing to do with a Web browser or a Java server program that has nothing to do with a Web server. Java will grow its own **language tower,** just as other languages, such as C++, Smalltalk, and BASIC, have. Such a language tower will include GUI builders, visual programming tools, distributed objects, extensive class libraries (for instance, database and transaction access), test tools, version control, team programming support, and integration with upper CASE tools. We expect Java will continue to be ported to run in a variety of environments, from special embedded devices to mainframes running under the control of TP monitors to database stored procedures.

The challenge is to preserve Java's benefits while growing the language quickly

The challenge for Java is to preserve the benefits of the language while growing it at a tremendous rate. For example, portability is a key attraction of Java today. As Java extends to run in various environments and access data and legacy systems, its portability will be increasingly difficult to maintain. For instance, embedded devices and mainframe servers clearly don't support graphical user interfaces, so any program using the standard Java Abstract Windowing Toolkit (AWT) will not be portable to those environments. Similarly, a Java server program that relies on special services unavailable on the client will not be portable to the client. Such portability issues can arise even among clients. For example, a Java client program that accesses special devices such as audio and video cannot be expected to work on another client without those devices.

Various vendors will extend Java in different ways to differentiate their offerings—for example, to provide unique class libraries and functions unique to specific platform or virtual machine implementation. This makes the portability issue even more complicated. Fortunately, Java is not the only language in computing history that has faced such problems. Many languages, such as C++ and Smalltalk, have gone through similar growing pains and accumulated a lot of experience in handling the issues. As Java grows, those lessons will surely come in handy.

Many popular languages have gone through similar growing pains

ActiveX Components In addition to Java applets, Microsoft is also promoting the ActiveX technology to ship code across the network. An ActiveX component is a piece of executable code that can run on Windows platforms. Because all ActiveX components conform to the COM standard, they can be loaded and executed by a container that understands how to deal with COM objects. Microsoft has enabled their Web browser (the Internet Explorer) to do just that. The Web and the Internet still provide the distribution mechanism; the target execution context is a browser that knows how to deal with ActiveX components.

ActiveX download— the Microsoft way

Compared with Java applets, ActiveX components have a unique performance advantage because they are compiled to the native executable format. This makes them just like any other programs that run on top of the native operation system, which gives them access to the full platform functionality (for instance, files, memory, hardware and software system controls) unavailable to a Java applet.

ActiveX components have unique performance and access advantages

ActiveX components also have drawbacks.

ActiveX drawbacks include portability . . .

- Portability: Because it is compiled to the native executable format, the same ActiveX component needs to be compiled for all platforms that it is intended to run on. Depending on which platform the browser is running on, different versions of the executable would have to be downloaded. This contrasts with the applet executables that run on all the platforms.

. . . and safety

- Safety: Because the ActiveX components have full access to platform services, they can be versatile. On the other hand, they can also be used to do great damage to a system (such as deleting important files). Microsoft's answer to the safety issues is a verification mechanism that allows the receiver of an ActiveX component to verify that the component comes from a trusted source. The assumption is that if a component is supplied by a trusted source, it should be safe to execute. (Such techniques can also be applied to applets to make them even more secure.)

The problem with such approach is that, to be safe, a user surfing the net would have to reject all ActiveX components not signed by an authority, which is not a common practice. Also, even if a user can verify that an ActiveX component comes from an identifiable source, there is still no way to tell if executing the component will cause damage. A user can always hold the source liable for any problems caused by a component. However, by that time, the damage has been done, and it may not be reversible.

Partitioning also happens at the data level

Data Partitioning Vendors with strong data partitioning and replication technology are getting into the game by adding Web capabilities to their existing products. Lotus Domino is a good example. Lotus Notes has been famous for its data replication support. The new Domino client not only can access both Notes servers and Web servers, but also has the capability to replicate and cache data on the client side. This pushes the partitioning point into the data area, as shown in Figure 8-7.

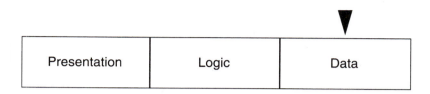

Figure 8-7 Partition
point for Lotus
Domino and the
Webcasting/push
model

Other software programs that fall into this category are those following the push model. **Webcasting** software, such as PointCast,
Intermind Communicator, and other push media, push the contents that fit your interest profile from the server to your computer. Their architectures split the application in the data section,
as well. The server contains the complete data while the client receives a subset of the server data that you are interested in. The
presentation and logic components of the application also reside on
the client side in order to intelligently display the data. Most Webcasting software uses proprietary protocols to replicate and synch
up the data between the client and the server.

*The Webcasting
model splits the data
component*

Figure 8-8 summarizes the partition schemes discussed in this section. For the Web as a whole, the initial partitioning point is controlled by the HTTP protocol. That protocol is expanding to satisfy

*More client/server
solutions are finding
their way onto the
Web*

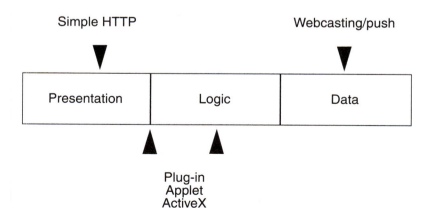

Figure 8-8 Summary
of Web partitioning
points

more requirements, and many vendors are trying to add value to the Web by providing additional protocols and technology to work alongside HTTP. As the Web is used to address more of the business computing requirements that client/server technology has been addressing, more of the existing client/server solutions are going to find their way onto the Web. It is no surprise that the application partitioning aspect of the Web is already similar to that of client/server systems.

Web Server Evolution

A Web server is an HTTP server plus additional services

Web server used to mean *HTTP server*—the daemon that runs on the server machine listening to the HTTP traffic and serving pages. However, the industry is adding functionality to the Web server every day. As a consequence, there is no longer a simple and crisp definition of what a Web server is. Many Web server solutions now claim HTTP server independence. That is, their Web server can plug into any HTTP server on the market as a back end. We define a Web server as the combination of the HTTP server and the additional services needed to execute and manage Web applications.

Web servers have followed a three-stage evolution

Web servers have evolved from a static publication vehicle to a provider of dynamic contents to a medium for enterprise applications. Figure 8-9 shows these three phases of evolution. The following sections detail these phases and discuss more general issues related to Web server evolution: performance, robustness, the transaction model, and coexistence of the three phases.

The first stage is static publication

Static Publication At the beginning of the Web era, Web servers were used to publish hypertext documents composed of static HTML pages stored in the file systems. This is still an important aspect of the Web. The word *publishing* is used because there is a clear distinction between Web page authoring (development time) and publish-

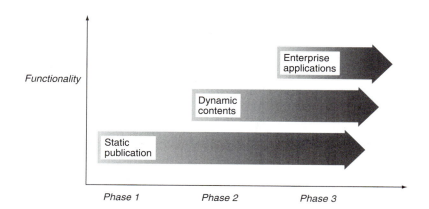

Figure 8-9 The three phases of Web server evolution

ing (runtime). Web page authors develop the pages and then publish the entire hypertext document. In this way, Web page publishing is similar to the final compile/build step in software development.

Dynamic Content Web servers are being enhanced to handle content that is more dynamic. The Olympics Web site is a good example. While the Web server was publishing the Olympic results to the world, further results kept coming in from the arenas. The server posted new results and changed team standings dynamically, based on the results from each round of competition. Multiple real-time authors updated the contents of the Web server at the same time.

Example: The Olympics Web site handled dynamic content

An inventory counter in an electronic commerce page is another example. It can change after every purchase to reflect how many items remain in stock.

Personalized Web pages are another example of dynamic content. Personalization enables the Web server to provide you with pages based on information it has collected on you. For instance, based

Example: personalized Web pages

on the pages you've visited and the keywords you put into the search dialog, a Web server can include advertisements related to your interests.

Dynamic content blurs the line between development time and runtime

With dynamic content, the line between development time and runtime gets blurred. There is no longer a single point when someone can push a "publish" button and build the entire Web site. The contents of the site are evolving and multiple parties can contribute changes. With dynamic content, using file systems to store pages becomes impractical. The solution calls for database-like functionality that can handle complex structures and concurrent updates from multiple users.

Dynamic content can use database-like services

Groupware databases, such as Lotus Notes, are also being enhanced to support collaborative types of Web applications. Most database vendors now offer their databases as platforms for Web servers. Databases also offer better system management functions (such as logging, backup, and access control) than simple file systems.

Dynamic HTML enhances the dynamic nature of the user interface

When contents need to be dynamic, various mechanisms are introduced to enhance the static HTML so that it becomes dynamic. Dynamic HTML extensions allow a scripting language embedded in a Web page to reference and modify HTML tags in that page. Using dynamic HTML, developers will be able to create a Web page that can respond dynamically to user-generated events (such as mouse clicks) by doing such things as expanding an HTML table, changing the attributes of a font, and moving a graphic across a page. All of this can be done without going to the server or relying on plug-ins or Java applets. Dynamic HTML puts more UI logic in the Web page, which simplifies certain types of application development and gives users the perception of greater bandwidth. The essential result is a more dynamic Web user interface.

To move beyond the dynamic user interface, various server-side mechanisms are introduced to support dynamic contents. The HTTP server can invoke programs to generate the HTML pages—for example, CGI programs and servlets can generate dynamic contents. Another mechanism is to introduce the capability to invoke programs from within an HTML page. For example, the Microsoft Active Server Page allows the mixing of JScript and VBScript statements in the HTML file. Those statements can invoke arbitrary logic (often packaged as ActiveX objects) to generate dynamic contents. Netscape, Sun, and IBM also have similar server-side scripting mechanisms that use Java and JavaScript as other scripting languages. Java servlets can also be invoked directly or from within an HTML page to provide the dynamic capabilities.

Various server-side techniques can support dynamic content

Enterprise Applications In the enterprise applications phase, people are creating and using real business applications with the Web as a front end. Instead of spending most of the time on composing and enhancing the page layout, equal or greater amounts of time go to constructing the business logic and data processing. Such applications must be able to integrate with critical enterprise back-end transactions and data. The internal corporate networks (intranets) are the initial proving ground for these enterprise Web applications. Later, as issues such as security and inter-corporation data exchange get addressed, enterprise Web applications will push into the Internet.

In the third phase, enterprise applications use the Web as front end

Performance As more users connect to the Web and more people use it to do serious business, Web server performance will continue to be an important issue. In general, server performance concerns are related to either the server's front side or its back side.

Web server performance is getting attention

- The front side has to do with managing large numbers of client connections and the efficient use of networking resources. **IP spraying** is a technique to present a single server IP address (*www.olympics.com,* for example) while having multiple machines with different IP addresses working together as the Web server. The client requests are "sprayed" among the servers to balance the load. More advanced systems, with geographically dispersed server machines, could calculate the distance between the client and the servers and assign the closest server with the greatest bandwidth to serve the client.

• The back side has to do with efficient use of server resources. Once requests are received, how does the server schedule and dispatch them to achieve good response time and high throughput? Some initial enhancements are being delivered by vendors. For example, instead of executing the CGI program as a separate process and incurring the cost of starting a brand new process every time, some servers provide the option of running the business logic in the same process/address space as the HTTP server itself.

Web servers must be reliable enough to trust with real dollars

Robustness For Web servers to provide the robustness to handle serious processing with integrity, they must be reliable enough for people to trust them with real dollars. For example, a mission-critical Web server may be required to run 24 hours a day, 7 days a week. A glitch in an individual program should not affect other programs or the server itself (an obvious performance concern when running the application in the Web server's address space). And if a Web server program tries to update two databases and crashes between the two updates, the data integrity should not be lost.

Web server issues are the same issues faced when TP monitors were first developed

Toward the Transactional Model As server providers worked toward enhancing Web server robustness, performance, and scaleability, they realized that the issues are familiar. They are the same issues people faced 20 years ago when TP monitors were first developed. The system must support large numbers of connected users and provide high-performance processing, maintaining the integrity of system and data alike. As Web technology evolves, it is logical to expect more transaction server functionality in it, shown in Figure 8-10.

Coexistence The three phases of the Web server are not exclusive. As the Web continues to evolve, we expect to see a mixture of static publishing, dynamic content, and enterprise applications coexist in most Web sites. A good Web server solution should support all three of them and provide smooth progression paths from phase to phase. As in the evolution of all other servers, object technology will be central in dealing with change and complexity. We also expect end-to-end OO development environments to emerge that support the development of applications spanning the enterprise and the World Wide Web in a unified fashion.

A Web server solution should support all three phases of evolution

The Internet and OO Client/Server Computing

So far, the Web has been the primary focus of our Internet discussion because it is one of the most exciting and pervasive applications of the Internet. Web implementations are an important subset of OO client/server computing on the Internet, but they are only a subset. The Internet is more than the Web, and Internet

Internet client/ server computing reaches beyond the Web

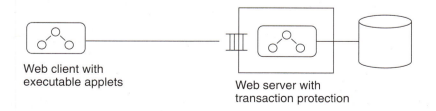

Web client with
executable applets

Web server with
transaction protection

Figure 8-10 Transaction server functionality on the Web

client/server implementation can reach well beyond the boundaries of the Web. We will look at using the Internet to download the client portions of client/server programs and then using the Internet as the infrastructure to run those programs. Last, we will look at what the future holds for objects on the Internet.

Downloading Client/Server Front Ends

The Web can be used to download a client for any client/server application

With the Web's extensive reach and its download capability, it has become clear that people can download much more than just HTML pages—not only the plug-ins and applets we have discussed, but also executables unrelated to the Web browser. People can start by using the Web as a search mechanism. When the application that a user wants is found, the user can initiate a download to obtain and install the client portion of the application. This means that all client/server applications that know how to use TCP/IP as the transport service can be used in the Internet instead of just the ones specifically designed and built for Web browsers.

Many client/server protocols can be used

With this downloaded client model, the Internet becomes a client/server platform. The Web browser is one of the key user interface elements in such a platform and it supports a specific protocol, HTTP, very well. Other client/server protocols (for instance, CORBA, DCOM, ECI, SQL) and their corresponding client-side and server-side programs can be used on top of the Internet. A client can choose the best protocol and easily download the corresponding software to access the server, as shown in Figure 8-11.

This model brings full-function client/server applications to the Internet

This model is compelling because the current HTTP-based Web middleware is not suited to handle many types of client/server traffic. For example, the one-way stateless RPC of HTTP would not provide good support for an application that requires two-way messaging. Also, when the client side would like to submit units of work to a CICS server transaction, it is important that middleware,

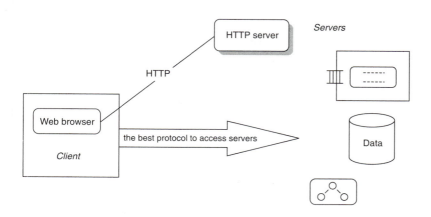

Figure 8-11 A client choosing a server access protocol

such as ECI, is used to guarantee the transaction ACID properties. Going through the ECI, protocol directly is also a faster path to CICS than going through the Web server in order to invoke the transaction. Other similar examples are Webcasting software and SQL clients that interact with a database server.

If the size of the downloaded client is significant, the downloaded client model is better suited for interactions that happen regularly. Occasional users will probably not want to spend a long time downloading a large and sophisticated client executable (for instance, an applet or an ActiveX component) for a one-shot interaction. However, for frequent users of an application, it may be well worth the initial download and setup time to get better service and performance in the long run.

The downloaded client model is suited for interactions that happen regularly

The client portion of an Internet client/server application does not always have to be downloaded from scratch. As the commercially available Web client packages expand, they include more of the client-side plumbing, so fewer services have to be downloaded. It is possible to bundle applications into the Web client package, which would make it even more similar to a traditional client implementation. The trick is to strike a balance between the compactness of

The model still raises issues such as client compactness

the Web client and the pre-loaded functionality (whether the functionality comes with the Web client package or is downloaded). One of the perceived attractions of the Web is the thin-client notion. If too many pre-loaded services are bundled with the Web client, it may no longer be thin and attractive.

Safety is another issue

Other issues need to be addressed as they come along. For example, downloaded executables (including Java applets) are often hard to verify in terms of safety. This has led to the growth of services, such as those offered by VeriSign and the U.S. Postal Service, that can authenticate a server and secure the download process.

The Internet as Infrastructure

The Internet is a platform for client/ server applications, of which the Web is one

So far, this chapter has focused on the Web, demonstrating that it can be comfortably described and discussed within the client/server architecture models that we have already established. Although the Web is an important application running on top of the Internet, it is not synonymous with the Internet. Rather, the Internet is a super-large platform that hosts many client/server applications, including the Web. All of the OO client/server architecture models and associated issues we've discussed apply to the Internet as a platform for the Web, as well as for more advanced client/server applications yet to come. As it has done throughout its history, the Internet will continue to support multiple protocols that satisfy different requirements.

The Internet can extend existing IS infrastructures

Many corporations see the Internet as a natural extension of their existing IS infrastructure in two important ways.

- The Internet as a medium to extend services to the customer
- The Internet as a medium for collaborating with organizational partners

An example of the Internet as a medium to extend services would be online banking. One example of the Internet as a medium for collaboration would be a project shared between two research institutes. Another example is the interaction between a merchant and the bank of a customer who purchased something with an online banking card. Both collaborating and extending services require extending the exiting IS structure so that it can interface and work with Internet contents.

In addition to its size, the Internet has other unique characteristics that differentiate it from the typical corporate network.

- It has a unique unifying protocol (TCP/IP). Users, application developers, and system administrators can depend on the ubiquitous underlying protocol to make their work portable and to potentially simplify their tasks.

- It spans multiple organizations. This generates opportunities because it connects businesses. It also generates challenges because the Internet is not controlled or supported by any single organization.

- The configuration, user population, content, and infrastructure of the Internet all change constantly. And both above and below the TCP/IP layer, complexities abound. Underneath, networking technologies, such as the asynchronous transfer mode (ATM), are being introduced to enhance the performance. Up on top, a variety of new applications and higher-level protocols are being introduced; even the IP itself is changing. A new version of the IP standard (version 6 of the Internet protocol, often referred to as IPv6) is ready to be deployed soon.

Object technology, which has helped traditional client/server computing, applies well to the Internet because many issues, such as change and complexity, are similar. The Internet's size provides additional incentives to managing complexity. With such a heteroge-

The Internet has unique characteristics: It has a unifying protocol

It spans multiple organizations

It changes dynamically and is complex

Object technology provides a lot of the needed benefits

neous community participating in the Internet, encapsulation is a valuable way to insulate changes. Integrating with legacy systems through the wrappering provided by objects is also a forte of object technology.

Internet clients and servers move quickly toward object technology

It's no surprise to see Java (an OO language) being accepted by the Internet community at record speed. Internet clients and servers are moving toward object technology at the same pace as the rest of the client/server world. Glue is no exception, with OO glues being introduced by all the vendors.

Distributed objects fit in well

Using the downloaded client model, distributed objects can easily be introduced to the Internet through the Web, as shown in Figure 8-12. Client objects are retrieved from the HTTP server. Once the client objects are downloaded to the client machine, they interact with the object server through an OO glue (such as an ORB supporting IIOP).

As is typical with OO client/server computing, multiple glues support distributed objects.

Figure 8-12 Introducing distributed objects to the Internet

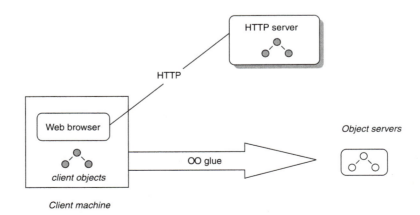

- At the common middleware level, there are two prominent solutions: Microsoft's DCOM and OMG's CORBA. The Microsoft solution leverages the significant market share of the Windows operating systems to deliver support for its distributed object component infrastructure (ActiveX). CORBA leverages the Java implementation of its Internet Inter-ORB protocol (IIOP) to enable every Web client to access any ORB server.

- At the common language level, Java supports remote method invocation (RMI). Java is bundled with Web clients and, thus, is extremely pervasive across the Internet. Because many Web server applications are likely to be written in Java, situations in which client and server can take advantage of the common language model can occur quite often.

Future Evolution

The evolution of the Internet and the Web has followed patterns similar to those of OO client/server computing. Because the two areas have so much in common, we can easily look to the future by analyzing the past. A few trends are worth mentioning.

Internet and Web evolution follows existing patterns

Ongoing Merger From a user's perspective, the Internet is another platform for conducting business. The application functions common in private networks are mostly still desirable on the Internet. Instead of reinventing several wheels (technology and solutions) specifically for the Internet, we are seeing an infusion of OO client/server technology to help develop Internet applications.

OO client/server will continue to merge with Internet computing

Another reason for the ongoing merger is that the Internet is becoming essential to the existing corporate network and IT infrastructure. If a corporation is to be successful in the new era of Internet computing, it has to successfully bridge the gap or, better yet, merge its existing IT systems with the Internet. Leveraging the established practices (such as OO client/server technology) provides a more efficient and less risky path to extend the IT world into the new Internet world.

The Web client will integrate with the desktop

Integration of Web Client and Desktop The Web client will integrate closely with the desktop. The Web browser will cease to be a stand-alone application. We expect that compound document frameworks like ActiveX/OLE will componentize the Web browser functionality and treat the display of Web pages as simply the display of one of the desktop components. This process will also enable desktop components to be included in Web pages, resulting in even richer Web pages than we have today.

Web servers will evolve into transaction and database servers

Evolution into Database and Transactions Servers Web servers will continue to evolve from native servers into database servers and transaction servers, as we discussed before. The movement is generated by the need for some architectures to address certain problems and for the technology providers to leverage what they already have invested. The current Web server implementations will continue, leading to a proliferation of types of Web servers.

Common middleware and common language glues will be important

Support for Different Glues Both common middleware and common language glues will be important. The common middleware glue will continue to be prominent, as it is in general OO client/server computing. However, as users demand more tool support and a higher level of abstraction, they will look for a common language model supported by the tool providers. The model is very promising because the Java language has become ubiquitous on both sides of the wire.

Objects will be uploaded from clients to the server

Uploading Objects to the Server This originates with the idea of mobile software agents. A software agent is a piece of software capable of accomplishing tasks on behalf of its user. If an agent is capable of moving around some network, it becomes a mobile agent. Downloaded applets can be thought of as mobile agents dispatched by the server to the clients. If clients are enabled to send objects (agents) to the server, as well, the server becomes much more dynamic in satisfying the clients' needs. In certain cases, a significant performance advantage can also be achieved by executing client-submitted code on the server. (This is similar to the performance benefits of stored procedures except that the procedures are submitted dynamically at runtime.)

Uploading objects from client to server is equivalent to supporting true dynamic partitioning on the fly. From a general architecture perspective, it is the one aspect that will make the architecture complete. However, for security reasons, it has not yet become pervasive in OO enterprise computing. Remember that the server community is necessarily more conservative than the end-user community. Running user-defined agent objects on the server sometimes amounts to changing server code on the fly. This is a taboo for many people and organizations because it can create situations that are difficult to control and debug. The move toward this feature will have to be driven by compelling business and application needs.

For security reasons, this is not yet pervasive

Coexistence of Different Models As in other areas of OO client/server computing, we don't expect any single model of protocol, server, or glue architecture to dominate. This is because they address different problems and there is no one-size-fits-all solution. The future of Internet computing will most likely continue to be a heterogeneous world with models coexisting and interoperating as they do throughout the OO client/server world.

No single model is expected to dominate

We commonly hear that a Web year is three calendar months. The pressure is on for participants to move fast or else become obsolete. As technology providers struggle to keep pace with the changes in the Internet and the Web, they will need to leverage

Existing technology can help to keep up with the pace of Internet evolution

existing technology assets and make them applicable to the new environment.

Evolution is preferable to revolution

Businesses also have a need to evolve their IT infrastructure instead of completely replacing the existing systems with new ones. Leveraging OO, client/server, and other more-mature technologies makes it possible to skip some of the early technology adoption risks. This is why an evolutionary approach, fast as it may need to be, is preferable to a revolutionary one.

Synergy between OO client/server technology and Internet computing is strong

For all these reasons, we see a strong synergy between object technology and client/server computing on the Internet and the Web. We expect the synergy to strengthen as these two technologies are increasingly used to meet the challenges of the Internet.

Summary

The World Wide Web is an application running on top of the Internet. Both Web and Internet are growing exponentially, paving the way for fundamental changes in how we use and view computers. The Internet makes information and services available to internal and external sources alike, and the architectural differences between internal and external networks are diminishing.

The Web is evolving to meet the more sophisticated requirements of organizations doing business on it. The evolution of partitioning on the Web has been similar to its evolution in client/server computing.

- Plug-ins provide additional processing on the client side.
- Downloadable applets add flexibility and more dynamic partitioning.

- ActiveX components have performance and access advantages but raise issues of portability and safety.
- The Webcasting model splits the data component.
- Downloading client/server front ends extends full client/server capabilities to the Web.

The Java language has potential for strong growth in two directions: as a Web language and as a general-purpose OO programming language. The challenge is to preserve Java's benefits as it grows.

Web servers have followed a three-stage evolution: static publication, dynamic contents, and enterprise applications.

The future evolution of the Internet and the Web will likely follow patterns similar to those of object technology and client/server computing. The Internet client and server are quickly moving toward object technology, including distributed objects. The Web client will integrate with the desktop, and Web servers will evolve from native servers into transaction servers and database servers. No single model of protocol, server, or glue architecture is expected to dominate.

9

End-to-End OO Enterprise Development

In this chapter, we will discuss tool issues related to developing an OO enterprise system. First, we will look at development models that have evolved over the years and how they apply to enterprise development. Starting with the "first generation" of client/server computing, it becomes important for tools to have the capability for developing OO enterprise components. This leads into a discussion of the advantages of objects from the development and tools perspective.

This chapter focuses on the development aspects of enterprise systems

The second half of the chapter takes a look at the general architecture of the tool suites required to develop end-to-end OO enterprise systems. To do this, we provide a template to help development organizations evaluate such tools. As an example of how the template works, we show how it applies to three of today's development tool suites.

It also provides a template for evaluating OO development tools

We believe that because enterprise customer requirements point toward an end-to-end view of the system, the industry trend is to provide tools for developing the system as a whole instead of piecemeal. The tool suites we consider all support end-to-end development to one extent or another. They all have support for Web and Internet application development as extensions of their existing functionality. This support corresponds to the needs of many businesses that want to extend the reach of their business information systems to the Internet.

The tools we look at support end-to-end development

The Development Models

The "waterfall" model made it hard to correct errors from earlier stages

The software development process has come a long way from the early days of computing, when the "waterfall" model was in common practice. In this model, requirements gathering, application specification, analysis, design, coding, testing, and maintenance are carried out one after another, leaving little room for feedback that would enable you to correct errors from earlier stages. For example, the test phase might discover an error that was due to faulty application specification, but it would be difficult to go back and respecify that part of the application; instead the testers would have to develop a workaround the best way they could.

Models such as the spiral model overcome the waterfall model's limitations

The waterfall model was used in the early days to develop programs that we would now consider relatively simple. As program requirements became more complex and executables mushroomed in size, the model ran into limitations. In working to overcome these limitations, development organizations began to discover the value of incremental and iterative development processes. Models such as the **spiral model** came into use. You design a little, develop a little, integrate a little, and test a little throughout the development cycle. This has become a common practice for many OO development projects.

Developers can minimize risk by uncovering potential problems early

The key to developing better programming practices is to recognize that problems in the late stages of a project are costly and difficult to recover from. By using a variety of project techniques, developers can attempt to uncover and correct potential problems early in the project cycle. (To learn more about these techniques, consult the books and articles on the subject in our list of references at the end of this book.) These techniques seek to minimize the risk of a project not achieving its objectives in the areas of schedule, budget, and quality.

Client/Server Development

In Chapter 1, we looked at the evolution of client/server comput- ing. It goes without saying that as the runtime model evolved, the development tools also evolved. This section looks at the changing concerns of the runtime model in order to establish a context for understanding the OO development environment.

As the runtime model evolves, devel- opment tools also evolve

Figure 9-1 summarizes the changes in the runtime model over the years. The arrows indicate the changing location of the partition between client and server as client/server computing evolved from the centralized mainframe (a) to front-end screen scraping (b) to the data server model (d and e) to the various split logic models represented by (c).

The First Generation Client/Server

Screen scraping represents the beginning of client/server develop- ment. However, it is not that much different from the old central- ized mainframe development. As indicated by (a) in, most of the work is done on programming the host server using traditional methods. Such architecture is really more an extension of the cen- tralized development model rather than true client/server. It was popular in the late '80s, but most organizations have been moving away from it, so we will not elaborate on it.

Screen scraping marked the start of the client/server movement

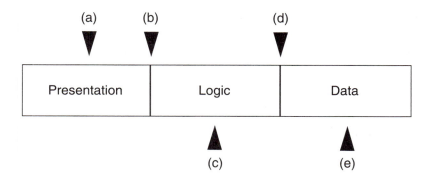

Figure 9-1 The changing location of the client/server partition

First-generation client/server systems were mostly database-oriented

The generation after screen-scraping client/server development focused on the data server model with connected fat clients. Together with screen scraping, they are often referred to as the first generation of client/server systems. In developing such a system, most of the concerns fall into two categories: database and client.

Schema mapping and performance are database concerns

Database Concerns The two main concerns are 1) mapping between the data schema and the object schema and, 2) the database tuning that obtains appropriate performance. Stored procedures and techniques like de-normalizing relational tables are commonly used. Because the clients and the server run at different locations, data caching and data replication (represented by partition point (e) in Figure 9-1) are also used to enhance performance. Often database optimizations can be transparent to the client programmers. For example, client programmers do not need to know whether they are referencing records in a local replica of a remote master database or going after the real record in the master database.

Client development focuses on GUI, application logic, and client/server interaction

Client Concerns Concerns related to the client are the design and implementation of the user interface, the application logic, and the interaction of the client with the database. There is one concern about application logic—because the logic no longer runs under the control of a TP monitor, the application programmer cannot assume that a transaction manager exists on the client side to take care of crash recovery or update coordination at commit/rollback. The application code has to either handle these transaction protection issues or recognize and avoid the risk.

Developers need to optimize for client database access

Client interaction with the database raises other interesting concerns. Because the database is most often remote, going to the database to get data becomes expensive. Developers employ various techniques (discussed in Chapter 7) to enhance the response time. For example, when retrieving and displaying a large table, the code may decide to get the first 50 rows and immediately display them on the screen instead of waiting for the whole table (which may have thousands of rows). In other cases, the database access code may decide to get more rows, so if the user decides to scroll down, the needed rows are already in the client memory. Essentially, the issue is how much data to get per trip to the server and how much to cache.

The Second Generation Client/Server

As discussed in Chapter 4, the model that includes a fat client with a database server runs out of steam when faced with the requirements for some of today's applications. Developers started to seek a client/server partition that would be balanced from a business logic perspective (Figure 9-1 (c)). Tools that support partitioning of business logic often refer to themselves as second-generation client/server tools to distinguish themselves from the first generation, which lumped together screen-scraping and fat-client tools. Because most second-generation tools are object-oriented, we will discuss them later when we talk about OO enterprise development.

Second generation tools seek optimal partitioning of the business logic

The Web Generation

As discussed in the previous chapter, early Web implementations tended to move the client/server split from logic and data back into presentation. The majority of today's Web applications have partition points between (a) and (c) in Figure 9-1. Partitioning the application back toward the client side provides the opportunity to leverage much of what we have learned in the early days of mainframe and client/server development. As the partition points move toward Figure 9-1 (c), (d), and (e), much of what we have learned during the client/server evolution can also be leveraged.

Early Web implementations moved the split from logic and data back into presentation

Client/Server Integration

Traditional client/server systems are developed in a two-track fashion

No matter where the client and the server split, they always have to be integrated so that the application can work. Traditional client/server systems are developed in a two-track fashion. Server development includes database management and transactions; client development includes the user interface and some business logic. Server pieces are often designed and developed separately from client pieces, by different teams or even different organizations. Glue development tends to be a client-side task. However, both client and server teams are responsible for creating, or at least accounting for, some portion of the glue.

Glue-related issues are addressed when the two halves are integrated

When both client and server halves are ready, the team responsible for integrating the code brings them together. (This is often part of the client team.) At this point, it becomes clear whether they will connect and form an integrated system. The integration team exercises the glue, so issues related to networking, middleware, and cross-process performance are uncovered and tackled at this stage.

These issues can introduce changes late in the development cycle

The integration process is a high-risk area in traditional client/server development. Glue-related issues can affect the overall project by introducing late changes in the development cycle. For example, because of sluggish performance, the architect may be forced to move some of the code on the client side to execute on the server side as either stored procedures or transactions. This requires a rethinking of the partition boundary, with corresponding changes to the glue.

The wholistic model calls for developing the whole system iteratively

To mitigate the risk, development teams tend to move away from this waterfall-type practice and turn to iterative and incremental principles. This leads to the wholistic model—developing the whole system iteratively instead of doing the pieces separately and integrating later. In other words, it is now a goal to integrate the glue throughout the development process.

Other reasons also drive the need for the wholistic model. For example, in today's rapidly changing business climate, requirements often change during the development cycle, requiring changes in design or even in the overall architecture. Using the wholistic model, developers can understand the impact of such changes more easily. They can determine the affected pieces and the ways to change them earlier in the cycle and, thus, increase the chances of success.

This model helps developers manage changes in requirements

OO Enterprise Development

The introduction of object technology does not change the fundamental characteristics of client/server development. However, it does make it easier to apply the wholistic development model. As we saw in Chapter 3, objects can be integrated into an enterprise system at a number of levels, providing benefits within client or server components and also within the glues that connect them. If a system follows an OO architecture, the benefits of objects transcend process boundaries to apply to the system as a whole.

Object technology makes it easier to apply the wholistic model

Integrating objects into enterprise systems provides benefits for developers, as well as for users. As with users, these benefits depend on the extent to which objects are integrated into the system. The major benefits are

Objects provide benefits for developers as well as users

- Easier mapping from design and analysis to implementation
- Better and earlier overall view of the system
- More flexible system partitioning
- Opportunities for better tool support

Doesn't this Require OO Tools?

To develop OO systems, the tools themselves do not have to be implemented with object technology, although they frequently are. It is not uncommon for a vendor to implement a suite of tools that contains some OO components and some traditional components, depending on what works best for a development situation. An analogy might be a collection of power tools for a home workshop. In selecting a new tool, such as a drill, you would be most concerned about the drill's features, capabilities, and performance. Whether its casing was made of steel or plastic would be a minor issue. Likewise, in choosing application development power tools, you will be more concerned about their performance and features for developing OO applications than about whether the tools themselves are constructed of objects or procedures.

OO enables business objects to map more clearly to software objects

Easier Mapping to Implementation Less translation is needed between analysis/design and implementation if they share the same paradigm—namely, objects. This benefit becomes clear when we think back to the video store model we developed in Chapter 2. The objects of interest in the store—videos, sections, customers—map directly to software objects. In contrast, in a conventional architecture, developers would have to map the business domain into a structured programming paradigm and implement the business objects and their interactions as procedures.

Straightforward mapping makes the design and the code easier to understand

Not only does traditional mapping cost more in the first place, but it also demands more effort to keep up with requirement changes from the business. In general, the more straightforward the mapping, the easier it is to understand the design and the code. We all know that software developers come and go during the life cycle of an application. The easier it is to learn the system, the easier and quicker it is for a project to bring new people up to speed.

Better and Earlier Overall View As we discussed earlier, the iterative and wholistic model that object technology encourages has the
benefit of giving the developers an earlier and better view of the
entire system end-to-end. By using encapsulation, object technology enables complex systems to be viewed with unnecessary complexity hidden. Even when there are legacy components, OO still
helps. As discussed in Chapter 2, one of the ways to integrate OO
and enterprise computing is to objectify the conventional architecture by wrappering the legacy system with OO interfaces. With
such an approach, the legacy components of a enterprise system
can be treated as objects, which allows the system as a whole to be
viewed, understood, and managed with the object paradigm.

*Object technology
controls complexity
and fosters wholistic
development*

Flexible System Partitioning The encapsulation of objects provides
an ideal abstraction for distribution. Objects are a lot more mobile
than data structures and procedures because they encapsulate both
the data and the behavior in a single entity that can be relocated
quickly. This enables more flexible and dynamic system partitioning.

*Encapsulation of ob-
jects enables easier
partitioning*

One benefit of flexible partitioning is its potential for enhancing
system performance. Often, a client/server system's performance
can be enhanced by positioning frequently interacting objects close
to each other. For example, if an object frequently calls the database, locating the object and the database on the same machine
may prove to enhance performance.

*One benefit of flexi-
ble partitioning is
enhanced system
performance*

Control of information assets is another common reason for repartitioning a system. For example, in some environments, the client
hardware is not secure and thus the software running on the
clients cannot be trusted. Because the servers are often secured and
can be trusted, a system administrator may want to move code that
manages sensitive data onto the server.

*Another benefit is
better control of in-
formation assets*

Systems can be partitioned based on the frequency of updates

Also, systems can be partitioned based on the frequency of updates to the various components. Synchronizing and coordinating updates to a few server machines is often easier than doing it for the large number of client machines. If a system administrator finds that some client components need to be updated frequently, OO technology enables the components to be easily relocated from the clients to the servers, where they can be more easily updated.

Changing business needs can require repartitioning

Note that the factors that determine the partitioning are dynamic. This is true in many cases where applications must be repartitioned after they are implemented. Business needs can change quickly, and meeting those needs can require rapid repartitioning of applications. For example, in the insurance industry, adjusters now carry many functions on their field machines that were once the province of mainframes. In other words, the need for mobile user support requires that many server functions move onto the client.

So can the change from two-tier to three-tier hardware architecture

To take an example from the other end of the spectrum, an enterprise may decide to go from a two-tier hardware architecture to a more flexible three-tier architecture, a change that often requires that the server code be repartitioned among the two server tiers. These and many other examples show why the flexible partitioning supported by OO technology becomes crucial in contemporary enterprise systems.

The more similar the client and server, the more a tool can do for the user

Opportunities for Better Tool Support Using object technology on both client and server helps not only the application developers, but also the tool providers. As we mentioned in Chapter 6, the more similar the client and the server, the more the tool can do for the user and the more easily such tool functions can be implemented. Having objects on both sides increases the similarity and facilitates benefits linked to better tool support. Let's look at two benefits: more-seamless application partitioning and distributed debugging.

The closer the entire end-to-end system resembles a seamless network of objects, the easier it is for development to occur on a single machine. This enables the developer to verify the code with local simulation and then partition and push the code out onto multiple machines. Within a local program written in an OO language, objects naturally form a seamless local network, and if client and server programs follow the same model, then seamless interactivity between them is at least theoretically possible. Most of the discontinuity appears at the glue level; different glues support different degrees of seamlessness. The common language glues support a higher level of seamlessness than the common middleware glues, which in turn support a higher level than the common buffer glues. If the local OO program uses a two-way messaging model (often the case), then two-way messaging glue can provide a higher degree of seamlessness than the one-way messaging glue.

Different glues support different degrees of seamlessness

Client/server application development raises more complex issues of application verification and debugging than stand-alone application development. Suddenly, distributed debugging becomes necessary. Figure 9-2 shows that distributed debugging is not the same as remote debugging, which is support for debugging a piece of code that resides on a remote machine. In contrast, distributed debugging means debugging the entire client/server system as a single unit.

Distributed systems require distributed debugging

A thread of execution in a client/server application may run through multiple machines on the network. With a distributed debugger, the developer uses a single debugger with one window to view and manipulate a composite calling stack composed of the individual stacks on each network machine. This contrasts with remote debug support, which in this case would require multiple remote debuggers open on multiple target machines. The developer is responsible for piecing together the thread of execution—in

This contrasts with remote debugging

Figure 9-2 Remote
debugging vs. dis-
tributed debugging

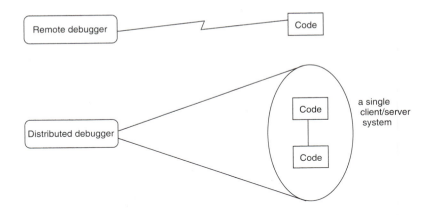

other words, tracking down which processes and objects on which machines are invoking processes and objects on other machines, and then deciding which remote debugger corresponds to which.

The OO benefits lead to more rapid application development

Easier mapping from design and analysis to implementation, better and earlier overall view of the system, more flexible system partitioning, and opportunities for better tool support naturally lead to more-rapid development. This enables the enterprise systems to better keep pace with the rapidly changing business requirements.

OO Enterprise Development Tools

This section takes a look at several OO development tool suites

In this section, we examine several second-generation OO client/server development tools to illustrate the concepts introduced in this chapter. Most of the tools strive to provide end-to-end development support; the goal is to provide this support over the full range of client/server application types. We will look at the features of these tools that are fundamental to the OO enterprise development process.

First we will present a template for looking at them, then we will discuss each one. The template serves to focus our discussion on the architectural aspects of the tools, not their minor features and implementations on various platforms with various communication plumbing configurations. These details tend to change more quickly than the overall architectures of the tools.

We will focus on the architecture aspects instead of basic development support

The tools we discuss include basic client/server development support, such as GUI building and relational database access. However, we will not spend a lot of time on these aspects of the tools, which are common even in first-generation client/server tools.

Visual programming is one of the benefits that object technology as brought to application development. Many of today's tools now also include a visual programming component as an extension to the GUI builder. However, visual programming is not fundamental to the architecture of second-generation client/server development; rather, it is a valuable shortcut that, used correctly, can greatly speed certain phases of the development cycle.

Visual programming is a valuable shortcut but not fundamental to OO development

A Template to Look at Development Tools

Our template for development tools is intended to bring focus to the essential issues that determine what tool is best for the job. The idea is to apply the template when choosing the tools that your organization will use. As an example of how to do this, we take a close look at three development tools, Microsoft's Visual Studio, Forte Software's Forte, and IBM's VisualAge.

Our template focuses on the essential issues

We don't want to get too specific about the tools themselves because they change so frequently. Therefore, we don't provide a list of features to look for because in making a long-term commitment to a tool, you need to see beyond the current features into the in-

Visual Programming: Hype and Reality

If we can express and comprehend our computer applications more clearly with a few lines and drawings than we can by writing down many lines of code, the benefit is obvious. However, the big word is always "if." When visual programming was first introduced into the commercial client/server market, it was promoted as the solution for many things, such as low productivity and a scarcity of skilled programmers. It enabled vendors to produce sexy demos that gave people the illusion that a client/server application can be constructed "without writing a single line of code." Over the years, people learned that visual programming is good for certain things but not all, and it's by no means a panacea.

The fundamental attraction of visual programming is the principle that human beings can comprehend and manage visual notations effectively. In GUI construction, a picture can be worth a thousand words. Take a simple push button, for example; with a GUI builder, a developer can position and size it with a few mouse clicks. Achieving the same effect with textual code would require calculation and specification of multiple screen coordinates. The visual programming is a more expressive notation for telling the computer system what the user wants.

Some vendors have tried to push visual programming further into client/server development by extending the GUI tools into the back end. Inevitably, they hit the "visual programming wall." As soon as they venture out of the GUI domain, they encounter the business logic, which requires conditional statements and looping. Trying to express these visually can make both the tool and the visually programmed artifact too complex. Even without the addition of such constructs, today's visual programming can result in complex diagrams that can be difficult to comprehend and debug.

So, is there hope to leverage visual programming in other aspects of client/server development? The answer is, yes. For example, domains like application partitioning and system management can use visual techniques. Building a visual programming tool is relatively easy. The hard part is defining the tool's domain and matching it up with the right notation (in other words, what are the right semantics for the graphical elements like boxes, circles, and lines).

We believe in picking the right tools for the job. If the problem domain renders itself well to visual notation, then use visual programming to help. If textual, voice, or gesture techniques are the best for the domain, then use them. In the foreseeable future, we expect the world of client/server programming will continue to mix the textual and the visual. In the end, it's not whether one can create an entire application "without writing a single line of textual code." What counts is productivity and the manageability of the resulting code reflected in overall cost and time.

trinsic architecture issues that cannot easily change. In using the template, think of the following items as areas of concern, not necessarily as features.

- Language and reusable components
- User interface and visual programming
- Server programming
- Distributed glue
- Distributed application specification
- Verification
- Internet/Web support
- Build and team support
- System management

The key questions about language support are straightforward and relatively easy to answer—but also essential. What programming languages does the tool support? Does it support a single language or multiple languages? Proprietary or standardized? Are there any

Language

unique language characteristics? Do vendors provide comprehensive class libraries and reusable components for the tool's language?

User interface and visual programming

Assuming that most of today's tools provide a visual GUI builder, how far does it go beyond constructing user interfaces? How mature is the tool support for visual programming compared with textual programming? Visual programming is still programming, and people can easily write visual spaghetti code. Without good tool support to help understand, debug, and manage it, the visual component is often limited to simple GUI construction.

Server programming

What server platforms does the tool support? Is it specific to transactional servers, data servers, application servers, or can it work with more than one type? What's the programming model and the tools to support it? Does it provide a simulated workstation development environment?

Distributed glue

What are the glues that it supports? At what level of abstraction (common buffer, middleware, language)? One-way or two-way messaging?

Distributed application specification

What tools support the design of the distributed applications? Are there tools to help analyze the traffic across the network? Is there tool support for iterative code partitioning? Does the environment provide the ability to capture the distribution design together with the code and place both under version control?

Internet/Web support

What tools support the development of Internet applications? (See the sidebar below for a conceptual framework for Internet application development.) How integrated are the Internet/Web tools with the other tools in the suite? How open is the underlying architecture for other tools to integrate with the suite?

What means are provided for developers to verify their applications? Does the tool support simulated distribution that can test some aspects of the application without actually distributing it? What's the debugging support in each case? Do the tools support true distributed debugging or simply remote debugging? (See page 229 for an explanation of the difference).

Verification

What kind of team programming support is available? Is it tightly integrated with the environment or is it loosely coupled so that it can be provided by a third party. What build capabilities are supported? Do the tools support cross compilation or can they compile remotely? (Cross compilation produces executables for multiple target platforms on a single machine; remote compilation produces executables by invoking compilers on the target machines remotely.)

Build and team support

Is there software distribution support to deliver the developed system to the distributed network? Is there an integrated system management tool or do the tools work with existing system

System management

Internet Application Development

From an enterprise computing perspective, the Web and the Internet are new platforms that can be used to extend the reach of the business system. To successfully develop an Internet application (we define Web application as a subset of Internet application), new components need to be implemented to tap into the existing applications and data. In addition, the existing code may have to be modified to support the new requirements. This makes Internet application development (AD) a superset of traditional client/server application development. It includes all the existing client/server development support and adds two new categories of tools: content authoring and Web site development.

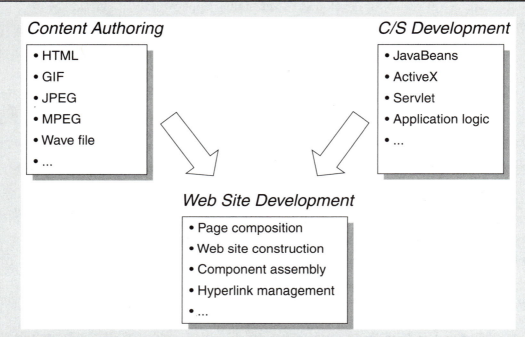

Content authoring tools are used to create and manipulate the variety of multimedia content found in today's Web-based applications. Standard content types include text, images, animation, audio, and video. These tools provide the raw contents required by the Web site development tools. Content authoring tools focus on enabling designers and graphic artists to render content efficiently and professionally.

Client/server development tools produce applets, servlets, ActiveX components, JavaBeans, and objects in a variety of languages to implement the application logic and to connect to the enterprise information systems.

Web site development tools support content assembly and content management. The content assembly tools take active contents, such as JavaBeans and applets, and compose/ script them together with static contents, such as HTML and multimedia, to form a cohesive Web page. Multiple pages are combined to form a complete Internet application.

> **Content management tools** provide the ability to identify and manage the resources that make up the Web site: HTML files, media files, Java classes, JavaBeans, plug-ins, ActiveX controls, URLs, and so forth. These tools also aid in managing the execution environment. They include Web server-specific tools that deal with such aspects as broken links and site structure visualization.

management solutions? If there is an integrated system management tool, how comprehensive is the support? (For example, are there tools to perform post-deployment tasks at the application level, such as status reporting and performance monitoring?)

Case Study: Visual Studio

Microsoft Visual Studio is a comprehensive suite for creating multi-tier and Web applications and for integrating client/server and Internet technologies. It includes Visual C++, Visual J++, Visual Basic, Visual InterDev (for Web applications), and Visual FoxPro (for database applications).

Introduction

Both C++ and Java are considered nonproprietary OO languages, although Java doesn't have an ANSI standard yet. C++ is one of the most popular OO programming languages, built on a hybrid of procedural and object-oriented concepts. For Internet development, Microsoft has also added scripting languages, such as JScript (a Microsoft version of the JavaScript language).

Language

Java provides a syntax similar to C++ but without as much complexity. However, under the covers, it shares characteristics such as garbage collection and single implementation inheritance with the other major OO language, Smalltalk.

Reusable compo-
nents

A large set of COM/DCOM-based reusable components is available from Microsoft and third-party vendors. Because COM is a cross-language mechanism, the components can be implemented and used by any Visual Studio language.

Note that additional factors affect the usability of these components. Reuse also requires effective debugging of the resulting application. Debugging across language boundaries has proven to be difficult and requires specialized skills (including knowledge of both the calling and the called languages and of the cross-language mechanism). Reuse within a single language is easier than reuse across languages. However, even in this case, a component packaged with the cross-language component technology will still require the user to know both the language and the cross-language mechanism.

User interface and
visual programming

Visual Studio supports GUI building for Windows clients and Web clients. So far, there has been little attempt to extend the visual programming paradigm much beyond UI construction. The Microsoft builder is very user friendly, and many reusable components are available from third-party vendors.

Server programming

The Microsoft tools support Windows 95 and Windows NT as the only server platforms. The tools are currently optimized for developing database servers. However, the native server support found in the Visual Basic Enterprise Edition is likely to find its way into the C++ and Java tools. With the emerging Microsoft Transaction Server, COM components can also be transactional, leading to support for object TP monitor servers.

Visual C++ and J++ support data server glues such as ODBC and JDBC. Communications occur at the level of common middleware. (See Chapter 6 for a full discussion of communications levels.)

Distributed glue

Additional glue support for native and transaction servers is provided by Distributed COM. The Java Remote Method Invocation (RMI), a common language-level service, is supported, as well.

The data server glues support only the one-way messaging model. The rest support two-way messaging through DCOM.

Visual C++ provides tools for the user to examine SQL Server databases, tables, and views across the network from within its Developer Studio. Developers can edit SQL Server stored procedures and issue SQL commands directly to remote databases. They can also use the integrated remote debugging to step from the client-side C++ source code to an SQL Server stored procedure executing on a server machine, set break points for debugging triggers, and examine local and global database variables.

Distributed application specification

There is little support in these tools today for partitioning design and analysis of either the data server or the native and transaction servers.

Visual InterDev provides one of the most comprehensive suites of tools for Internet application development. All three categories of tools (content authoring, Web site development, and client/server development) are well covered by the Microsoft offering. The tools are also well integrated. Web-related multimedia contents can also be managed by Visual SourceSafe, and all tools provide a single consistent user interface to interact with Visual SourceSafe. Be-

Internet/Web support

cause the tools focus on supporting the Microsoft Active Server Page architecture, which depends on ActiveX, they are not very useful on non-Microsoft platforms.

Verification

Data server verification occurs through a live connection to a database (in contrast to the VisualAge single system image verification discussed below). For all server types, debugging is at the remote debugger level (the debugger allows users to debug a single program remotely). There is no distributed debugger yet.

Build and team support

The Microsoft Visual SourceSafe is a file-based check-in/check-out tool. It can store both source files and binary files (such as complied executables). It is not a repository based on an information model that describes the stored software artifacts for sharing among tools. It is integrated with Visual Studio tools, so Visual SourceSafe commands can be issued directly from within the Developer Studio. Because only Windows platforms are supported, there is no need for cross-compilation. As the Microsoft repository technology, which is currently shipped only with Visual Basic, becomes more mature, it is expected to assume the role of Visual SourceSafe. It can provide services beyond file-based check in/out, such as meta information services for objects stored in the repository.

System management

Microsoft provides its own Systems Management Server. The linkage between the Systems Management Server and Visual SourceSafe is at the file exchange level. Application management support (such as application-level performance monitoring) can be obtained from third-party system management vendors, such as Tivoli.

Summary

The key strength of the Microsoft Visual Studio lies in its cross-language support, integration of tools, and the large number of reusable ActiveX components. The server development story is weaker than the client story. Application partitioning support is also weak.

Case Study: Forte

The Forte Application Environment is an integrated set of object-oriented tools for building, deploying, and managing high-end client/server applications. Forte is considered by many analysts to be the technology leader in the 4GL OO client/server tools market.

Introduction

Forte uses its own proprietary "object-oriented 4GL," called TOOL (Transactional Object-Oriented Language). It is a derivative of C++ but easier to use and with single-inheritance only (similar to Java). It supports garbage collection and has no concept of pointers.

Language

Forte supports both synchronous and asynchronous execution. Events can be defined within a class to support event-triggered execution.

The code can be executed by a client-side interpreter with GUI capabilities. On the server side, you can use the interpreter or compile the code to get better performance.

In comparison to the other tools evaluated in this chapter, fewer classes, libraries, and reusable components are available for Forte, either through Forte itself or through third-party vendors.

The Forte GUI builder is a screen painter and makes no attempt to provide visual programming support beyond screen layout. Developers must capture UI events by writing an event loop for each window.

User interface and visual programming

Forte supports NT and most major UNIX varieties as server platforms. The tools are optimized to develop objectified native servers

Server programming

with distributed transaction support. Server logic is written with the TOOL language, which is supported by the Forte development environment. TOOL statements can be executed with the interpreter on the development platform. There is no server programming support for third-tier mainframe platforms, such as CICS and IMS/TM. Nor is there simulation support on development platforms for the mainframe platforms' resource managers.

Distributed glue

The main glue model Forte supports is the transactional distributed object model surfaced through the TOOL language. Communications occur at the common language level. However, not all the local services are supported across the network. For example, Forte does not support distributed garbage collection or distributed deadlock detection. This decreases some of its local/remote transparency.

Forte uses the two-way messaging model, which is implicit in its programming language.

Distributed application specification

Developers can generally specify applications without regard to their eventual distribution topology. Once an application is developed locally, the developers can create partitions as the unit of distribution. A drag-and-drop partition tool enables developers to specify the network node where a specific partition should run. The distribution design and the code are stored in a repository.

Internet/Web support

Forte provides an optional Web SDK (software developer's kit) that enables Web clients to access the Forte services. This kit provides tools to convert existing Forte windows into appropriately formatted HTML pages for Web clients. The kit also supports Java applet access to Forte server objects. Because the approach is to extend and support the existing Forte architecture, the tools and the generated code are only useful in a Forte environment.

Developers can verify the application locally and also after it has been distributed. Simulation support is limited to relational databases. Remote or distributed debug support is not available at the time of writing but should not be hard to provide, given the common language communications level of Forte's 4GL environment.

Verification

A program repository is tightly integrated with the development environment. This is based on a check-in/check-out model, but does not provide version control at this time. Developers can use remote compilation for the code that runs on target platforms.

Build and team support

Forte provides a proprietary, tightly integrated system management tool that supports software distribution and some application monitoring after deployment. It is not as robust as the tools from system management vendors like Tivoli and Computer Associates. Because system management is normally broader than the services a single tool can provide, we expect Forte will need to make efforts to work with system management vendors.

System management

Forte's key strength is in its integrated environment, based around its proprietary language. All tools necessary for developing an OO client/server application are well-integrated. This is the typical strength of any 4GL system. Forte also inherits the drawbacks of 4GL. The proprietary language and closed environment limit developers to the tools and services that Forte and its business partners can provide.

Summary

Case Study: VisualAge

IBM's VisualAge is a family of application development tool suites based on different OO programming languages. Each language-based tool suite is a complete development environment, with components such as the visual composition editor shared across the family. Each tool suite provides extensive class libraries and ro-

Introduction

bust tool support, but the precise tool support varies from language to language.

VisualAge seeks to provide a single tool set for multiple languages

VisualAge is heading in the direction of providing a single tool set for multiple languages—for example, the VisualAge visual builder is already used across the languages. The obvious benefit of tool consolidation is that language-independent skills, such as database design and GUI construction, are transferable among projects developed in different languages. However, because of the realities of technology integration and the marketplace, such consolidation cannot be achieved overnight. It will likely continue over the next few years.

Language

The IBM VisualAge family supports a "language of choice" strategy, supporting the largest number of OO languages available from any single vendor: C++, Java, Smalltalk, and OO COBOL. It also supports a proprietary 4GL.

Reusable Components

The number of reusable components is significant but fewer than Microsoft's. IBM's attempt to introduce cross-language reuse through SOM has not been as successful as Microsoft's COM efforts. Currently, most of the VisualAge reusable components are language-specific, which results in lower accessibility but higher usability.

User interface and visual programming

The VisualAge composition editor reaches beyond standard GUI construction into the domain of visual programming. The result of a visual programming session does not necessarily have to be visual screens. Business objects on the other side of the visual programming wall can be programmed textually but wrapped and presented to the visual builder as "nonvisual parts." They can then be manipulated visually and with dialog boxes and participate in visual connections to the GUI. Access to common services, such as relational databases, can also surface as nonvisual parts, which provides ease of use.

Most VisualAge consultants advocate the use of the composition editor primarily as a GUI builder. As discussed in the sidebar "Visual Programming: Hype and Reality" (page 232), further technology and research breakthroughs are necessary before visual programming reaches the level of textual programming.

Although its client programming side is at least the equal of most other tool suites, server programming is considered a particular strength of VisualAge. It supports all three major server types and almost every server platform. Server support is especially strong for mainframe platforms, such as MVS, CICS, and IMS.

Server programming

The simulated workstation-based development environment allows interactive development of server code without connection to the actual target platforms. CICS, IMS, VSAM, DB2, and other legacy data stores are also simulated on the workstation. Remote debuggers give access to both mid-tier and mainframe servers.

VisualAge supports glues for all three server types. The common middleware support focuses on the CORBA standard. Common buffer support is used for interfacing with legacy systems. As with Visual Studio, data server access uses one-way messaging while the other server types use two-way messaging.

Distributed glue

C++, Smalltalk, and Java versions of VisualAge provide strong common language support for communications. For example, Smalltalk supports distributed garbage collection, a feature that no other OO development tool suite currently provides.

Distributed applica-
tion specification

VisualAge does not require explicit specification of the execution platform while the application is being specified. Because of its extensive server programming simulation, VisualAge enables development in a single address space, followed by verification, partitioning, and deployment. The tools capture the partition design, version it, and store it with the code in a program repository.

Program analysis tools—including a strong program visualization component—help developers determine the optimal logic partitioning for their applications. VisualAge is a leader in this new technology area. For a detailed description, see the sidebar, "Program Visualization in Distributed Computing."

Internet/Web
support

VisualAge for e-business, the newest member of the VisualAge family, supports Internet/Web application development. Its coverage is good in the client/server and Web site development categories but not in the content authoring category. Instead of relying on its own product to deliver all the content authoring tools, IBM takes an open stance and leverages the other industry providers. Because tools come from multiple providers and there is no single repository, the IBM suite is not as well integrated as the Microsoft suite.

Verification

VisualAge provides **single system image** verification. A client/server application can be verified with simulated data and services on the workstation without actually being partitioned and distributed. This is especially true for the common language case. Once the application is partitioned and distributed to the different target platforms, the distributed or remote debuggers enable debugging of the entire application across the network.

Languages provide different levels of debugging support. In the Smalltalk version, a single distributed debugger window

---

Program Visualization in Distributed Computing

Program visualization techniques represent objects, machines, and program modules graphically and enable developers to analyze their behavior with a variety of views. Many program visualization techniques can be useful in distributed computing. For instance, a *cluster view* can be used to show the natural proximity of objects in a system. Real or simulated input can be used to drive the program associated with the cluster view. The program visualization interface shows icons representing objects attracting each other if they communicate frequently and repelling each other if they don't. Given a representative set of input, an equilibrium state indicates the optimal logic split.

Additional program visualization techniques include visual specification of the client/server topology and *pinning* of certain objects at certain locations (for example, it makes good sense to pin GUI-related objects to the client partition). The tools can suggest a default partitioning for program entities that touch either the UI or the database. Object modules, represented by icons, can be manually moved from one location to another.

Like visual programming, program visualization is good for program artifacts that are easier to analyze and manipulate when rendered graphically. It is not the solution to all programming problems.

---

displays execution stacks from multiple machines as a single contiguous stack. This allows a user at a single location to set breakpoints and modify code on all machines spanned by the enterprise application. Other languages use remote debugging.

VisualAge uses two repositories: Envy and TeamConnection. Both support team programming and version control. Work is ongoing to integrate the two into a single solution. The development tools

Build and team support

can leverage the repository for tool integration. For example, through the repository, a design tool is able to change its diagrams based on code changes in the program editor.

The build tool supports distributed compilation through its ability to kick off compilation of different client/server components on different platforms.

System management   VisualAge is strongly integrated with the Tivoli system management tools. The VisualAge program repository is integrated with the Tivoli software distribution tool; this enables the delivery and installation of the software components to the network from the repository. The entire client/server system can be controlled from a single point. In addition to application monitoring and error notification, VisualAge leverages the Tivoli tools to collect runtime application performance information. VisualAge also works with system management tools by vendors other than Tivoli, though the strong integration capabilities are missing.

Summary   The key strength of VisualAge is its breadth of language and platform coverage. It provides all the tools necessary to deliver and maintain applications for enterprises that deal with heterogeneous systems. Another strength is VisualAge's extensive development support for servers and distributed applications. The key weaknesses are the lack of integration of the many elements in the solution family (especially across language boundaries) and the room for improvement in the user friendliness of the tools.

Summary

As the enterprise computing runtime model has evolved, development models and development tools have also evolved. First-generation client/server development was mostly database-oriented. In the second generation, client/server development tools seek optimal partitioning of the business logic. The Web generation initially pushed the partition point toward the client but is following the path of client/server computing to offer all the partition possibilities.

Client/server integration is a major issue in traditional development. Glue-related issues often are not tackled until the two halves are integrated, which can introduce changes late in the development cycle. The wholistic development model addresses these integration issues. It calls for developing the whole system iteratively. In applying object technology, visual programming can be a valuable shortcut but is not fundamental to OO development.

Our template for evaluating development tools covers the key characteristics of the tools.

- Language and reusable components
- User interface and visual programming
- Server programming
- Distributed glue
- Distributed application specification
- Verification
- Internet/Web support
- Build and team support
- System management

By applying the template to three representative tool suites, we bring the concerns of the chapter into focus and give organizations a model for evaluating their development tool needs.

10

Performance

We often hear that performance is one of the major issues of any system. In developing OO enterprise systems, it is critical. Introducing object technology into an enterprise system affects the overall system performance in a number of ways. OO features such as encapsulation, polymorphism, wrapping, and automatic garbage collection require additional layers of indirection and computing at the level of programming language implementation. These tend to have a negative impact on performance. However, object orientation also introduces new ways of looking at and solving problems, which results in different design and architecture. This can have a positive effect on performance.

Performance is a major issue in any system

For example, componentizing desktop services (such as a spelling checker) reduces the overall footprint of the system, which in turn decreases the disk access by the swapper and allows better performance. The advent of OO glues has also had a positive effect on performance by allowing more flexible application partitioning. ODBMSs are an example of how a new architecture introduced by object technology can drastically improve performance for a specific domain.

OO architecture and design can improve performance

This chapter starts by looking at the two major criteria for measuring client/server performance—throughput and response time—and at some guidelines for optimizing them. Then we turn to a more detailed discussion of performance as it relates to the four major areas of client, server, glue, and data. We end with a discussion of load balancing. As we go, we note the aspects of performance that are specific to object technology.

Throughput and response time measure client/server performance

Throughput and Response Time

Throughput measures the amount of work done per unit of time

Throughput is a measure of the amount of work done in a unit of time. It is a server-oriented measurement. In traditional OLTP systems, such as CICS, throughput is often measured in the number of transactions processed per second. Such a performance number is meaningful only when the transactions are clearly defined. This is because the amount of work done in a transaction is system- and application-dependent and can vary widely. For example, in an online transaction processing system, transactions are often programmed to finish in milliseconds, while in a decision support system, a transaction may run for several minutes. Various applications also give different amounts of work to their transactions.

Throughput can also measure batch processing

Throughput is also used to measure batch-oriented processing. A batch job is often composed of multiple units of work (sometimes also called transactions). The faster a system can complete the entire batch job, the better the performance. A **batch window** is the period of time allotted by the system administrator for a system to complete batch jobs. Because many systems have online processing duties during the day, they tend to run batch jobs at night so that the online and batch jobs do not affect one another's performance. Having good enough system performance to run the batch jobs overnight (or over the weekend) within batch windows is important.

Response time comes between the initiation of a request and the system response

Response time is a measure of system performance from the user's perspective. It measures the amount of time a user perceives between the initiation of a request and the rendering of the system response. This includes client processing time, network time, and server processing time. As with throughput, response time is also application-dependent. Because response time measures the user's perception, techniques that manipulate that perception can improve system responsiveness. For example, rendering partial results to the user while the system is still computing can give the user the perception that the system has a fast response time.

Throughput and response time are often related. A client/server system with high throughput usually has better response time, and vice versa. However, the two are not necessarily directly coupled. Here is an example of how a system with slower throughput can have better average response time with intelligent job scheduling.

Throughput and re-sponse time are re-lated but not necessarily coupled

Figure 10-1 shows a system with a throughput of five units of work per second. Two users of the system are submitting requests at the same time. The request from User 1 takes 1,000 units of work to process and the request from User 2 takes only one unit of work to process. As shown in the figure, User 1's request is processed first. It's completed in

A system with greater throughput . . .

1,000 / 5 = 200 seconds

and the perceived response time is 200 seconds.

User 2's request, submitted at the same time as User 1's, takes

1 / 5 = 0.2 second

to process. However, the response time is

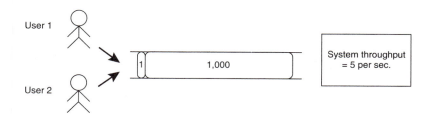

Figure 10-1 System with a throughput of five units of work per second

User 1

User 2

1   1,000

System throughput = 5 per sec.

0.2 + 200 = 200.2 seconds

because it represents the total time the user has to wait between submitting the request and getting the result back. The average response time of the system is

(200 + 200.2) / 2 = 200.1 seconds

. . . can display
slower response time

Figure 10-2 shows the second system with 20 percent less throughput (four units of work per second) than the first system. The same requests are submitted by the same users. However, User 2's job (the smaller one) is scheduled to execute first. It's completed in

1 / 4 = 0.25 second

and the perceived response time is 0.25 seconds.

User 1's request takes

1000 / 4 = 250 seconds

to process. The response time is

0.25 + 250 = 250.25 seconds

The average response time of the system is

(0.25 + 250.25) / 2 = 125.25 seconds

**Figure 10-2 System
with a throughput of
four units of work
per second**

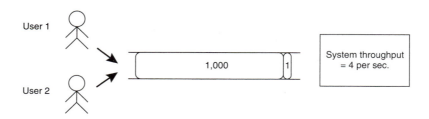

Although the first system runs faster and has higher throughput, its average response time is worse than the system with a lower throughput. By scheduling the jobs more intelligently, the system with lower throughput gives the impression of better performance. This helps illustrate that performance tuning is not simply getting faster components. Smart use of system resources is also important.

Performance tuning is more than having fast components

Sophisticated mathematical models based on queuing theory can be built to analyze system throughput and response time. The parameters of the models include

Queuing theory analyzes throughput and response time

- The probability distribution for request inter-arrival time
- The probability distribution for server processing time
- The number of servers being modeled
- The maximum number of requests allowed at any time

The details are beyond the scope of this book, but interested readers can consult the references listed on Operations Research and Queuing Theory for more information.

Optimization

Whether we are talking about throughput or response time, the performance of a client/server system is limited by the bottlenecks caused by slow components. In other words, a system can perform only as fast as its slowest component. For example, Figure 10-3 shows a typical client/server processing time line. It starts with an end user submitting a request through the client. The client requires processing time to present the user interface and perform local logic, such as entry-field checking. The request is then sent to the server via the network, which involves the hardware and software stacks of the LAN, the bridges and routers between the LAN and the WAN, and the WAN. When the request reaches the server, the server executes the server-side logic and accesses the data

A system can perform only as well as its bottleneck

store. The return result traverses the same components in reverse order and eventually is rendered to the user.

Identifying bottle-
necks is the first step
to optimization

Identifying the bottlenecks is the first step in optimizing any system. A common pitfall is to optimize what one is familiar with instead of the true bottlenecks. The scale and complexity of an enterprise system make it easy to lose the right perspective. For example, client programmers often look to optimize the client code first and server programmers do the same with the server code, when the real problem may be in the glue. Such an approach can easily waste time and fail to produce results. Worse yet, optimization can often introduce complexity that makes the software difficult to maintain later on. Blindly introducing optimization can corrupt the integrity of the system architecture and increase the defect rate and maintenance cost.

If a slow network
creates a
bottleneck . . .

To illustrate the importance of identifying the bottleneck in optimization, Figure 10-4(a) shows the unit of time a specific client system spends in client, network, and server processing. The system bottleneck is a slow network: 80 percent of the overall pro-

Figure 10-3 Typical client/server processing time line

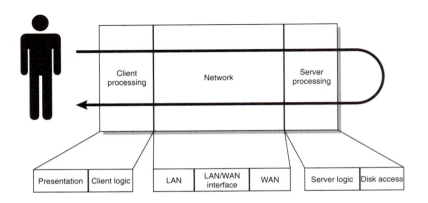

cessing time is spent on transferring the request and result between the client and the server.

Figure 10-4(b) shows an optimization effort to speed up the client processing by a factor of ten, say by getting a client machine that runs ten times faster. Though the client processing is 1,000 percent faster, the overall system sees only a 9 percent reduction of processing time. This is because client processing was not a bottleneck to begin with. (In fact, even if one could make the client processing infinitely faster and thus reduce client processing time to zero, the overall performance improvement is only 10 percent.) Figure 10-4(c) shows the result of optimizing the true bottleneck, the network. By doubling the network speed, the entire system enjoys a 40 percent reduction of processing time.

... optimizing the client won't help

To optimize an enterprise system, one must examine the end-to-end system as a whole instead of looking at individual system elements. Optimization becomes a series of modifications to eliminate bottlenecks. This is an iterative process. As one bottleneck is removed, another one is likely to emerge. The entire system must be examined again to identify and eliminate. This iteration continues until the performance objective is achieved.

Optimization is a series of bottleneck elimination actions across the system

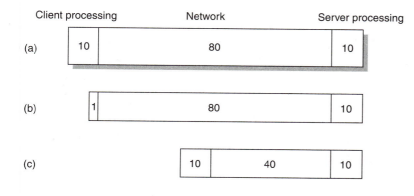

Figure 10-4 Comparison of optimizing in different areas

Client Performance

Client performance issues center around workload, speed, and user perception

Performance issues for client, server, and glue all tend to center around the same questions: How much work does the component do? and How can we make it faster? The client side faces the unique issue of: How does the user perceive the response time?

We'll take a look at how OO clients deal with these issues and then turn our attention to the server and the glue.

Client Workload

It's important to strike a balance between client and server workload

A client's workload can vary quite a bit. A fat client might handle all presentation, business processing, and persistence mapping. In contrast, a thin client might deal only with part of the presentation processing. Fat clients can get too fat, run slowly, and require more client-side resources than the system can provide. Thin clients can get too thin to fully use available resources and then create too much network traffic to the server. Therefore, the key to obtaining the best client performance is striking a balance between client and server workloads.

Client Speed

There are multiple ways to make the client process the work faster. Adding hardware (a faster CPU, more RAM and disk capacity, a faster graphics card) is the obvious one. However, several other techniques are also effective.

Smaller client-side executables are more responsive

Reducing the Size of the Client-Side Executable can increase responsiveness by speeding program start-up time. It can also eliminate the annoying pauses caused by virtual memory swapping between the hard drive and RAM.

Manage Memory for Transient Objects During execution, an OO client can sometimes create a large number of short-lived objects. Proper management of the memory for these objects can enhance performance. For languages with automatic memory management (garbage collection), properly tuning the parameters, such as heap size and space allocations for generational garbage collectors, can often enhance performance. For languages that do not have a garbage collector, it is even more important to follow the correct programming guidelines to ensure that there is no memory leak and that memory is allocated and returned to the system appropriately.

Proper management of short-lived objects enhances performance

Moving Some Computation to a Different Time can also help performance. Most client programs interact with the user for a long time (usually minutes or hours). A user may not notice that program start-up time is a few seconds longer while an increase of even one second to the sub-second response time during user interaction may be quite an annoyance. Moving computation from interactive time to start-up time can result in better user perception of performance. For example, instead of creating the next screenful of GUI objects in response to a user action like pressing a button, the program can pre-compute those objects at start-up time. Note, however, that such techniques can use more system resources, such as memory, to hold the pre-computed objects.

Pre-computing objects helps performance but uses more resources

Increasing Concurrency is also helpful in many situations. If a client needs to issue I/O requests to multiple sources (such as a database and a communications socket), it's more efficient to send out multiple requests concurrently than sequentially. An efficient client application allows other processing (such as user interaction or preparing other requests) while waiting for an I/O request to return. Not blocking on I/O is a typical way to enable this.

Increased concurrency can also help

Nonblocking I/O and Native
Operating System Threads

Nonblocking I/O does not necessarily require surfacing the native operating system threads to the application programmer. In fact, most application developers are not trained to do preemptive native-thread programming. Also, the semantics of native operating system threads can vary widely from platform to platform.

With the advent of multiple-processor workstations, some operating systems map the threads to multiple processors to leverage the parallelism supported by the hardware. In such a situation, the application code is not portable from platform to platform. There can also be tricky synchronization and locking problems that are hard to track down.

As a consequence, vendors often support higher-level notation, such as the language-level thread support in Java and asynchronous callout in some Smalltalk implementations, to make it easy to do nonblocking I/O without involving low-level native threads.

Web browsers often take advantage of concurrency by opening multiple TCP/IP connections to retrieve multiple files from the server concurrently.

Concurrent execution threads can further the effect of other optimizations

Concurrent threads of execution can also be used to further the effect of other optimizations. For example, instead of pre-computing all the presentation objects at initialization, which would require the user to wait before starting the first interaction with the system, the client can do such pre-computation concurrently in the background, with a lower priority than the user interaction activities. That way, the user can start interacting with the system quickly, while the CPU cycles during user pauses are picked up for the precomputation.

Cache Objects and Data If the client machine has sufficient resources and the application semantics allow it, caching server objects and data can also enhance performance. A typical example occurs when a user scrolls through a large database table on the server. Instead of discarding the rows that have been scrolled out of the display window, the client can cache them to avoid trips across the network when the user decides to scroll back.

A client machine can cache server objects

Perceptions of Client Response

Effectively managing the user-perceived response time can have a big effect on system performance. The key is to keep the user occupied.

Render Partial Results Instead of waiting for the entire result to come in from the server, the client can start displaying partial results early. For example, in displaying a long list to the user, the client program can render the first few items to give the user something to read while the rest of the list continues to process. Many Web browsers employ this technique to render large images progressively, instead of waiting for the entire image to arrive.

A client can start displaying partial results early

Display Status Information Even when the request processing requires the user to wait for a long time without intermediate results, showing a progress indicator can make the wait more tolerable to the user. A moving slider or bar graph informs the user that the operation is progressing and maintains user confidence. As an example of this technique, consider the Web browsers that show the percentage of the document retrieved.

A progress indicator informs the user of the operation's progress

*Users are more toler-
ant if they can
switch to another
task*

Free the User Interface Allowing the user to do other things while
waiting for the result can enhance the user perception, as well. If
users can switch to another task, such as reading a document,
preparing another request, or checking on the result of a prior request, they are occupied and will tend to be more tolerant of the
time required for processing.

*Web clients use
many of these tech-
niques*

Remember that a user surfing the Web is interacting with a
client/server system. Because this interaction often involves retrieving files across a modem connection, which can involve longer
wait times than a typical client/server system, it's no surprise that
many of the techniques discussed in this section are used by Web
browsers.

Server Performance

*Speed and workload
are server issues, but
user perception is not*

Managing user perceptions is not an issue on the server side because the server does not interact directly with a human user.
Therefore, only two of the three fundamental client issues are relevant here: amount of server work and server speed.

Some of the factors affecting these issues are similar on both sides;
other factors are very different.

Server Workload

*Off-loading user in-
teraction can en-
hance server
performance*

In a traditional mainframe system, the server does most of the
work, including user interfaces. By off-loading the GUI processing
to PC clients, the server can speed up the processing of business
logic and data. Because a traditional system like CICS has to
process every screen the user sees, the savings can be significant.

*Screen scraping does
not add to perfor-
mance*

Note that screen scraping may be a useful presentation enhancement, but it does not save you anything on the server side. Because the same server transactions (including the UI processing)

are still being executed, the server is doing exactly the same amount of work.

It's also important to remember that performance optimization is a function of the end-to-end system, not the individual components. Doing everything possible to off-load computation from the server will not necessarily produce better performance because you can off-load so much to the client that the entire system performance suffers. The client becomes overloaded or the overall system spends too much time doing network I/O. For example, if a database server has stored procedures that frequently access the data, moving some procedures down to the client side may save on the server resources but cost more because of more frequent network traffic. Remember that the first principle of performance tuning is to identify the bottleneck. If the stored procedure processing on the server is not a bottleneck, moving it not only won't help the overall system performance, but it can make it worse by putting more stress on the existing bottleneck.

Too much off-loading can cause the whole system to suffer

Server Speed

As on the client side, faster hardware is the most obvious way to enhance server performance, but it is not the only way. Smart use of resources can play an even more important role than it does on the client side because server resources are shared and are usually highly stressed. A change in server performance characteristics can affect many clients. Let's look at some of the important server-side optimization techniques.

A change in server performance can affect many clients

Configure the System Properly An experienced system administrator typically monitors system execution and makes adjustments to system configuration to enhance performance. Many system parameters can be adjusted, ranging from hardware (for example, how many processors to assign to a certain class of tasks) to operating

Many system parameters can be adjusted

system and system services (for example, available swap space or how many worker processes should be started) to application software (for example, how much memory to allocate by a program or what code and data to make memory-resident). System administrators can use monitoring tools to find bottlenecks, then change system configuration parameters to either streamline the bottleneck or off-load work from it.

Short-running server programs can't afford long initializations

Reduce the Initialization Cost for Short Running Programs In contrast to client programs, many server programs (especially on OLTP systems) start, run for a very short time, and shut down. For these server programs, it does not make sense to do a lot of pre-computation at initialization because a long start-up time can affect system performance significantly. Although a client program can afford a few seconds to start, a server that processes hundreds of transactions per second often can not afford to have each transaction take even one-hundredth of a second to initialize.

Server programs can be set up to load strings or compute only as needed

Often, not all the pre-computed results will be used during real processing. This means that you can pay as you go by doing the computation on an as-needed basis to minimize the initialization cost. For example, a client program designed to run in several countries would usually do all nationalization chores at start-up, taking a few seconds to load message strings in the correct language based on information about the locale. For a server program, such an initialization time is often not acceptable. A solution is to have nationalization occur statically on the server side at development time. This eliminates that part of start-up computation altogether (provided the locale does not change dynamically). If such a solution is not possible, server programmers can still choose to have the program load a string only when it's needed, such as to report an error.

Another way to amortize the initialization cost is to make the program serially reusable. For example, under IMS/TM, a program can start, initialize, and process multiple client requests before shutting down. The start-up cost is amortized across the multiple transactions.

Reusing a server program spreads out the initialization cost

This technique does have a drawback. Because the application is not reinitialized for every transaction, application programmers must take care not to produce any side effects that can affect the next transaction execution. Likewise, programmers must design transactions so that they are not affected by any side effects of the prior execution. For example, a transaction could reinitialize global variables every time instead of relying on the existing values, which could have been set by the prior transaction execution. (Note that relying on programmer discipline to ensure the isolation in the ACID transaction properties is never as reliable as having the system enforce it.)

This technique requires that transactions be carefully isolated

Use a Single Address Space Most server functions are not monolithic. They consist of modules that invoke each other to get the job done. Running all the modules in a single address space reduces the cost of cross-address data transfer and eliminates some task scheduling, thus enhancing the performance. However, there are several other factors to consider in making such a decision.

Using a single address space enhances performance

- Running code modules in separate address spaces provides more protection and security. For example, a database running a stored procedure in a separate address space can control exactly what the stored procedure can access and can protect the rest of the system from a crash of the stored procedure. If the stored procedure runs in the same address space as the database manager, the execution speed may be faster, but if the stored procedure crashes, it can bring down the entire database.

Separate address spaces provide protection and security

Separate address spaces make updates easier

- System management is also a factor. If two components run in the same address space, it's difficult (if not impossible) to update one without taking down the other. Updating, protection, and security are three of the reasons why CICS supports multi-region operation (MRO), with which system administrators can run terminal control, logic, and data access code in separate address spaces.

Certain architectural benefits depend on multiple address spaces

- Running everything in a single address space may eliminate some of the benefits of modern server architecture. For example, in a multiprocessor server, running everything in a single address space may prevent the operating system from scheduling multiple processors for the job and thus lose the benefit of parallel execution.

Multithreaded execution offers the benefits of concurrency

Increase Concurrency By allowing the server to process multiple clients' requests concurrently, you can better utilize system resources and improve the throughput and response time. Multithreaded execution can be supported at different levels not only by the operating system. Surfacing the native operating system thread to the application may not help achieve the best performance. For example, CICS implements its own multitasking on top of MVS to achieve high-performance concurrent execution of multiple transactions. This is because the native MVS multi-thread support is too heavyweight, both in the switching speed and in the system resources allocated per thread. It is difficult to scale up to thousands of concurrent users with such a heavy-weight service.

Controlling the number of threads is important

Controlling the number of threads of execution is particularly important on the server side. A server with too many threads of execution can spend too much time maintaining and switching among tasks and too little time getting the real work done.

Why Use Native Operating System Threads?

People often believe that a good server environment requires the programming environment to surface thread support from the native operating system. In general, there are four reasons for wanting to use native threads.

- *Non-blocking I/O* This is the most common reason. By using a native operating system thread to issue the I/O calls, an application can avoid blocking its entire execution when doing I/O. Higher-level mechanisms, such as asynchronous call-outs, can also be used to address the issue, without the programming complexity of low-level threads.
- *True preemptive scheduling* Some programs require a true preemptive scheduler to run correctly. They can achieve this with native operating system preemptive threading support. When the threading models are language-supported (such as some implementations of Smalltalk and Java) or system-supported (CICS on MVS), sometimes they are not truly preemptive.
- *Leveraging underlying parallel hardware* Some multi-processor operating systems assign different threads to different processors. However, multithreaded programming at the application level is not easy, and relatively few programmers have experience with it. When the threads are running on top of true parallel hardware instead of multitasking in a single CPU, the timing and synchronization issues become even more complex and difficult to track down.

  A common alternative is to stay single-threaded at the application level and let the underlying system services leverage the parallel hardware. For example, TP monitors, such as CICS, can work with the operating system to schedule transactions on parallel processors without the application's awareness. Databases can also use the underlying hardware to perform parallel queries without application involvement.

- *Underlying system requirements* Some systems (such as Encina) attach special meanings (for example, transaction semantics) to threads. To leverage the service provided by such a system, one would have to use the native threads.

Various applications often have different reasons for wanting to use native thread support. It's important to understand exactly what the reasons are and consider all the available options. Native threading, which has certain associated cost, may or may not be the only answer, or even the best one.

Server-side caching is different than on the client side

Use Server-Side Caching This is significantly different than it is on the client side, and client programming techniques may not always apply. For example, most databases already maintain a cache of the data pages in memory. When the server program runs on the same machine as the database, accessing data via the cross-memory mechanism between the server program and the database is efficient. Instead of managing an application-level cache (as we often do when the code runs on the client side and must access the database remotely), it may be simpler and cheaper to take advantage of the database-managed memory cache and avoid any additional caching at the application level. This saves application cache memory and eliminates an extra buffer copy between the server application cache and the database cache.

TP monitors optimize the scheduling of system resources

Use a TP Monitor In addition to supporting transaction semantics, TP monitors often provide highly efficient scheduling of system resources. Putting a TP monitor in front of a database can sometimes enable the same hardware to support an order-of-magnitude greater number of concurrent users.

Keeping database connections open saves time

Keep the Database Connection Hot Opening and closing connections to a database can be a costly operation even when the database is local. Pre-allocating connections at system initialization time and keeping them open for subsequent accesses can eliminate this cost during execution of online transactions. This technique can also apply to optimizing Web servers that handle database contents.

Schedule Proactively Most people think of the server in a client/server system as passively sitting there, waiting for clients to submit requests. However, that does not have to be the case. A server can also optimize performance by actively scheduling the time for clients to send in their requests. For example, a file-backup server may not want to let clients decide the time to submit backup requests because many users might pick the same time. (A popular choice is 2 A.M.) If many PCs start backing themselves up at the same time, the server can quickly become overloaded (and so can the network). By having the server actively control when clients can submit backup requests, higher throughput can be achieved.

Servers can proactively schedule client requests

Glue Performance

The glue of an OO client/server system is often its most important aspect when it comes to system performance. With today's networking infrastructure, sending messages across the network is often several orders of magnitude slower than sending messages locally. Because the glue is often the bottleneck of the entire client/server system, it deserves special attention.

Without special attention, the glue can become a system bottleneck

Communication performance is also the most difficult aspect of the client/server system to measure. Not only are there fewer tools for the purpose, but the existing tools can be harder to use. The results of measurement can also vary from time to time, because of timing issues and other traffic on the network.

Communication performance is difficult to measure

Glue performance can be measured on throughput and latency. The throughput of a glue is the number of bits it can transfer per unit of time. Message latency is similar to response time. It measures the delay introduced by the glue on message sends. One factor that affects this latency is the actual network transport.

Glue performance is influenced by throughput and latency

Another is the networking software on both ends of the network that sends and receives packets and manages buffers. A third is the work, such as parameter marshaling, required from application runtime services to create remote messages out of local messages that are sent to a proxy.

As with the server, network performance tuning comes down to how much work the glue has to do and how we can make it do the work faster.

Glue Workload

The glue's workload is easier to change than its speed

The amount of work done by the glue (determined by data size and number of trips) is a lot more controllable by application programmers than the speed of the network. Therefore, we have more tips on how to reduce the amount of work done by the glue than we had for clients or servers.

The glue transmits data in increments of a certain buffer size

There are two measures of the amount of work by the glue: the size of the data and the number of trips. The size of the data transmitted across the network often does not have a linear relationship to the time it takes, as shown in Figure 10-5. This is because the networking hardware and software transmit increments of a certain buffer size at a time (for instance, K bytes).

Figure 10-5 Relationship of transmission time to size of data

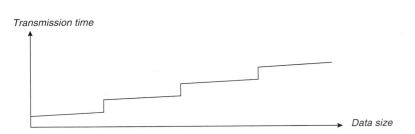

As long as the size of the data stays within the size of the buffer, transmission time for different amounts of data is roughly the same. (The slight slope for each increment shown in the figure is due to costs directly related to the size of the data that need to be moved in and out of the various buffers.) For example, with a 1K buffer size, a request that sends an 800-byte string may not take much more time than a request that sends a 1-byte string. In optimizing the size of the data, understanding where the buffer boundaries are can be more important than simply minimizing the quantity of data.

To optimize data size, it's important to understand the effect of buffer size

The number of trips across the network is usually the most significant factor in glue performance. Cutting down the number of network crossings has so much effect on glue performance that most experienced programmers look to optimize it first.

The number of trips is usually the most significant factor

Architecting the Application Differently In a traditional mainframe architecture, each business transaction (such as booking a trip through a travel agency) is composed of many technical transactions. Every time a technical transaction is executed, it means a round trip between the client and the server. With intelligent clients, one could architect the system so that the clients would talk to the server more at the business transaction level and reduce the number of network crossings.

Application architecture can affect the number of trips

Partitioning the Application Intelligently If application semantics allow it, repartitioning the application can sometimes produce significant savings in both the number of network trips and the overall data transmitted.

So can repartitioning

Figure 10-6 shows a partitioning design in which the message frequency between the client objects (C, D, and E) and the server object (B) is high. Moving Object B to the client, as shown in Figure 10-7, significantly reduces the message sends between client and server.

Moving a single object from server to client can reduce message sends

Figure 10-6 Partition with high message frequency between client and server

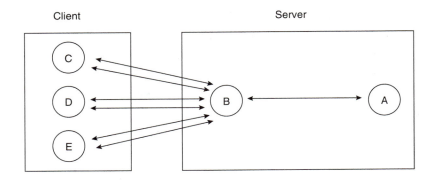

Figure 10-7 Partition with low message frequency between client and server

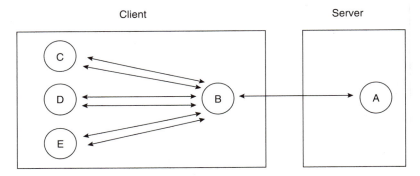

Batching message sends can also help

Batch Message Sends When application semantics allow, batching several messages into one can also reduce network crossings. Batching can occur at the application level. It can also be supported by the underlying glue system. For example, an underlying messaging system can detect that there are multiple messages targeted at the same network address and decide to combine them together in a single packet instead of sending them separately. However, batching must be applied judiciously, because it can sometimes slow down response time.

Caches can be located on the glue, as well as on the client and server

Caching a Copy of the Target of remote message sends locally can save many network crossings. Caches can be located on the glue (the middleware), as well as on the client and server. Figure 10-8 shows such an example. A corporation sets up a proxy server to

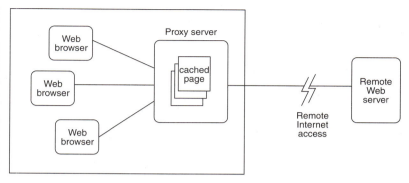

Figure 10-8 Data cached on a proxy server

Corporate network

issue HTTP requests on behalf of its internal Web clients. The proxy server (part of the glue), which is transparent to the Web clients, caches certain pages that it receives from remote Web servers. If an internal client requests one of the cached pages, instead of going across the Internet to get the page again, the proxy server simply returns the page in its cache. Note that the difference between caching and partitioning is that caching involves replication of data while partitioning does not.

Although caching can improve performance, it is not free. Synchronizing the cache with the master can require additional processing. For example, if the contents of Web pages cached in the proxy server are updated frequently, special care must be taken to avoid or minimize the probability of the proxy server handing out obsolete pages.

Caching can require additional processing

Glue Speed

Assuming the number of network crossings and the amount of data transmitted are fixed, there are still ways to get better performance besides buying a faster network. As always, the techniques are centered around intelligent, balanced use of glue resources.

Even if the amount of work is fixed, better performance is still possible

Networks can send concurrent messages

Increase Concurrency Instead of serializing all the message sends, networks can send them concurrently (when the application semantics allow). For example, if a client needs two pieces of information from the server, instead of asking for the first one and then the second one, it can fork a thread to ask for the first one and then ask for the second one before the first result comes back. In addition to application-level concurrency, which may improve performance, this technique also provides opportunities for the communication software to execute concurrently. The communication software stacks run on both the client and server machines. With sequential sends, only one stack on one machine can run at a time. With concurrent message sends, both stacks could run concurrently and increase the overall transmission rate.

Conversational mode yields better response time but pseudo-conversation supports more clients

Mix Conversational and Pseudo-Conversational Modes In general, conversational communication provides better response time because no time is spent restoring the application states and the connection. However, pseudo-conversation supports more clients because of its efficient use of system resources.

With OO programs, conversational communication can save the steep initialization costs

OO client/server programmers often develop server programs that embed large and fine-grained object models. These programs can include long-running business transactions that involve many message sends to the objects in the models. Because these programs can take a long time to start and initialize, conversational communication between the client and the server generally provides better performance by avoiding the start-up/initialization cost every time a message is received.

Pseudo-conversation is good for situations involving user think time

On the other hand, pseudo-conversation is good for situations involving a long user think time. While the user is thinking, the system resources are released to do other work. In a long-running business transaction, the pattern of alternating user think time with bursts of server interaction is common. In these cases, mixing

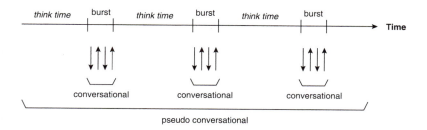

think time | burst | think time | burst | think time | burst | → Time

conversational

conversational

conversational

pseudo conversational

Figure 10-9 Combining conversational and pseudo-conversational communication

the conversational and pseudo-conversational styles provides a unique way to optimize the performance.

Figure 10-9 shows that the overall execution of a long-running business transaction can follow the pseudo-conversational style while the individual bursts of interaction can follow the conversational style. This enables the system to achieve good response time during the interactive period and good resource use and throughput during the think period.

A system can combine the two for best performance

Data Performance

In addition to the configuration and tuning of client, server, and glue, the location of the data has a big impact on overall system performance. Configuring the data to be close to where it is needed can reduce the network traffic and thus enhance the system performance. In general, there are three ways to do this:

Data location has a big impact on performance

- Data partitioning
- Data extraction
- Data replication

A combination of these techniques can be used in a single client/server system. Each way offers different performance gains and imposes different restrictions. Although most of these techniques were developed in the context of relational databases and

3GLs, they are applicable to OO enterprise systems and can make a significant positive impact on the overall system performance.

Data Partitioning

Data partitioning stores records on different machines

Data partitioning involves storing certain database records on one machine and storing other database records on one or more other machines. No single piece of data is stored in more than one place. There are two types of partitioning.

Horizontal partitioning groups information about a single business function

- Horizontal partitioning: The database is partitioned such that it stores in one location all the occurrences of the set of data elements that represent a given business entity. For example, Figure 10-10 shows how an order entry database might store information about orders in one location, information about customers in another, and information about inventory in yet another.

Vertical partitioning groups all information from a single geographical location

- Vertical partitioning: Different sets of occurrences of the same data elements are stored in different locations. For example, the orders, customers, and inventory information for each city are stored in the database located in that city, as shown in Figure 10-11. This technique is often used to optimize local per-

Figure 10-10 Horizontal data partitioning

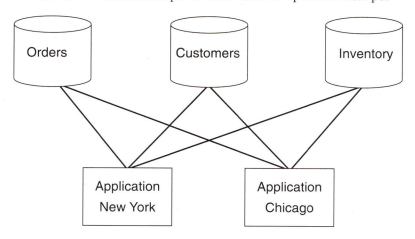

formance. For example, an application in New York can access all the information necessary to process an order from a local customer from the local city database instead of going remote.

Because no data is stored in more than one place with data partitioning, the update mechanism can be relatively simple. The challenge is to make data quick and easy to locate, data updates easy to coordinate, and give end users the appearance of a single logical database.

The challenge is to make partitioned data work as if it were not partitioned

Distributed Relational Database Architecture (DRDA) specifies four levels of distributed database access to manipulate remote partitioned data. They are progressively more complex and more difficult to support.

Remote partitioned data can be accessed in four ways

1. Remote request: A single SQL statement accesses a single remote database. This is the simplest form.
2. Remote unit of work: Each transaction can contain a series of related SQL statements that access the same remote database.

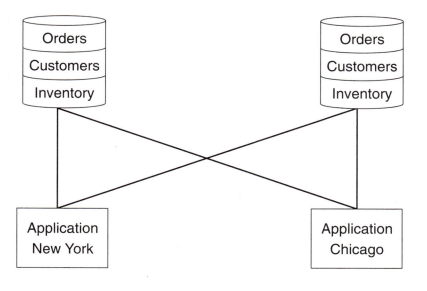

Figure 10-11 Vertical data partitioning

The underlying database software must be able to remotely coordinate the commit and rollback of all statements as a single unit.

3. Distributed unit of work: The transactions can contain a series of SQL statements that can each access a different remote database. However, each SQL statement still references only one database.

4. Distributed request: This is similar to the distributed unit of work except that each SQL statement can reference different databases, potentially residing on different machines. This requires the database software to support distributed join operations, which bring together information from multiple databases.

Only the first two are common in commercial systems

Implementation complexity increases as the underlying infrastructure does more work to make the data partitions appear as one single database. From a performance standpoint, such extra work decreases the gain obtained by data partitioning. Out of the four levels described above, the first two are most common in commercial implementations.

Data Extraction

Data extraction creates copies of data that cannot be updated

Data extraction creates copies of all or a portion of a database intended to be used on a read-only basis. These extracts can provide mechanisms that allow application programs to determine how outdated an extract is.

There are several ways to determine the currency of an extract

- An extract can contain no information that can be used to determine the validity of the extracted data.
- An extract can include side information, such as a time stamp. For example, a Web browser often caches downloaded Web pages on the client machine. When the user clicks on a cached URL, the browser can compare the time stamp of the cached

page with the page on the Web server to determine whether an updated page needs to be retrieved over the network.

- An extract can contain content-related information, such as an expiration date. Application programs can use this information to determine whether the extracted data is out of synchronization with the master and, if so, how to resynchronize them.

In addition to its uses on the Web, data extraction is also used extensively in decision support and data mining systems. To avoid affecting online performance, these systems often work on an extract of the operational database.

Data Replication

Replication is similar to data extraction except that the replica can also be updated. This makes synchronization management more difficult than with read-only extracts. Any data partition may have many replicas; it is necessary to ensure that updates to a data element value are eventually applied to all replicas that contain copies of that value.

Replicated data can be updated

Many mechanisms have been devised for bringing replicas into convergence. There are two general kinds of convergence policies: strongly consistent and weakly consistent. Strongly consistent servers must either produce the same results at all times or else not be available. For instance, an online trading agency must avoid selling the same commodity twice, so its replicated databases must be strongly consistent. Transaction managers, such as CICS, TUXEDO, and Encina, are commonly used to implement the strongly consistent policy because of their ability to coordinate transactions for multiple distributed resource managers. Such strong synchronous replication is often expensive because data is locked for a relatively longer period of time during update, and the

Strongly consistent replicas must produce the same results at all times

concurrency of the entire system suffers. However, if the application semantics require such strong policy, it's much better to have the correct result more slowly than to have the incorrect result faster.

Weakly consistent replicas are synchronized periodically

Frequently, it is sufficient to provide weakly consistent updates. The data might not be updated very often and might not have an urgent nature, or there might only be a small cost associated with the occasional use of obsolete data. For example, a Lotus Notes discussion database may have many replicas that are not completely in synch. The users can still use the replicas to participate in the discussion even though not all users will have the latest view of all the comments. When many users work with many replicas, updates to the replicas can easily conflict with one another. Such a system requires a conflict resolution mechanism (sometimes called a convergence function). The exact nature of this mechanism varies widely and often depends on system and application semantics.

Correct design is important for data replication mechanisms

Designing Data for Replication Programmers must take special care in designing replicated data so that the application functions correctly. For example, Figure 10-12 shows a typical configuration for a corporation moving from a centralized mainframe-based system to a client/server architecture. Relational databases have been introduced into the middle tier for OO clients to connect to. New data may be hosted by the relational databases, but the majority of the operational data (such as the customer database) still resides on the mainframe. The configuration calls for some of the data to be replicated to the mid-tier databases. Note that the following discussion is as valid for ODBMSs and objectified relational databases as it is for pure relational databases.

The update sequence can have a major effect

For this configuration to work, it must clearly identify the strongly and weakly consistent replicas and implement convergence functions for them. For example, an update to a strongly consistent

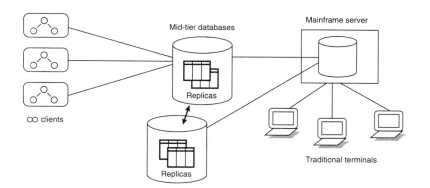

Mid-tier databases

Mainframe server

Replicas

∞ clients

Replicas

Traditional terminals

Figure 10-12 Configuration for an enterprise moving to a client/server architecture

replica must be propagated to the mainframe and other mid-tier databases holding the same replica before the operation returns. The mainframe database is likely to have legacy programs updating it in real time. Therefore, the best sequence of actions may be to update and commit the mainframe data first, then propagate the update to the mid-tier replicas. In the event of a conflict, such as two mid-tier replicas not agreeing with each other, the mainframe database becomes the arbiter and prevails over any replica.

The mid-tier database administrator also has to establish periodic refresh mechanisms for replicas so that the object clients won't be working on obsolete information. This involves determining when and how to synchronize the mid-tier replicas with each other and with the mainframe database.

Replicas require refresh mechanisms

When some of the data involved in a transaction is new and stored in the relational database and some of the data is in the replica, things can get complex quickly, especially when crash and recovery conditions are considered. This situation can require updating the mid-tier database and the mainframe database as a single unit of work. Unless the application programmer wants to implement complicated services, such as two-phase commit and write-ahead logging, in the application code, it's desirable to get a real transaction manager and use its services.

Complexity results when new data resides in the same mid-tier database as replicated data

A replica doesn't have to have the same format as the original

A replica doesn't have to be in the same format as the original data. For example, IMS data on the mainframe can be replicated in a relational database. However, changing the replica format does not change any of the replication issues discussed above.

With OO clients, it's often convenient for an OODB to host the replicas

A configuration often recommended by OODB vendors uses an OODB to host the replicas, as shown in Figure 10-13. The potential benefit is the lower impedance mismatch between the OO clients and the mid-tier data. Note that mapping between the object format and the mainframe data format still has to occur; it just occurs at a different place. When the mainframe data is relational, an OODB still can't collaborate with it as seamlessly as a relational database can. For example, in a totally relational scenario, instead of sending changed data, some convergence functions could send SQL commands between the replicas on the mid-tier and on the mainframe. An OODB couldn't support this because it cannot process SQL commands.

Figure 10-13 Data replication with a mid-tier OODB

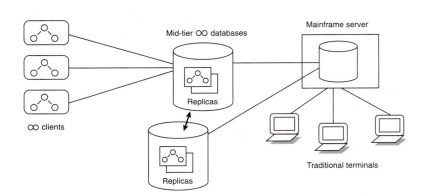

Load Balancing

Load balancing is another technique used to tune client/server system performance. The general idea is to spread the workload among the available resources so that the job can get done faster. There are two kinds of load balancing, shown in Figure 10-14: client/server (a) and server/server (b). Our preceding discussions on partitioning applications and data effectively cover client/server load balancing. This section focuses on server/server load balancing, where the load is spread across the available servers.

Load balancing spreads the workload among the available resources

Approaches to Server/Server Load Balancing

The common approaches to balancing the workload among servers involve client-side selection, centralized architecture, and distributed architecture.

Client-Side Selection This is the simplest load balancing approach to implement. The client contains a list of available servers, and for each request the client uses an algorithm to select a server process. The algorithm can be as simple as "round robin" or "random," or it can use historical data or additional system knowledge to choose the server. Experience shows that in many client/server systems, a

The client can select which server to go to

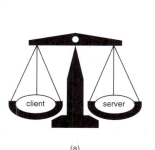

(a)

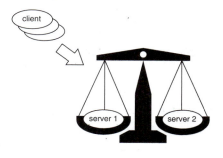

(b)

Figure 10-14 The two varieties of load balancing

random algorithm performs amazingly well. In the client-side selection model, the client is aware of the existence of multiple servers. However, this doesn't mean that the client *applications* need to know it. The server selection can be made by the underlying glue, which frees the applications from the task.

With centralized server architecture, incoming requests are weighed against server workload

Centralized Architecture Load balancing happens among servers within a single geographical location. It often involves a multi-processor machine or a cluster of server machines. The underlying system software (generally the operating system or TP monitor) can often present a single server image to the clients. From a client's perspective, it feels like it is dealing with a single server. Incoming requests are scheduled to execute on the processor or machine with the least workload at the time.

Centralized load balancing requires scheduling and state management

The challenges in centralized architecture are scheduling and state management. A good scheduler can ensure the workload is spread evenly. State management handles cases when the processing of a client conversation (real or pseudo) moves from processor to processor. An intelligent server system would transfer the server application state to the new processor transparently (that is, without the application being aware of it).

Distributed load balancing often involves a "matchmaker"

Distributed Architecture Load balancing happens across servers located in a cluster of server machines or in widely distributed geographic areas. As shown in Figure 10-15, there is often a **matchmaker** of some form or another that represents the server group. A client sends the request to the matchmaker (Figure 10-15(1)). The matchmaker uses an algorithm to find the best server (Figure 10-15(2))—for example, it can choose the one that's closest to the client, the one with the least load, or the one that specializes in the service the client wants). Once the server is determined, the client

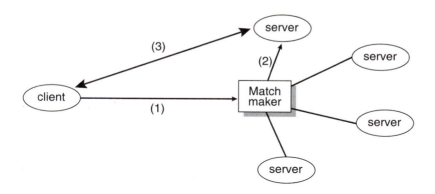

Figure 10-15 Distrib-
uted load balancing
using a matchmaker

and the server establish their own channel of communication (Figure 10-15 (3)), and the matchmaker gets out of the way.

Centralized load balancing and distributed load balancing are similar at the conceptual level. The key difference is that a distributed architecture usually makes no attempt to migrate the state to different server machines, because of the performance cost of such an operation. Once a client finds a server, it sticks with it until the request is completed (unless a workflow arrangement routes it to another server or certain error conditions occur).

Distributed load balancing does not migrate the application state

Matchmakers can come in different forms. For example, an IP sprayer that sits in front of a Web server can take an incoming request to a single IP address and redirect it to multiple machines. A TP monitor, such as TUXEDO, can dispatch request events to its servers in a balanced fashion while ensuring the transaction's ACID properties.

Matchmakers can take different forms

Using Load-Balancing Techniques

Load-balancing approaches are not exclusive; they can be mixed and matched to obtain the best results. For example, a Web site may use distributed load balancing by having an IP sprayer distrib-

Load-balancing approaches can be combined

ute requests to several multiprocessor machines. These machines can in turn do centralized load balancing among the various processors.

To evaluate load balancing, build and test a model of your system

Because the gain from load balancing varies from application to application and from approach to approach, the best way to evaluate it is to build a simulation model of your own system and test it with realistic request traffic instead of simply trusting the claims from the vendors.

Load balancing does not always deliver results

Note that load balancing does not deliver significant results in all cases. It works best if application execution naturally offers parallelism that can be exploited and there is no centralized bottleneck. For example, a load-balancing system can have multiple servers concurrently executing business logic. But if all of them have to access the same records in the same database, data access becomes a bottleneck, so it may not matter if you balance the load for business logic processing. Remember that optimization techniques (including load balancing) can be effective only when applied to system bottlenecks.

Don't let the load-balancing effort exceed the actual work effort

In choosing the dispatching algorithm, it is important to weigh the cost of load balancing against the cost of the work itself. This is especially true in a distributed architecture in which the algorithm needs to go across the network to gather information and negotiate. The effort to find the optimal balance can exceed the effort to do the work. In general, simplicity is the best policy because it costs the least and it's easiest to understand.

Load balancing contributes to reliability

Because of the redundant elements often introduced in implementing load balancing, it can contribute to the reliability of a system. Reliability is a large topic. We cover it in the next chapter.

Summary

Performance optimization consists of successively identifying and eliminating bottlenecks across the system. Performance issues for client, server, and glue center around workload and speed. In addition, user perceptions of client response time are important.

- Clients: The ways to make a client faster include smaller client-side executables, proper management of short-lived objects, pre-computing objects, increasing concurrency, and caching server objects. To improve user perception of client response, a client can display partial results early, use a progress indicator, and enable users to switch to another task.

- Servers: Off-loading user interaction can enhance server performance but off-loading too much can cause the system to suffer. To increase server speed, many system configuration parameters can be adjusted. Reducing program initialization also helps. So does reusing an initialized program. Single address space and multithreaded execution offer benefits but raise issues. Other techniques include caching, optimizing system resource scheduling (with a TP monitor), keeping database connections open, and actively scheduling client requests.

- Glue: The glue's workload is easier to change than its speed. Optimize data size according to the size of the data buffers; optimize the number of trips across the network with better application architecture, repartitioning, and batching message sends. Caches can be located on the glue, as well as on client and server. Even with a fixed workload, glue performance can improve with concurrent messaging or with mixing conversational mode and pseudo-conversational mode.

Three ways are available for optimizing data performance. Each offers gains and imposes restrictions.

- Data partitioning
- Data extraction
- Data replication

Load balancing optimizes performance by spreading the workload among the available resources, in particular among different servers. There are several approaches to load balancing.

- Client-side selection
- Centralized load balancing
- Distributed load balancing

Load-balancing approaches can be combined. Load balancing does not always deliver the intended results, particularly when the load-balancing effort exceeds the actual work effort.

11

The Scaleable OO Enterprise System

In this chapter, we discuss issues related to scaling up an OO enterprise system, particularly in the areas of reliability, system management, and legacy integration. Again, we start with issues that are relevant to all systems (traditional or OO) and introduce OO-specific issues in which they are relevant. As in many other aspects of enterprise systems, the ability of objects to manage complexity increases their value to systems as they scale up.

Four main issues affect system scalability

System performance, discussed in the last chapter, is normally seen as a major issue of scaleability; reliability is an equally important consideration. For a system to serve more users, the overall system needs to perform well enough to handle the increased workload. However, the system also needs to be reliable enough to stay operating most of the time. A high-performance system that can't run reliably when more users are added can scarcely be considered scaleable.

Reliability and performance are both important

In addition to performance and reliability, a third factor that affects scaleability is how well the system can be managed. As client/ server technology has become more pervasive, the increased complexity of system management has hampered many systems in their efforts to scale up.

A third factor is system management

Finally, scaling across time leads us to consider the issues related to overall system evolution: maintenance and legacy integration. This is arguably the area in which objects can be of greatest value.

Legacy integration is the fourth factor

Reliability and Fault Tolerance

Different factors can lead to system failure

Many factors can disrupt an enterprise system. The IEEE/ANSI Standard 982 defines the following failure terminology for software. In our discussion we extend the use of this terminology to hardware and networking.

- An **error** is a human mistake (for instance, operational problems, missing functionality, programming mistakes).
- A **fault** occurs when a component fails to function as required.
- A **defect** applies to errors in a product's requirements, design, implementation, and documentation. For example, a document defect can result in a user error. Not all faults are caused by defects. For example, an administrative error (too little swap space reserved) may cause a fault that is not related to any defect.

Achieving reliability means identifying faults and reducing their probability

Two general steps lead to achieving a reliable enterprise system: coming to understand the fault points and then reducing the probability of critical faults by applying techniques that enhance reliability. Identifying the critical fault points is as important to reliability as identifying the bottlenecks is to performance tuning. Optimizing the reliability of noncritical components may not have much effect on overall system reliability.

Types of Faults

Enterprise systems have many potential fault points. They fall into three general categories.

- Hardware: client and server machines, network, devices such as printers and tape drives
- System software: operating system, networking layer, databases

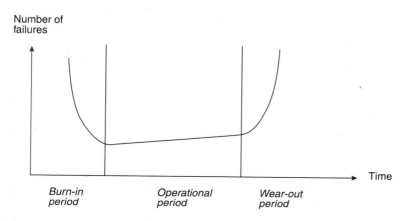

Figure 11-1 Hardware failure curve

- Application software: software written by the application programmers that runs on top of the system software

In general, the hardware failure rate follows the curve shown in Figure 11-1. After an initial burn-in period, the curve remains flat for a period of time until wear and tear come into effect.

Hardware failure follows a three-phase pattern

However, software has very different failure characteristics, shown in Figure 11-2. The failure rate tends to decline gradually and steadily over time, with periodic spikes that correspond to new releases and updates. The most important reasons for this are

Software failure declines gradually, with periodic spikes

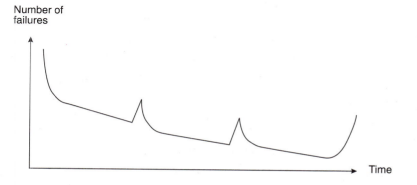

Figure 11-2 Software failure curve

Software contains a finite number of defects

- Software contains a finite number of defects after a build. Software faults are not due to software wearing out but to its defects turning up during processing. Note that users often learn to maneuver around the defects, so the number of failures can decline even without bug fixes.

Once a defect is removed, it cannot recur

- When a failure occurs, a maintenance programmer can remove the defect that caused the fault and, thereby, reduce the chances of failure in the future. However, the failure rate is also affected by the chance of accidentally introducing new defects when correcting old ones.

Change can introduce new defects

- New releases can introduce significant numbers of new defects (the spikes in Figure 11-2) in both the new components and the interaction between new and existing components.

Architectural integrity is required for software failures to decline

For the software failure to follow the declining curve in Figure 11-2, the architectural integrity of the software must be maintained by a well-engineered software process. If not, the defect rate can rise significantly because of unorganized patching of the original architecture and code and the serious re-architecting (the big changes) this might lead to, shown by the curve rising toward the end of the time axis. In general, the more change one introduces into a system, the more potential fault points one adds.

OO encapsulation helps ensure architectural integrity

Potentially, objects can be very useful in fault determination and prevention. The principle of encapsulation isolates objects in the system from the effects of changes to any object. Therefore, once an object is fault-free, it tends to remain fault-free. Faults that are introduced into a system must necessarily come from new, unproven objects or from the interaction of new and existing objects.

Availability of Components

One of the results of a fault is that the component it affects is not available. Availability is an effective measure of reliability. Having a clear understanding of availability helps in understanding the effects of different kinds of faults, as a precursor to minimizing their effects.

When faults occur, the time for which components are unavailable can vary greatly. We can calculate this time to get a measure of the availability of a component.

Availability is a function of time between failures and time to restore

A = MTBF / (MTBF + MTTR)

where

A = availability
MTBF = mean time between failures
MTTR = mean time to restore (time to respond, isolate, correct, and verify)

For example, if a component's MTBF is 30 days and the MTTR is 12 hours (0.5 days), the predicted availability of the component is

A = 30 / (30 + 0.5) = 98.36%

This would mean that the component could be out of service for roughly six days in every year.

The availability of individual components can be combined to arrive at overall system availability. We use a simple example to illustrate. Figure 11-3 shows a system with a network, a server, and a disk. In order for a client request to be successfully processed, all three components need to be available. Assume the availability of the individual components is

Overall system availability can be derived from individual component availability

A(network) = 80%
A(server) = 98%
A(disk) = 99%

**Figure 11-3 System
with three server
components**

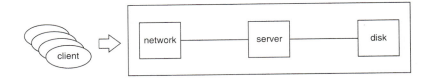

For real-world systems, these numbers can be obtained from the
manufacturers or derived from statistics gathered during past operation. The expected overall system availability is

$$A = A(network) \times A(server) \times A(disk) = 77.6\%$$

(For simplicity, we made several assumptions in the above computation, such as that failures are completely independent.)

*The availability of
the entire system
cannot be better
than its weakest link*

Note that the availability of the entire system cannot be better than
its weakest link. Therefore, to increase system availability, the best
place to start is with this weakest link, which, in this case, is the
network. The system administrator could decide to install a backup
network exactly like the existing one, as shown in Figure 11-4.
The availability of the network with the backup is

$$A(new\ network) = 1 - (1 - A(network))\ (1 - A(network))$$
$$= 1 - (1 - 80\%)\ (1 - 80\%)$$
$$= 96\%$$

And the overall system availability is now

$$A = 96\% \times 98\% \times 99\% = 93.1\%$$

*When improving
availability, consider
the system as a whole*

When looking at availability, it is important to consider the system
as a whole. It might not be worthwhile to upgrade a component if
it is not a major contributor to the availability problem to begin

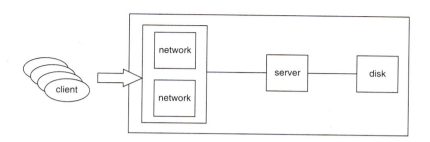

Figure 11-4 System with backup network

with. In our previous example, the system administrator could have decided to put in a mirrored disk instead of a backup network. The disk availability would increase from 99 percent to 99.99 percent. However, the overall system availability would still be

A = 80% × 98% × 99.99% = 78.4%

This approach yields an increase of merely 1.2 percent, in contrast to the 15.5 percent increase when a backup network is installed. Formulas exist that enable you to work with even more-complicated situations. For example, you could compute the availability of a system in which there are n redundant components and the system can tolerate the failure of up to x components. (We will not go into the details because the point is to illustrate the importance of finding the right components to work on. For further information, consult the Scaleability section of the references.)

Focusing on the weakest link yields the best result

These principles apply to OO systems. Instead of considering availability in terms of components that work together in a client/server system, we can consider it in terms of objects that communicate with one another in an OO application. It turns out that all the principles are still valid. For example, the expected availability of one service that requires services from ten other objects is the product of the availability of each of the objects.

Object availability is analogous to component availability

Increasing a System's Availability

To increase system availability, improve robustness or create redundancy

For a system to be reliable, it must be available when the organization needs it. (Organizations may vary in the degree to which they can tolerate an unavailable system.) There are two general approaches to increasing availability:

- Improve the robustness to prevent system failure.
- Create redundancy so that if system components fail, backup exists.

System robustness requires a four-pronged approach

Robustness System robustness requires a four-pronged approach: good design and coding up front, effective testing, isolation of components, and good exception handling. The first step is to design and code the system as carefully as possible. However, no matter how hard we try, we cannot achieve 100 percent reliability when designing and implementing a system of any complexity. It is impossible to eliminate all human errors and their resulting faults. The next step is to implement extensive testing, which can turn up faults for the application developers to fix before the system is deployed. The third line of defense is to provide isolation. Isolation prevents one faulty component from affecting other components in the system. For example, running different applications in different operating system processes can often prevent failures in one application from spilling over into another.

TP monitors provide a system-level approach to isolation

Transaction processing (TP) monitors provide the most popular system-level approach to isolation. Besides isolating transactions from each other, TP monitors also provide recovery services that can back out the effects when a transaction fails. A study of all software faults of large IBM systems over a five-year period showed that most bugs were benign—transient software errors that only appear occasionally and are related to timing or overload.[1] Gray and

---

[1] Edward N. Adams, "Optimizing Preventative Service of Software Products," *IBM Journal of Research and Development* 28:1 (1984), pages 2-14.

Reuter call these faults **Heisenbugs.**[2] Instead of requiring bug fixes that may introduce new bugs, many Heisenbugs can be fixed simply by restarting the program. TP monitors allow individual application programs with Heisenbugs to fail and to be restarted without affecting the rest of the system. This enhances reliability.

Good exception-handling logic at the application level can often mitigate problems such as network transmission errors, time-outs, and unavailability. This kind of logic can be designed into both the client and server sides of the application at the system or the application level. Because many network errors are also Heisenbugs, a retry can easily succeed where the original operation failed. For example, network congestion may cause the client to throw an exception. If the client contains the logic to handle this exception, it can retry the operation after a fixed time interval. The network congestion could easily be over by that time.

Exception-handling logic can mitigate errors

Redundancy As demonstrated in the discussion of calculating a system's availability, adding redundant elements, such as a backup network, can greatly improve availability. If redundant service providers are available, the requester can switch over to an alternative service provider when a service becomes unavailable because of a fault. This switching process is commonly called **failover.**

Redundancy enables a component to "fail over" to its backup

Failover support can be stateless or can preserve application states. A stateless failover mechanism does not attempt to carry over any computation states from the failing component to the new component. From the requester's perspective, everything that has been done using the failed service provider is lost. The requester starts from scratch with the backup service provider.

With stateless failover, application states do not carry over

---

[2] Gray, Jim, and Andreas Reuter. *Transaction Processing: Concepts and Techniques* (San Mateo, CA: Morgan Kaufmann, 1993).

Stateless failover can be fault-prone

Stateless failover is easier on the mechanism provider but harder on the user. Let's say the server of a client/server application fails in the middle of a conversation with the client. The client needs to detect the server failure, roll back its own states, and then connect to a different server to start the conversation all over again. This situation can be potentially fault-prone if the application logic is not carefully written to handle the failover. For example, a banking client might be trying to increase a customer account balance by $200. If the server is busy or the network connection to the server is slow, the client might erroneously fail over to another server with the same request. This could pave the way for the record to get updated twice, which would compromise the integrity of the business data.

Failover mechanisms that preserve states are harder to implement, easier to use

Failover mechanisms that preserve states are harder to implement but make the requester's job a lot simpler. For example, a server system with a hot backup configuration can have the backup server pick up the clients without creating the type of situation just described. A CICS system running on top of a multiprocessor mainframe can also switch a transaction execution from a processor in trouble to another processor. The transient states of the pseudo-conversation between client and server would be preserved and the client would not be aware of the failover.

Other Measures of Reliability

Reliability can mean things other than availability

Reliability doesn't necessarily mean that the system has to be up all the time. It can mean other things.

- The system is up at the scheduled time.
- System failure occurs gracefully.
- The system can recover quickly.

The System Is Up at the Right Times Often, this is a requirement for mission-critical systems and applications. For example, most mainframe users expect to have no unscheduled downtime at all. Note that this does not mean that a system must be up all the time. It just needs to be available at the scheduled time or the exact time it is needed. Consider a typical weapons guidance system. Most of the time the system is turned off to prevent enemy radar from locating it. However, when it comes time to turn it on and fire the weaponry, the system had better be available.

Many systems must be up at the right times

Such reliability—and customer expectations of such reliability—come about only when a system or technology has had extensive usage. Newer systems, such as ODBMSs, have to achieve technological maturity before they achieve a comparable level of reliability. It is also worth noting that vendors charge a premium for such reliability. For example, the operating cost of running a mainframe DB2 system is typically higher than that of a UNIX-based ODBMS.

Near-total reliability can occur when a technology has extensive usage

System Failure Occurs Gracefully This means that with the occurrence of a fault, the system or component degrades its service in proportion to the severity of the fault. Little problems should cause only a small degradation of service. A system that fails gracefully would also provide notifications to the system management software as its service degrades. Going down without any notice is not considered graceful.

A component can degrade its service in proportion to the severity of the fault

The System Can Recover Quickly Instead of implementing extensive defensive measures to keep the system up all the time (which can often decrease its performance), systems can be designed to start back up quickly after a fault, without losing integrity. The SABRE airline reservation system developed jointly by American

Some systems can go down and quickly restart without losing integrity

Airlines and IBM is an example of this approach. In the event of a failure, the end user may experience a short delay when the system is restarting. This is deemed acceptable, considering the performance gain during normal operation.

Final Thoughts on Reliability

Organizations need different degrees of reliability

Each organization has to determine the level of reliability it needs, on the basis of its business cost and return structure. In the case of a large bank, having unscheduled down time might result in being unable to serve millions of customers, thus losing both revenue and reputation. These losses can easily amount to more than the additional costs of hardware and software for a mainframe database.

Consider vendor claims of reliability carefully

Be forewarned about the claims of reliability offered by system and tool vendors. A system is only as reliable as its weakest component. In evaluating schemes that are supposed to make systems reliable, even before asking whether the scheme is effective, you must first ask whether it addresses the most critical component of the availability chain. It is not meaningful for a vendor to claim "Because we are the experts on component X, we know our new scheme will make it more reliable." Time and energy may be wasted if component X is not the weakest link.

A reliable system requires reliable hardware, system software, and application software

It is also important to realize that a reliable system must have reliable components in all three categories: hardware, system software, and application software. For example, one cannot declare the entire system to have a 99 percent availability just because the system software has a 99 percent availability. Such a claim would assume that the hardware and the application software are 100 percent available, which we know cannot be true.

System Management

System management is a critical element in enterprise computing because it represents a significant portion of work in running any enterprise system. A centralized computing environment typically contains relatively few components; monitoring and problem resolution are mostly done at a single location. However, as client/server systems expand across ever-widening geographical areas, management becomes increasingly complex. It is no longer feasible for the system administrator to walk across the hall to fix a problem. With increasing complexity, good system management practices become even more crucial for a system as it scales up.

As a system scales up, good system management becomes crucial

From a vertical perspective, systems require management at all levels: hardware (CPU, memory, disk), system services (networking, databases), and applications. The hardware and system services levels are well understood and documented. We will focus more on application management because it represents a key pressure point for client/server computing. The objective of application management is to enhance the availability, reliability, and performance of applications in a distributed computing environment. Because of the tremendous cost to the organization if this is not done properly, many people consider application management the Achilles' heel of client/server computing.

Systems require management of hardware, system services, and applications

From a horizontal perspective, client/server system management involves managing the client, glue, and server. Traditionally, the system administrator manages the glue and the servers and users manage their own clients. However, the industry has been moving toward an end-to-end perspective that includes the clients in system management; leaving clients out can be problematic. For example, if individual end users can install, remove, and configure their clients as desired, the system configuration will differ from

Client/server systems require management of client, glue, and server

user to user. When a help desk receives a call reporting that a certain client/server application is not working, it's extremely difficult to pinpoint the problem location. It could easily be in some unique aspect of the client configuration, which could make it difficult and costly to reproduce, fix, and verify. More important, it would be essential to make sure that the fix wouldn't adversely affect the clients with different system configurations.

Aspects of Management

Every aspect of system management tends to have associated services

To ensure a smooth operation, many aspects of the system must be managed. Each category of system management tends to have system management services associated with it. These services perform tasks or generate information that is used by the system administrator or by other system management tools.

- The **monitoring** service provides information on the status of components, as well as resources, such as file systems, printers, memory, and system processes (such as whether a Web server or database process is running).
- The **software distribution** service deploys the application software on the appropriate target machines. A client/server application can have multiple pieces that run on various machines and require different installation and configuration procedures. The software distribution service needs to address these requirements.
- The **inventory/configuration** service collects information on the software and hardware elements in the system. Such information can include the number of active or installed client machines, server machines, printers, available application software, and the software installed on each machine.
- The **security** service manages security-related aspects, such as user IDs, user groups, passwords, and public keys.

- The **licensing** service tracks and controls software usage for licensing purposes. For example, the licensing service could manage the number of concurrent users logged onto a database.
- The **data** service backs up and recovers files and databases.
- The **performance** service captures performance data on the overall system, as well as individual components. The performance management service can provide information on how much processing time is spent in various components and operations, such as client software, the network, server transactions, and database access.
- The **fault** service alerts the system manager to the occurrence of faults in the components and records sufficient data to allow further analysis and recovery from the faults.

What Roles Are Involved?

There are also multiple roles involved in making a system work. In general, five roles are relevant to client/server system management.

Five roles are relevant to client/server system management

1. Application system management administrators (the system administrator) have three areas of responsibility: preparing the environment for management, distributing and installing the applications, and actually managing the system.

   Application system management administrators

   While the system is being configured, the administrator performs several tasks: defining software distribution procedures, determining the aspects of the system to monitor, installing system management agents on monitored resources, and configuring the licensing and inventory services.

When the system is in service, the administrator responds to events, collects system execution data, analyzes the data to improve future execution and to plan for future requirements.

End users

2. End users use the client/server application. The role of the end user in system administration is mainly to receive informational messages and act on system events that require intervention. For example, a dialog box might pop up when the number of concurrent users reaches the licensed limit, and the user might have to wait until someone else stops using the application. Other system events might require the user to call the help desk with problems.

Application developers

3. Application developers invoke system management APIs in the application code to enable the client/server application to be managed. Such calls enable the application to report its status (such as when it starts or stops, or when some application error occurs). The calls also enable the system management services to interact with the application to manage its performance, licensing, fault, security, and so forth.

AD environment administrators

4. Application development environment administrators manage the development environment that the application developers use. They ensure that the developers use the right level of libraries to create the applications so that they can be managed. They also collect the application packages and package descriptions and feed them to the software distribution services.

Help desk

5. The help desk diagnoses and resolves problems. In addition, it monitors system performance, updates status messages, and monitors the fulfillment of service level agreements. (For example, a service level contract might guarantee subsecond response time on certain transactions.)

Application Development Support
for System Management

In the past, system management has meant management of the
hardware and the system software, but this is changing. Faults
often occur in application software, and as applications become increasingly complex, it becomes necessary to bring application software under the umbrella of system management. Although
yesterday's calculator application was not a candidate for system
management, today's complex enterprise application is. It can consist of several components (for instance, clients and servers) that
need to be deployed on heterogeneous platforms. To manage such
an application effectively, the system management software and
administrators need to have access to information that describes
the application architecture and layout. Mechanisms to specify and
transfer that information are required.

*Application software
increasingly comes
under system
management*

The current approach by vendors is to provide tool support to enable application-level system management. System management
vendors and application development tool vendors jointly offer
toolkits to assist developers in this process (as part of the overall
application development). Application providers can specify information that tells administrators how to distribute and install the
application on a variety of platforms. The application providers can
also specify software and hardware dependencies that must be met
by the target systems in a production environment before the application can be successfully deployed. Applications can invoke the
libraries in the toolkit to report the start and the finish of execution, various application-level statuses during execution, and error
events. The resulting application can be managed by the same system management system that manages the hardware and system
software. We expect this trend of integrating application development and system management will prove fruitful.

*Vendors provide AD
tools that support
application-level sys-
tem management*

System Management and Object Technology

The phrase *OO client/server system management* has two contrasting but equally valid meanings. It can apply to managing OO client/server systems or to using OO client/server technology to implement system management functionality. Clearly, these two aspects are related. Organizations often use OO system management technology to manage their OO client/server systems.

Agent/manager architecture is commonly used in system management

In looking at the relationship of OO technology and system management, we can start by looking at the **agent/manager architecture,** which is commonly used in system management. An agent represents a managed resource (such as a disk) and the manager uses the agents to control the resources. As you can see in Figure 11-5, the software manager is managing the printer and the PC through their respective agents. In a distributed environment, the management software is itself implemented as a large client/server application. Both agents and managers can logically relate to each other as clients or servers. The manager gathers information from the agents and displays the results in some useful fashion to the system administrator. The manager can poll agents periodically for their current status, or the agents can actively volunteer information.

OO technology can handle the complexity of implementing system management

Many system management vendors use OO technology to tame the complexity of implementing large and complex system management systems. System management software must provide a model for the world it manages so that the system administrator can monitor and interact with the world through its software model. Object technology allows system management software to model the world as a set of managed objects. For example, most managed devices, when modeled as objects, require methods that can start, stop, and reset them. Using OO techniques, the developer of a system management tool can create a superclass containing start, stop, and reset methods and have the agents for all the devices inherit

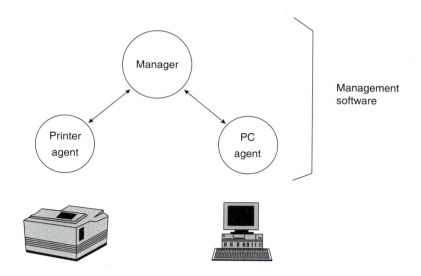

Figure 11-5
Agent/Manager
architecture

Management
software

these methods. Management applications have been among the early adopters of distributed objects, and system management standards such as SNMP (Simple Network Management Protocol) and CMIP (Common Management Information Protocol) often advocate OO concepts.

It should come as no surprise that it can be easier to make OO enterprise applications manageable (at the application level) than many 3GL applications. Because the system management software wants to manage the world as objects and the OO application is already structured as objects, there is little impedance mismatch between them. In contrast, in managing a 3GL application, some objectification (wrapping the 3GL entities) is necessary in order to identify and create objects that can be recognized and managed by the system management software.

OO enterprise applications can be easier to manage than 3GL applications

Just because it is easier to *make* OO applications manageable does not mean that those OO applications *are* easier to manage. Object systems tend to introduce many more fine-grained objects and data types than equivalent procedural systems, which tend to aggregate individual objects (for instance, videotapes) into larger-grained artifacts such as database tables (for instance, a videotape table). The number of entities to be managed in OO applications tends to be more than that in 3GL applications, which adds to the complexity and effort in system management.

The Impact of the Web and the Internet

The Web does not remove the need for client management

Some argue that the Web reduces the need for client (thus, end-to-end) system management. Web browsers make the clients thin and uniform, which theoretically means that some client management issues disappear. This is true to a certain degree if the client is rather static and its purpose is to browse published contents (in other words, if the Web browser is used like a 3270 terminal). However, this does not seem to be where the Web is headed. With client-side plug-ins, down-loadable applets and ActiveX controls, and various Web browsers supporting different functions, uniformity and simplicity can quickly vanish.

Users depending on the Web for business functions need reliable service

Web browsers increasingly provide user interaction beyond just browsing documents. Particularly in corporate intranets, Web browsers are used to access the business system, performing the functions previously covered by traditional GUI clients. While casual Net surfers are willing to tolerate a document's unavailability, a user depending on the Web to perform business functions will not tolerate unreliable service.

Plug-ins and applets need management as much as traditional applications do

Furthermore, plug-ins, ActiveX controls, and applets are not magic; they are code that needs to be downloaded, installed, and managed on the client, similar to traditional client code. This means that most of the management issues remain with us. The Web browser may change the protocol for downloading and make downloading available on demand, but it does not change the fundamental need for system management. The flexibility and dynamic nature of the download capability can actually make system management harder.

For example, when a user calls the help desk to complain about a browser problem, it's unlikely that the help desk knows which plug-ins, ActiveX controls, and applets are currently running on the user's machine. Those components are often installed by the user rather than the system administrator, and the user can change them at any time. Without such basic configuration information, identifying and solving problems becomes very difficult.

The real change introduced by the Internet is the change of perspective from centralized system management to distributed management. With centralized management, system resources are controlled from one point within a single organization. Over the years, this has worked well for many internal corporate computing environments. However, it is clearly impossible for one organization to own and manage the Internet. Though the system management of the Internet is usually reasonable for its current uses, more work will have to be done as Internet use expands.

The real change is from centralized to decentralized system management

For example, in the current situation, if a URL does not respond when you click on it, there is not much you can do about it. The server might be down, the router providing access to the server may have failed, the domain name server may be under scheduled maintenance, or the owner of the target page may have gone bankrupt. There is no easy way to analyze and address the problem. However, in order for people to use the Internet for serious business, such as trading stocks, it is necessary to provide the same level of system management support that currently exists in corporate networks.

There is no easy way to address Internet system management problems

The challenge is to coordinate among many parties

The challenge is to deliver a level of management function that is typical of a centralized organization to the more loosely organized Internet. This will have to be done by some sort of confederated entity composed of interested parties. Many social, business, and technical issues have to be resolved to achieve this objective. Although the Internet and the Web may make some things easier, the new territory they open up includes new system management challenges.

Network Computing

Network computing offers better manageability

Network computing, sometimes also referred to as thin-client computing, gives the client the role of network access device. For many organizations, the appeal of network computing comes from its better manageability and the ability to stop employees from tampering with their client systems. Thin clients can take several forms.

- NetPC: A typical PC in a sealed case, centrally managed with Microsoft's Zero Administration Windows Tool Kit (ZAK). It uses the currently existing infrastructure and can run almost all existing applications.

- Network computer: Web browser client that runs applications off a server and has a new infrastructure based on the Java download capability. Because of the new infrastructure, it needs new applications written in Java.

- Windows terminal: Can run Windows applications on a server and display the result on the client. It is similar in architecture to X terminals.

Manageability of thin clients comes at the expense of flexibility

Thin clients do simplify some system management issues. However, there is a trade-off between flexibility and manageability. In most cases, manageability is not the result of making the client thinner, but of restricting what the user of the client can do. After all, a thin client can do nothing that a real PC can't do. If PC users are willing to live under the restrictions defined by a thin client, they can receive the same system management benefits.

Maintenance & Legacy System Integration

A scaleable OO enterprise system must also be able to scale across time. This means that the system must be maintained. Maintaining a system is more than just fixing the defects. It also means evolving the system to satisfy new requirements, which requires integrating older, legacy portions of the system with newly developed components.

To scale across time, a system must evolve and be maintained

It would be a mistake to equate legacy systems with the centralized mainframe applications and data of the past. As a system evolves over time, today's new development becomes tomorrow's legacy. In thinking about the difficulty of dealing with the mainframe legacy, we should seriously imagine what it will be like ten years from now to deal with a client/server legacy system that is even more complex and brittle than the mainframe legacy systems today.

Today's new development becomes tomorrow's legacy

Two major factors affect the ease of maintenance: complexity and level of change. The more complex a system is, the more difficult it is to maintain. The more change that needs to be introduced into a system during the maintenance process, the harder it is to do the job.

Complexity and level of change affect the ease of maintenance

Very few of us have the luxury of building an enterprise system from scratch. Most client/server systems we build have to interface with legacy systems. One way to approach legacy system integration is to think of it as one of the maintenance tasks. The legacy elements can be as small as a data record accessed by a COBOL

We can think of legacy system integration as a maintenance task

program or as large as the entire mainframe system. In either case, the task is to evolve the system from a centralized architecture to client/server and from 3GL to OO while maintaining the functions and data of the 3GL system as long as necessary.

The ability of objects to encapsulate function simplifies legacy integration

The ability of objects to encapsulate function, no matter how large or small, simplifies this task. Earlier in this book, we discussed various legacy integration techniques, such as screen scraping and object scraping. The basic strategy is "surround and conquer." The first step is to surround the legacy elements with objects. This makes it possible to continue using the 3GL elements as long as necessary and to re-implement them with object technology in a phased and gradual way.

Objects help a system become more maintainable over time

Using objects to manage the complexity of legacy integration helps to prepare the system for tomorrow's maintenance tasks. By phasing objects into the legacy system today, the existing system can become more maintainable over time.

Good software engineering practices are essential

As for new development, although object technology helps manage the complexity, it is no silver bullet (as we have stated all along). Good software engineering practices make a system scaleable and maintainable—things like documenting the system well, having a good automatic regression test suite, and maintaining architecture integrity during rework. Only with these practices firmly in place can a system reap the benefits of objects.

Summary

In addition to performance, which we discussed in the previous chapter, the factors affecting scaleability are reliability, system management, and maintenance.

Achieving reliability means identifying faults and reducing their probability. You can increase a system's availability by identifying the weakest link and then improving robustness, using one or more of the following practices.

- Good design and coding
- Effective testing
- Isolation of components
- Effective exception handling
- Creating redundancy

Reliability can mean other things in addition to availability. Some systems must be up at the "right" time; some systems need to degrade their service in proportion to the severity of a fault; other systems can quickly recover from a crash without losing integrity.

Good system management is crucial as a system scales up. There are several main categories of system management services: monitoring, software distribution, inventory/configuration, security, licensing, data, performance, and fault. Application software is increasingly coming under system management, and vendors are providing AD tools that support application-level system management. OO system management technology is also increasingly used to manage OO client/server systems.

The advent of the Web browser does not remove the need for client management. The manageability of thin clients comes at the expense of flexibility. The real challenge to Internet system management is making the transition from centralized to decentralized system management.

Last, to scale across time, a system must evolve and be maintained. We can think of legacy system integration as a maintenance task. Object technology enables easier system maintenance.

12

Security

Security has always been a major concern for client/server systems. As system complexity increases, security becomes more difficult and effective security techniques become even more important. This chapter starts by looking at general concepts of client/server security. We define computer security and then examine the risk assessment required in the early stages of determining the kind of security measures to implement. We look at security boundaries and the security techniques that can be applied within those boundaries. These concepts of client/server security establish the context for the concerns added by the introduction of objects into a system.

With increasing use of OO and client/server technology, security becomes more complex

An Overview of Client/Server Security

Briefly, security protects an information system from unauthorized attempts to access information or interfere with its operation. It controls the disclosure, modification, and transfer of information. A good security system has the following characteristics.

Security protects an information system from unauthorized use

- Information is disclosed only to users authorized to access it.
- Information can be modified only by users who have the right to do so, and only in authorized ways.
- Information can be transferred only between intended users and in intended ways.
- Users are accountable for actions related to system security.
- The use of the system cannot be maliciously denied to authorized users.

Client/server security is difficult for a number of reasons. The chief reason is that the many elements of the system (clients, servers, and network) present multiple points of entry to the system. For

Client/server security is difficult for several reasons

example, caching the server database data on the client side improves performance, but it also creates an entry point for hackers to get at the data. Because it is often difficult to secure and manage all the hardware elements, most systems rely on software-level security services. However, software-level security is not any easier because both the security software and the application software can have bugs that allow people to break in.

When systems span multiple policy domains, security is even tougher

As the Internet becomes pervasive, many client/server systems are now spanning multiple enterprises. These systems are likely to have multiple security policies, enforced by a range of security mechanisms. Although standards organizations, such as the Open Group and OMG, are working hard to provide interoperating security mechanisms, security policies dictated by the business needs of corporations are likely to remain different. Mismatched policies can lead to complex management issues and vulnerabilities.

The human element is hard to manage

In addition, the human element in system security is difficult to manage. For example, a system may require its users to change their passwords frequently. The security challenge is to ensure that users actually make these frequent changes and that they use passwords that are difficult to guess but are still memorable, so users won't be tempted to write them down.

Security has associated costs

Security can be expensive. It is not only expensive in terms of the cost of hardware and software, but also in performance, administration, and user inconvenience. Given enough time and effort, almost every security system can be cracked. Security mechanisms are mainly there to slow down the attack. In general, the more secure the system, the less convenient it is for authorized users to access it and the greater the performance and management cost.

Therefore, before an organization implements a security policy, it must strike a balance between the cost and the benefits.

Risk Assessment

You can apply the techniques of risk assessment to find the balance point between security and its cost. These techniques enable you to calculate the risk exposure for various elements of your system, and by comparing this information with the cost of effective prevention, you can make informed judgments in the design or update of a security system.

Risk assessment helps balance security and its cost

In assessing a system's risk exposure, you need to start by listing all corporate assets. This can include physical objects such as PCs; logical objects, such as a client/server application; and data. This will help in planning the scope of a security system.

Risk assessment starts with accounting for system assets

Threats to the System

You also need to consider all the possible threats to your system and your corresponding **vulnerabilities.** As defined by OMG, vulnerabilities are system weaknesses that leave the system open to one or more security threats. Each system is subject to a unique set of threatening events, such as:

The next step is to consider threats and vulnerabilities

- Information compromise: the deliberate or accidental disclosure of confidential data (for example, spoofing or eavesdropping on a communications line)
- Integrity violations: the malicious or inadvertent modification or destruction of data or system resources (for example, a virus attack)
- Denial of services: the curtailment or removal of system resources from authorized users (for example, the effect of network flooding)

- Repudiation of action: failure to verify the identity of an authorized user and to provide a method for recording and proving the actions performed by the user (for example, a hacker who denies sending an e-mail message)
- Malicious or inadvertent misuse: active or passive bypassing of controls by authorized or unauthorized users

Security threats can come from a number of sources

Threats can come from a variety of sources, such as hackers, corporate espionage, disgruntled employees, or natural disasters. Note that security threats do not always come from the outside. Often, a security breach is caused by a well-meaning end user who leaks or erases information by accident. Software tools, such as SATAN (Security Administrator's Tool for Analyzing Networks) can probe a network and report common network-related security problems.[1]

Risk Exposure

We need to assess risk exposure for each potential threat

Once we have a comprehensive list of potential threats to the system, we can assess the risk exposure for each threat. Risk exposure (RE) is defined as the product of risk probability (RP) and risk cost (RC).

$$RE = RP * RC$$

RP is the probability of a successful attack

RP is the probability that a potential threat will lead to a successful attack on the system. The main factor contributing to the RP is system vulnerability, but other factors also contribute, such as value of the assets. A highly vulnerable system with no valuable assets normally does not attract many attackers and can have a low RP.

---

[1]For a good discussion of SATAN, see J. Levitt, "Not the Devil Incarnate," *Information Week* (April 3, 1995), page 15. The SATAN Web site currently has useful information on network security issues and links to a number of other sites relevant to security: http://www.fish.com/satan/

RC is the estimated cost to the affected parties if a successful attack occurs. This can be the cost in terms of financial impact to the business, as well as the effort and time required to recover lost information assets.

RC is the estimated cost if an attack occurs

Once we can estimate the RP and RC for each perceived threat, we can calculate the RE for that threat. Figure 12-1 demonstrates the relationships among these three factors. The vertical axis indicates the rising probability of risk; the horizontal line indicates the rising cost of the risk. The risk exposure for a threat to the system is the product of probability times cost, which can be any point on the quadrant.

RE is the product of risk probability and risk cost

The three curving lines in Figure 12-1 indicate the product of RP * RC—in other words, the relative levels of risk exposure (RE). The left-most line indicates a relatively low level; the center line, a moderate level; and the right-most line, a relatively high level.

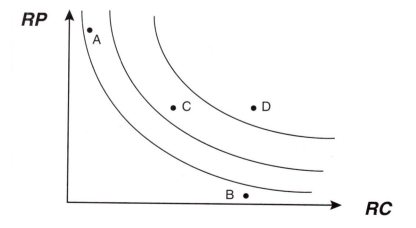

Figure 12-1 Relationship between risk probability, risk cost, and risk exposure for four sample situations

Low-profile items can become high risk-exposure items

A look at the four data points on the graph indicates the value of focusing on the risk exposure. People often focus on risk factors having either a high probability (Item A) or a high potential cost (Item B). However, because risk exposure is the product of probability and cost, a factor that is high in only one of these dimensions may not represent a key exposure. Relatively low-profile items, such as C and D, can become high risk-exposure items because they combine moderately high probability and risk cost.

It is necessary to consider exposure for all threats to a system

The completeness of the risk assessment is critical to the security of a system. A system's security is only as strong as its weakest point, and an incomplete risk assessment can provide the crack an attacker needs to bring down an entire system. This is why we must account for all the system assets and all the potential threats as a first step in assessing risk exposure.

Risk Prevention

Once we identify risk exposure, we can plan system security

This section discusses security boundaries and the various security functions that can be implemented inside those boundaries. Once we have identified the risk exposure for the various threats to a system, we can begin to plan system security. The first step is to determine the security boundaries we want to enforce and then determine what security functions to implement.

Security Boundaries

Security boundaries protect system assets

Security boundaries (also known as security perimeters) are established to protect system assets. In a traditional system, the boundaries are established as you see them in Figure 12-2(a).

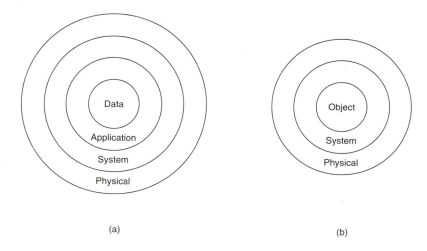

(a)

(b)

- The physical security boundary: controls physical access to the system hardware. In a client/server environment, it's usually difficult to have strict control over the client hardware. In that case, the system security boundary must be relied on to provide the protection.

  Physical access to the hardware

- The system security boundary: controls who can logically log onto the system. For example, most operating systems and networking environments (such as LAN Manager) currently provide built-in logon support to control access to the system.

  Logon

- The application secure boundary: controls who can execute an application and the functions they can perform within it. While the system security boundary is usually based on unique user identifiers, the application security boundary often uses groups or roles. For example, in a banking system, access to certain applications may be specific to roles such as bank teller, branch manager, and underwriter.

  Application use

- The data security boundary: controls who has access to the data and their level of access, such as read-only or read/write.

  Access to data

The database often provides this boundary. In some cases, such as when a TP system sits in front of a database, the TP monitor provides adequate protection for the data.

In OO systems, object-level protection replaces application and data security

In an OO system, the picture is conceptually simpler, as shown in Figure 12-2(b). Because objects encapsulate both data and behavior (application functions), object-level protection essentially subsumes the roles of application and data security boundaries. Object data is accessed through the methods of the object. Security measures implemented at the method boundary are sufficient to safeguard both the methods themselves and the data.

Implementing Security Functions

A variety of security functions can be implemented at a security boundary

A variety of security functions can be implemented at a security boundary. We will discuss these functions in the following sections.

- Identification and authentication
- Authorization and access controls
- Auditing and surveillance
- Privacy and encryption

It is important to weigh the cost of prevention against the cost of possible loss

In determining what functions to implement, it is important to weigh the cost of prevention against the cost of possible loss. There is no point in implementing an expensive function if the losses it protects against are relatively low cost. Note that system management and maintenance can present significant costs and should always be considered.

Identification and Authentication

Authentication means proving a principal is who it claims to be

Authentication means proving that a **principal** is who it claims to be. A principal is a human user or an object that needs to operate under its own rights. Client and server applications can also be considered principals. Every principal has at least one, and possibly several, identities (depending on the roles it assumes)—for example, an audit administrator might have an audit identity that is anonymous to everyone but himself and an access identity that can be used to obtain access to protected objects.

In a highly secured client/server system, the user, the client, and the server all need to authenticate themselves. A principal can be authenticated by:

A principal can be authenticated in several ways

- What it knows—for example, a login name and a password
- What it has—for example, a software credential, a smart card
- What it is—for example, recognizable voice, fingerprint, or retina

Single Authentication In a distributed environment with multiple nodes, each node can handle authentication independently or a network-wide service can provide single authentication. The file transfer protocol (FTP) common on the Internet provides an example of each node authenticating the user independently. The user provides an ID and password to each node. In contrast, the Distributed Computing Environment (DCE) provides a single logon for a group of nodes, called a **cell.** When users gain access to the cell from any node, they are authenticated for all nodes in the cell. The industry trend is toward this kind of single authentication because

The industry trend is toward systems that provide single authentication

- Multiple accounts and passwords are inconvenient to users and can slow them down.
- Managing multiple accounts and passwords is difficult for the system administration.
- Security holes can occur with multiple accounts. For example, changing passwords on multiple systems is tedious, which can deter users from changing their passwords often enough. When users must memorize multiple identifiers and passwords, they are more likely to use trivial, easily guessed passwords or, worse, write them down.

Multiple accounts and passwords can create problems

Sniffer programs allow hackers to collect remote logon information

Common Threats to Authentication **Sniffing** and **spoofing** are common threats to authentication. A hacker can set up a **sniffer** program that monitors the network traffic. The sniffer allows the hacker to trap remote logon information and collect user IDs and passwords. With this information, the hacker can access the system as freely as the "sniffed" users. This practice has become so widespread that CERT (Computer Emergency Response Team, an Internet security agency) issued a general advisory about it in 1994.

In spoofing, a hacker creates a fake principal to collect information

Spoofing is the other common authentication attack. In this kind of attack, a hacker creates a fake principal in order to collect critical information. Figure 12-3 shows an example of server spoofing. A fake server advertises itself to clients and collects the authentication information intended for the real server. Later, the hacker can use this information to access the real server.

Server, client, and IP spoofing can all occur

Another form of spoofing is **client spoofing,** in which the hacker installs a fake client to collect authentication information sent by the server to the client. (Remember, in a highly secured system, not only does the client have to authenticate itself to the server, but the server also needs to authenticate itself to the client.) A third form is **IP spoofing,** in which IP source addresses of data packets are forged. This enables a hacker to fool a security mecha-

Figure 12-3 Server spoofing

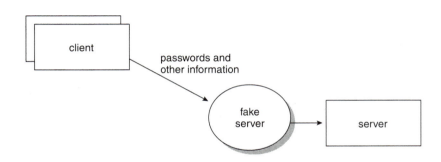

nism by using the IP address to determine what service to render. For example, to enforce the corporate firewall, a server may only respond to requests from machines whose IP addresses indicate they are internal machines. With IP spoofing, an external machine can masquerade as an internal machine and get the server to provide service to it.

A good security system must guard against these common attacks by making it difficult to sniff and spoof. For example, encryption techniques (discussed later) can be used to secure the password exchange. Or time stamp information can be included in critical network packets so that even if security information is intercepted by an attacker, the time stamp mismatch would prevent the attacker from reusing it. Another way to guard against common attacks is to be more vigilant toward suspicious events, using some of the techniques discussed later, such as auditing and surveillance.

A good security system guards against sniffing and spoofing in several ways

Authorization and Access Controls

Authorization and access controls determine whether a principal can access a particular object. To reduce the number of access relationships that need to be administered, aggregation techniques are commonly used.

Access controls determine whether a principal can access an object

Aggregation techniques are often used

- Principals can be aggregated into user groups.
- Objects can be aggregated into security groups.
- A security group can contain an access control list (ACL) that associates principals or user groups with access rights to objects contained in the group.
- Multiple methods on an object can be aggregated so that a principal with a single right can invoke them. For example, a videotape object could allow the clerks to invoke the ordinary methods (for instance, check in/out) but only allow the accountants to access the accounting methods.

Firewalls

Some networks use firewalls like some people use condoms. However, not enough people use either correctly.—Stephen Cobb[2]

A firewall is a means for protecting a private network from intrusion. Firewalls normally have two principal functions: to block specific traffic from gaining access to the protected network and to allow certain classes of traffic through.

Most firewalls work at the network or application level. Network-layer firewalls usually involve routers (typically hardware) that filter traffic passing through them based on source addresses, destination addresses, and port numbers. If a packet has a valid (trusted) IP address, the router forwards it to its next stop. Modern routers are becoming smarter. They can be programmed, usually through specifying rules in a table, to examine packets for suspicious characteristics.

Application-level firewalls provide additional security over the network-level firewalls. An application-level firewall can more closely examine the traffic that passes through it and interpret the headers on specific application level packets. This gives the firewall more information to use in deciding whether to forward these packets. Application-level firewall software is typically a modification of a well-known Internet service, such as TELNET, FTP, SMTP (e-mail), or HTTP, and is often acting as a **proxy server.** A proxy server shields a target server by inspecting incoming requests and authenticating their validity. Valid packets are forwarded to the protected server. Application firewalls are more expensive and are harder to configure than network-layer firewalls because you need a firewall program for each application on your network. In practice, network and application firewall mechanisms are installed in combination because their characteristics complement each other, thereby making the firewall more secure.

---

[2]"Internet Firewalls," *Byte* 20:10 (Oct. 1995), pp. 179–180.

A common firewall mechanism that operates between the application and the network level is the **SOCKS** mechanism. It is designed for protecting clients and servers that communicate via TCP/IP. To achieve this, the application client makes a request to SOCKS to communicate with the application server. Typically, such a request comprises information about the address of the application server, the type of connection (active or passive), and the user's identity. On behalf of the application client, SOCKS sets up a proper communications channel to the application server and relays the application data between client and server. During the connection setup, SOCKS can perform various functions, such as authentication, negotiation of message security level, and authorization.

To avoid a false sense of security, it is important to understand the limitations of firewalls. For example, if an intruder is inside the organization, the firewall cannot do much to stop an attack. Though firewalls can prevent information from being accessible to an external network, they cannot prevent someone from walking out of an office with sensitive information on disks or tapes or from sending such information via e-mail.

Firewalls also cannot protect a network from unauthorized modem connections to outside sources like the Internet. These types of accesses to or from the network are often called **back doors** and must be controlled by the organization's overall security policy. The easiest solution is to prohibit modem access to or from the network.

A firewall does not protect against viruses or data-driven attacks because firewalls do not interpret data. Nor do they protect against careless users who reveal sensitive information over the telephone or paste their passwords to their terminals with sticky notes.

Firewalls provide coarse-grained access control

The firewall mechanism can be considered a coarse-grained access control mechanism. It has two user groups—one that consists of principals inside the firewall and one that consists of principals outside. Objects inside the firewall are all in a single security group, which can be accessed only by the user group inside the firewall.

A shared file system is finer grained

A shared file system is a finer-grained example. File system users are often aggregated into user groups. Files (objects) in a directory are naturally aggregated as a security group. ACLs can be associated with the directories and the individual files to control who can access them and what methods (such as read, write, and delete) can be invoked.

To invoke a method, a principal's access rights must meet the requirements

The concept of "object" can be used to model access control mechanisms, both coarse-grained and fine-grained. Principals, assets, user groups, security groups, and other security notions can all be represented as objects. In a typical OO access check, the security system compares the required rights for a method being invoked with the access rights granted by the target object's security group to the principal. In order to invoke the method, a principal's access rights must meet or exceed the required rights.

Auditing and Surveillance

Auditing and surveillance involve monitoring, recording, and analysis

Security auditing and **surveillance** consist of monitoring, recording, and analyzing the security-relevant events in the system. This helps with the detection of actual or attempted security violations. Depending on the implementation, recording an audit event may involve writing event information to a log, generating an alert or alarm (such as e-mail to the security authority), or temporarily blocking suspicious users from accessing the system.

Auditing and surveillance can apply to the entire enterprise or to a specific application. System-level security events often include authentication of principals, changing privileges, and success or failure of object accesses. Application events depend on application semantics. For example, an application that handles money transfers might audit the identities of principals in the transfers and how much money is involved.

They can apply to the entire system or a specific application

Audit logs usually contain large numbers of events and take up a lot of disk space. Audit policies can be established to restrict the types of events and the circumstances under which they are audited. One parameter for audit policies is the success or failure of the event. Most of the time, failures are significant. For example, the failure of a user to provide the correct password in repeated attempts may point to an intruder. Other parameters include the type of event (for example, invocation of a particular object's method), the object being accessed, the audit ID of the principal for whom the event occurs, the time of day, and attributes of an event deemed significant by the application (for example, if the money amount exceeds $1 million in a transfer).

Audit policies restrict the types and circumstances of logged events

Note that security auditing and surveillance are a system management activity and should be integrated into the broader context of system management. For example, it is best to integrate the collection of security events with the collection of other events relevant to system management, such as component status events.

Auditing and surveillance are part of system management

Privacy and Encryption

In a secured client/server environment, **privacy** means that a message can be read and understood only by the intended receiver. Because network traffic is easy to intercept and read, various **encryption** techniques have been developed to ensure privacy.

Encryption techniques are used to ensure privacy

Because most encryption algorithms are well known, encryption systems do not depend on the secrecy of their algorithms. Instead, they require both an encryption key and the algorithm to be present to decode an encrypted message. Even with the knowledge of the encryption and decryption algorithms, a hacker still cannot crack the message without the key. The brute force attack, which tries every possible decryption key until the message is decoded, often takes too long even with the most powerful computer. That's how encryption protects privacy. Encryption techniques are frequently classified as being either *public key* or *private key.*

In private key encryption, sender and receiver know a single private key

Private Key Encryption requires that both the sender and the receiver know a single key that is private to them. The key is typically a large number carefully selected to conform to the requirement of the particular encryption algorithm used. Figure 12-4 shows a typical example: Mary encrypts the message, "Msg," with the key and the encryption function E. The encrypted message (EM) then travels across the network to John. John has the same key and he uses the decryption function D to extract the message from EM.

The bigger the network, the less practical private keys become

The Data Encryption Standard (DES) is the most common private key method. The primary weakness of private key encryption is secure key distribution. Every pair of principals that need to communicate require a separate private key. A large client/server network, containing c clients and s servers, would require $c \times s$ keys. The bigger the network gets, the less practical the private key method becomes.

Figure 12-4 Private key encryption

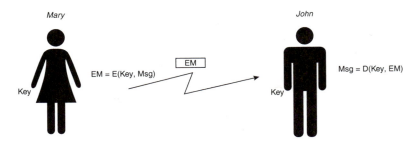

Private key encryption also requires that the two parties agree on a key. Because they can't communicate the key over the network, they need to find a secure means to do so. The Kerberos security system adopted by DCE minimizes this problem by requiring that all parties communicate their keys through a trusted third-party server.

Systems such as Kerberos alleviate the private key problem

Kerberos requires only this security server and one key per principal. The server generates a new session key for each unique client/server session. The private keys associated with the client and the server are used to deliver this session key. Once the client and the server receive the session key, they use it as the common private key for their communication. Note that this scheme potentially requires $c \times s$ session keys if every principal communicates with every other principal. The advantage is that they are generated on demand instead of being pre-issued.

Kerberos requires a trusted third-party server and one key per principal

Public Key Encryption The growth of the Internet has made public key encryption increasingly common. With public key encryption, the number of keys required is only $2 \times (c + s)$. Every principal has two keys: a private key (Pr) known to no one else and a public key (Pu) that is available to everybody. Data sent to a recipient is always encrypted using the recipient's public key. The encryption is designed to be one-way. It is not computationally feasible to decrypt the message using the same public key. The only feasible way to decrypt the message is to use the recipient's unique private key, which is mathematically related to the public key.

With public key encryption every principal has a private key and a public key

As shown in Figure 12-5, Mary uses John's public key (J.Pu) to create the encrypted message (EM) to send across the network. John then uses his private key (J.Pr) and the decryption function to quickly extract the message from EM. The encryption algorithm is designed to ensure that even if someone managed to intercept

The message is encrypted with the public key, decrypted with the private key

Figure 12-5 Public key encryption

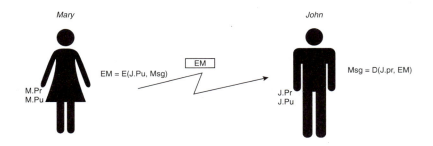

the message and tried to decrypt it with John's public key (available to everyone), it would take a very long time (say, several hundred years) even with the help of the most powerful computer on earth.

The best known public key system is RSA

The best known public key system is RSA, named after its inventors (Rivest, Shamir, and Adleman). RSA uses results from number theory to create encryption and decryption functions in which the private key can be figured out only by factoring the product of two very large prime numbers. There is no known way to do this quickly. However, public key encryption is from five to twenty times slower than private key encryption. In addition, it is not without weaknesses. For example, a hacker might figure out a way to spoof a public key database. The hacker could masquerade as the trusted database and give out the wrong public keys. If a sender uses the wrong public key to encrypt a message, only the hacker can decrypt the message, not the intended receiver.

Public and private key techniques can be used together

Public and private key encryption techniques are not mutually exclusive. In fact, they can be used together. For example, at the start of a communication session, the initiator can use the receiver's public key to encrypt and send a DES key. After the receiver decrypts the message and obtains the DES key, both parties can use the private DES key for better performance in encrypting and decrypting further messages.

Secure sockets layer (SSL) is a widely available network privacy mechanism at the TCP/IP socket level. It was originally designed to link browsers to a Web server, for passing information such as credit card transactions over the Internet. Because it doesn't actually assume the existence of the browser and the Web server, it can be used to secure communication between any two programs connected by sockets. SSL uses public keys to authenticate the client and the server and can encrypt the traffic between them.

Privacy mechanisms can be implemented at different levels

DCE security and the OMG object security services can provide privacy at a higher level. Instead of controlling the traffic at the socket connection level, they provide control at the RPC and object messaging level. The system designer does not need to be concerned about the connection and disconnection of sockets, as with SSL. Control is associated with higher level entities, such as 3GL procedures and CORBA objects.

Security in an OO C/S Environment

All of these security measures are effective with OO enterprise systems. However, the complexities of these systems can compound system threats and vulnerabilities. This section discusses some inherent characteristics of distributed object systems that can affect security issues, including the complex security delegation issues common to many OO systems. All these issues do not mean that OO client/server security requires drastically different measures. Rather, they point to a need to extend and adapt existing security technology to the more dynamic, complex, and fine-grained OO world.

The complexities of OO enterprise systems can compound threats and vulnerabilities

OO Characteristics that Affect Security

Several object characteristics affect security

The main characteristics of distributed object systems that can affect security are

- System dynamics
- Number of entities
- Legacy integration
- Complex administration

Object system flexibility makes it more difficult to ensure system security

System Dynamics One attraction of a distributed object system is its dynamic nature. Objects can be added, deleted, and modified with relative ease to react to changing business requirements. However, such flexibility makes it more difficult to ensure system security. For example, in a large distributed object system, it would be more difficult to update the security policy for all objects at one time. The system could often be in a state in which some objects were using the new policy while some were using the old.

The sheer number of objects can expose vulnerabilities

Number of Entities As discussed earlier, object systems tend to introduce many more fine-grained objects and data types than equivalent procedural systems. The effect, in a distributed object system, is often a network populated by a large number of objects of varying degrees of trustworthiness. The sheer number of objects and object types increase the chances of placing unjustified trust in some system component, thus exposing a vulnerability. Security mechanisms must ensure that necessary checks are performed to enforce the security policy on objects while supporting appropriate performance.

Security boundaries can encompass groups of objects

A common approach to this situation is to establish security boundaries around groups of objects. Objects belonging to a group are assumed to trust each other, and their interactions need not be mediated by security services. Interactions across boundaries may be subject to controls. Security services can establish a trusted relationship among objects across protection boundaries.

Legacy Integration The newly emerging OO systems cannot stand alone. They must interface with existing legacy systems, which often have well-established security measures. Instead of replacing the old security systems, the OO systems often must seek to extend them. In other words, if a legacy system uses established access policies, the goal is to leverage those policies to control access to the same resources through the object system. In most cases, it is not desirable to respecify access policies. Otherwise, for a single legacy system, there would be two sets of policies: the original one and the one associated with the new OO access paths. Keeping these policies synchronized would become a challenge.

Instead of replacing legacy security systems, OO systems must seek to extend them

Complex Administration With the increasing complexity of system dynamics, number of entities, and security policies in the OO client/server system, as well as the issues of legacy integration, security administration effort also increases. For example, an innocent change to a principal's access rights to an object could expose a serious vulnerability in a connected security domain. Security administration can require the cooperation of administrators across multiple policy domains, who might not see eye to eye or who might even be mutually suspicious. Such problems also exist in the 3GL world. However, object systems tend to amplify them.

Increasing complexity also affects security administration

Delegation

In an OO client/server system, delegation of access authority often becomes an issue. Typically, a client object sends a message to a server object to perform an operation. But the server object often does not complete the operation itself; it calls on other objects to do so. This usually results in a chain of calls. Security decisions

Chains of OO calls can require security delegation at every step

may be required at each point in the chain. Access control information is needed to check which objects in the chain can further invoke operations on other objects. Different authorization schemes require different access control information.

Delegation includes client, intermediate, and server objects

Figure 12-6 shows the general delegation model by looking at the relationship of three adjacent objects. Although a typical chain can contain many objects, the rest of the chain can be analyzed by applying the same principles.

The client offers its security credentials to an intermediate object

The client object invokes a method on the intermediate object. The client's security credentials enable the intermediate object to determine whether to grant the client's request for execution of its methods. After that, several variations are possible to determine the credentials (represented by the question-mark box) that would be used to access the server object.

- No delegation of credentials: The intermediate object does not use the client credentials when invoking the next object in the chain. In this case, the question-mark box represents the intermediate object's own credentials. There is no delegation of credentials from the client to the intermediate object.

Figure 12-6 General delegation model for an object system

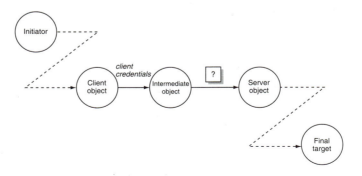

- Simple delegation: The intermediate object uses only the client credentials, not its own, to invoke the server object.

- Composite delegation: The client credentials and the intermediate object's credentials are combined in various ways to be used when invoking the server object. The combination can involve simply sending both, creating a single credential to represent both, or applying an established combination policy.

Note that the security delegation issue is not unique to OO systems. It can also happen in a remote procedure call (RPC) situation. In OO client/server systems, however, the problem does surface more frequently. It requires a more systematic treatment to architect and maintain adequate delegation mechanisms.

Security delegation requires systematic treatment

All of the above issues do not point to the need for drastically different measures when it comes to OO client/server security. We need to work hard to extend and adapt the existing technology base to scale up to the more dynamic, complex, and fine-grained OO world.

Summary

With increasing use of objects and client/server technology, security becomes more complex. Systematic security risk assessment and risk prevention are crucial.

Risk assessment promotes informed judgments on security systems. It starts with accounting for all system assets. The next step is to consider threats and vulnerabilities for the various assets and then, for each potential threat, assess the risk exposure.

Risk prevention determines security boundaries and implements security functions. Conventional systems have physical, system, application, and data security boundaries. In OO systems, object-level protection replaces application and data security. At each security boundary, a variety of security function, such as authentication, access control, auditing and surveillance, and encryption, can be implemented.

Several characteristics of objects affect security. Their flexibility makes it more difficult to ensure system security, and the sheer number of objects that need to be managed can expose vulnerabilities. In general, instead of replacing legacy security systems, OO systems must seek to extend them.

13

Business Systems

Business systems involve the interaction of information systems, business processes, and the people who work with those systems and processes. So far, our discussions have focused on information systems. In this chapter, we expand our view to encompass factors beyond information systems themselves, through the examination of two technology areas: **groupware** and **business systems engineering.**

Groupware and business systems engineering are factors beyond the information system itself

Groupware is a type of client/server system that enables people in an organization (or across organizations) to collaborate in their work efforts. Lotus Notes, Netscape Collabra Share, and Microsoft Exchange are common examples.

By business systems engineering, we mean the activities and techniques an organization can use to create and change its business practices, factoring in computer systems, processes, and people.

In talking about business systems, we are not talking about the ways in which business decisions and technology decisions affect one another. The decision to adopt or extend a technology depends on many factors outside the scope of the technology itself—for example, the degree of commitment to the existing technology, the capital available for change, and management attitudes toward the new technologies. Although these issues are important, we view them as more management-oriented than technological, which puts them beyond the scope of this book. Our hope is that the technical information we present can lead to effective management decision making.

This chapter is not about the relationship of business decisions to technology

Groupware

Groupware is applied to a wide range of products and functionality

Groupware is one of the most ambiguous terms used in the industry today. It is applied to hundreds of products with a wide variety of functionality. Groupware also goes by the names of collaborative computing; workgroup computing; and in academic circles, computer-supported collaborative work (CSCW).

What Is Groupware?

Groupware supports use of nonstructured information for collaborative activity

According to Orfali, Harkey, and Edwards: "Groupware is software that supports the creation, flow, and tracking of nonstructured information in direct support of collaborative group activity."[1] A typical groupware system enables users to share information of different kinds through a number of interconnected applications including

- E-mail
- Shared document databases
- Workflow
- Scheduling and calendaring
- Discussion groups and conferencing
- Telephony
- Internet access

E-mail provides messaging among users and system components

E-mail is the backbone of most groupware systems. E-mail provides messaging not only among users, but also among the system components. For example, groupware systems like Netscape's Collabra Share and Microsoft Exchange use an e-mail service to replicate data between the servers. (While Lotus Notes supports e-mail, it uses a proprietary RPC mechanism for replication.) Most products support multiple e-mail APIs, such as Vendor Independent Messaging (VIM) from a coalition of vendors (including

---

[1]Robert Orfali, Dan Harkey, and Jeri Edwards, *Client/Server Survival Guide*, 2nd ed. (New York: Wiley, 1996). p. 326.

Lotus/IBM, Apple, Borland, Oracle, and Novell), Microsoft's messaging API (MAPI), and X.400.

Shared document databases provide a way for the groupware users to store and retrieve the artifacts they create jointly or individually. These artifacts can include such things as text documents, spreadsheets, and even multimedia items. Replication between client and server or among servers can enhance performance and document accessibility. For example, replicating the address book from a remote server to a local server allows quick access to the address book and makes the address information available even when the remote server or the network is down. Replicating such information to the client allows even faster response time and operations in which client and server are disconnected.

Shared document databases provide storage and retrieval for shared artifacts

Workflow applications help route forms and documents through the users who are involved in completing a process. These applications are built on top of the e-mail and shared document database infrastructure. Note that the workflow support in groupware is generally people-oriented. Human users are an essential part of carrying out most workflow tasks. It would be unusual to have a groupware engine controlling a manufacturing workflow, in which the tasks are carried out by machines and software.

Workflow applications route forms and documents to users

Schedule and calendar applications manage the calendars of the people using the groupware system, as well as resources such as conference rooms. These applications enable users to schedule group activities intelligently.

Schedule applications manage calendars for people and resources

Discussion groups and conferencing provide structure and support for ongoing discussion on specific topics. They capture a "group memory" as the discussion goes on. A typical discussion group application enables groupware users to view comments of

Discussion groups and conferencing enable online discussions

other users and add comments of their own. This goes beyond simply sharing documents, as in a shared document database. When we push this practice into a real-time mode, the result is a conferencing application. Initially, conferencing applications, like "chat rooms" on the Internet, depended on written messages. Currently, vendors are adding multimedia capability to their products to support voice and picture teleconferences.

Telephony applications integrate phone mail and fax

Telephony applications integrate phone mail and fax features into the groupware system as a whole. For example, an e-mail message can contain a phone mail message or information that has been faxed. A voice message can be delivered to a user's e-mail box, and when the user double-clicks on the message, it is played back using the multimedia functions on the user's machine.

Internet access and Web capability are integrated into groupware products

Internet access plays a growing role in groupware, as Web capabilities are increasingly integrated into groupware products at the level of both user interface and database access. An example of the integration of Web capability and groupware is the ability to access a Web site directly from a URL in an e-mail message instead of having to open a Web browser and cut and paste the URL into it. Many vendors also support Web client access to their shared document databases.

Groupware products offer different features

Note that groupware products offer different features. Not all the features discussed above are available in a single product. Most vendors are currently working to round out their offerings by building more functionality into their existing products or by forming alliances with other vendors.

Certain features of enterprise computing are not groupware

To get a clearer perspective on what groupware is and isn't, consider some features of enterprise computing that are commonly considered beyond the reaches of groupware:

- Highly structured database: Groupware databases are not designed to support highly structured data and complex queries
  in the same way that relational databases do.

  Highly structured databases

- Real-time access to data: Although relational databases maintain a single consistent version of the data at any given time,
  groupware databases often allow different versions of a document to exist across the network. A change made to one
  replica is often not visible until it has been propagated to the
  other replicas. (See Chapter 7 for a general discussion of data
  replication.)

  Real-time access to data

- Online transaction processing: Most groupware engines don't
  know how to spell ACID. There is little support for functions
  commonly supported by a transaction processing system, such
  as locking and two-phase commit.

  Online transactions

- Complex business logic: Scripting support in groupware products is not designed to handle large programs on the order of
  several hundred thousand lines of code, developed by large
  teams of programmers.

  Complex business logic

Groupware in the OO C/S Landscape

Groupware fits into the OO client/server world in two ways. First
groupware products are client/server software themselves, and
they are increasingly OO. Second, groupware provides a platform
for building other applications that will fit into the OO client/server
landscape.

Groupware fits into the OO client/server world in two ways

From the groupware provider's perspective, the groupware system
is a client/server application. As shown in Figure 13-1, the document database supports persistence and knows how to replicate itself. The groupware server handles e-mail, workflow, and other
server functions. The clients connect to the servers and provide the
user interface.

Groupware products are client/server applications

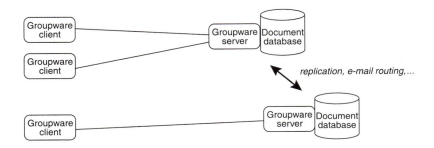

Figure 13-1 Group-ware client/server architecture

replication, e-mail routing,...

Groupware systems face many typical client/server issues

As groupware products grow in sophistication and scale, they en-counter many of the same issues that any other typical client/server system faces, such as complex user interfaces, perfor-mance, system management, program partitioning, and reliability. Because object technology provides a lot of value in addressing these issues, it is not surprising that many vendors have adopted object technology to implement their groupware products.

OO APIs help to handle the complex-ity of groupware ap-plications

At the same time, vendors are also using OO languages to surface their groupware development APIs. This helps developers handle the complexity of groupware applications while reaping the other benefits of OO. For example, Lotus supports Lotus Script, which is an objectified version of BASIC. Microsoft supports ActiveX as the component model for its Exchange product.

Groupware must be integrated into the enterprise computing system

From an enterprise perspective, groupware represents an impor-tant piece of the end-to-end client/server landscape. Like any other component in the information system, groupware applications nor-mally do not stand alone. They need to be integrated with the en-tire enterprise system to achieve full functionality.

Like any client, a groupware system can access external functionality

Figure 13-2 shows a typical scenario. The functionality external to the groupware (relational databases, transaction programs, and so forth) is accessed through the groupware back-end access support, which can be made transparent from the groupware user's per-

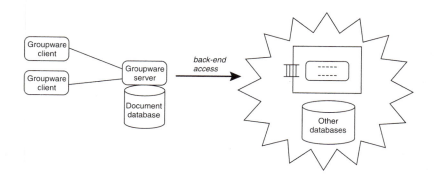

Figure 13-2 Groupware accessing enterprise functionality

spective. Just like any typical client, a groupware application can use client-side APIs to access other servers. For example, it can use ODBC to access a relational database, ECI to access CICS, and APPC to access IMS. It can also participate in distributed computing through the use of an ORB, message queue, or RPC.

From an architecture perspective, a groupware server is a type of database server with weak transaction semantics. The data it manages are documents and e-mail. The server-side scripts are its stored procedures. Update coordination and data integrity can be guaranteed only on the data that it holds. It is good at tasks such as data replication, but it can be dangerous for things it is not intended for, such as transaction coordination. For example, writing a groupware server script to access two external databases at once, expecting them to be committed as a single unit of work, is going outside the intended purposes and can potentially compromise the data.

Architecturally, a groupware server is a database server with weak transaction semantics

The groupware service can also act as a server to other components. Figure 13-3 shows the greater picture, in which other applications in the enterprise system can access the groupware server. Most groupware servers now publish APIs that allow external ac-

It can act as a server to nongroupware components

**Figure 13-3 Group-
ware servers ac-
cessed by other
enterprise applica-
tions**

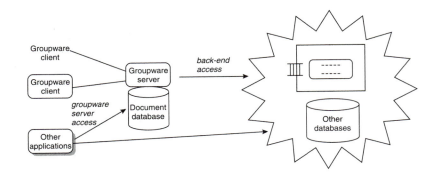

cess to their document database and to services such as e-mail and
calendar functions.

*The groupware
trend is toward OT
and better integra-
tion with the Inter-
net and AD tools*

In summary, groupware serves the essential business needs of
human collaboration and supporting less structured data. We anticipate that the groupware trend is to move toward more extensive
use of object technology, better integration with the Internet, and
better integration with existing application development tools. In
this way, groupware will continue to be an important part of the
end-to-end enterprise computing picture.

Business System Engineering
and Realization

Business systems involve three principal elements and their interactions (see Figure 13-4).

1. The business process that defines the flow of activities and the
   roles involved in carrying out tasks
2. The people and organizations that constitute the resources required to perform the tasks in the business process
3. The information system, composed of the computing infrastructure and the applications that facilitate execution of the
   business process by the people and organizations

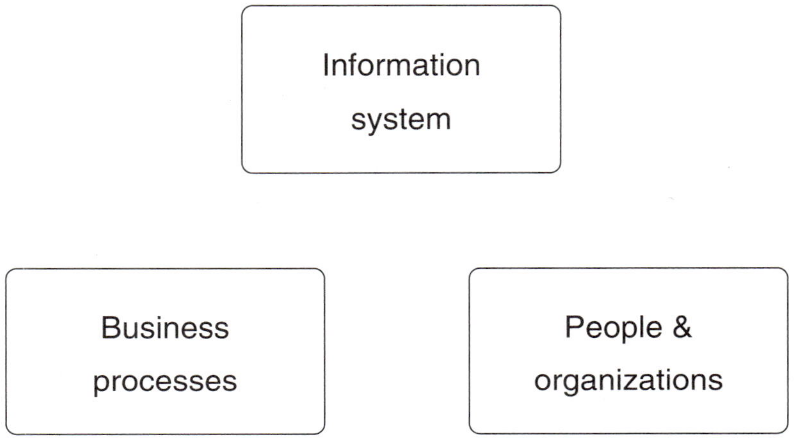

Figure 13-4 The three elements of a business system

We use the term **business system engineering** to denote the activities involved in creating and operating a business system to achieve the goals of an enterprise. The word *business* is used in a broad sense to cover a variety of activities. For example, business goals could involve entertainment, academic research, and so forth. Business system engineering involves many activities. For example, business process reengineering (BPR), software development, personnel training, and system management are all part of business engineering. Considering that any OO enterprise system is developed to achieve some business objectives, you could say that all the subjects covered in this book are part of business system engineering.

Business system engineering means creating and operating a system to achieve an enterprise's goals

Business system engineering drives the need for software development, and OO client/server technology facilitates that development. In that sense, business system engineering creates the context for software development and OO client/server technology. The problems in today's business engineering present some of the greatest challenges and opportunities for object-oriented client-server technology.

Business system engineering creates a context for software development and object technology

The executable business model is a promising solution

Our discussion of business system engineering starts with the need for reduction in two areas: application backlog and the excessive transformations currently required between initial requirements gathering and the eventual implementation. This discussion leads us to the executable business model, a promising solution that integrates business process reengineering with application development. The executable business model draws heavily on object technology.

Our discussion of the executable business model is somewhat speculative

At press time, a gap exists between the proposed model and the infrastructure needed to support it. Therefore, our discussion of the model is more speculative than in other parts of this book. Portions of the model can be applied to today's systems, and as the technology advances, we expect the full model to increasingly become a reality.

Application Backlog versus Business System Backlog

Application development backlog has been a well-known problem

Application backlog has been a significant problem since the early days of computing. As a software industry, we have not been able to develop applications fast enough. The term *software crisis* is often used to depict the severity of the problem. IS organizations have commonly been identified as bottlenecks in rolling out new business initiatives.

Changing business requirements require changing business systems

Today's business people face a similar problem. A fundamental change has come over the business world—it has become much more dynamic. Change is now the norm rather than the exception. A corporation that simply wants to do business the same way year in and year out cannot survive the new business climate. Corporations that can quickly react to change, or better still, create change, have come to dominate the business scene. For example, a bank that deploys a new type of loan program six months ahead of the competition can enjoy a tremendous market share and huge profits.

Creating change like this requires a corporation to have the ability to change its business system quickly. In our banking example, the speed with which the new loan program can be rolled out depends on the speed with which the bank can change its business system to provide the new services to its customers.

Business systems must be able to change quickly

One factor that complicates the ability of a business system to change is the fact that, in general, a business system is the synergistic combination of its people, processes, and information system. Business system engineering must encompass all three elements, as shown in Figure 13-5.

A business system combines three elements

In terms of the information system, it is easy to understand that the more dynamic nature of today's business climate makes the application backlog problem worse. However, experience has shown that just finding ways to develop information systems faster does

Changing a business system requires changing all three elements

Figure 13-5 A business system in the context of business system engineering

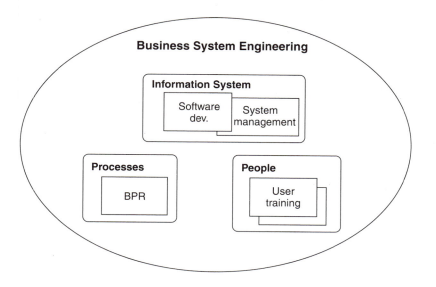

Business System Engineering

Information System

Software dev.

System management

Processes

BPR

People

User training

not solve the business problem. Changing a business system requires changing all three of its elements—new processes need to be defined, people and organizations need to be trained to perform the new tasks, and the information system needs to be changed to support the work.

Speedy implementation of the wrong process can lead to disaster

Speed is important, but not everything. Faster ways to change the three elements are always helpful, but the changes have to be made correctly and in a synergistic way. Otherwise, the new business system can easily fall apart. For example, even the best new software application is not useful if it does not support the business process well. A speedy implementation of the wrong process, or a process that the people in the organization cannot accept, can only lead to disaster.

Reengineering attempts often fail to deliver the intended results

Too Much Transformation Traditional ways of changing a business system can be ineffective and risky. According to Hammer and Champy, 50 percent to 70 percent of reengineering attempts fail to deliver the intended dramatic results.[2] Many factors contribute to these failures. One significant factor related to computing is the large number of transformations required in changing a business system.

Traditionally process reengineering and information systems development are separate

Figure 13-6 illustrates the traditional way of changing a business system. The requirements for change come from external competition or from an internal desire to improve. The first step is to go through the exercise of business process reengineering (BPR) to determine a new and improved business process. The result of the

---

[2] Michael Hammer and J. Champy, *Reengineering the Corporation: A Manifesto for Business Revolution* (New York: HarperCollins, 1993), p. 217.

exercise is often a series of paper documents that capture the process and its potential benefits. Executives in the company then make a go or no go decision on whether to implement the new business process. If the decision is to move forward, the next step is to transform the information system, people, and organizations to implement the new business process.

Note that business analysts and consultants are generally the ones who do the business process engineering, while it is programmers who modify the information system. Often, they do not share the same language and cannot communicate well. There is a good chance that information can get lost or misinterpreted during the transformation. The result could be a new (and costly) information system that does not correspond well to the desired business process.

Business profession-
als often have trou-
ble communicating
ideas to the pro-
grammers

If we drill down into the IS-related activities noted in Figure 13-6, we find that even more transformations have to happen en route to deploying the system. Given the new business process as the input to the IS department, Figure 13-7 shows a traditional sequence of transformations in an iterative information system development.

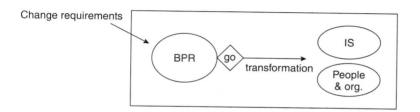

Change requirements

Figure 13-6 Tradi-
tional way of chang-
ing a business
system

Figure 13-7 Transfor-
mations in informa-
tion system
development

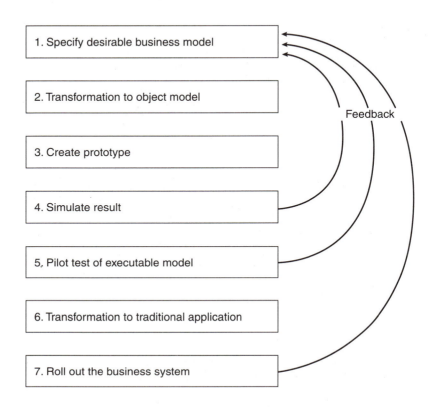

The seven stages of required transformation are

*Traditional IS devel-
opment requires
seven stages of trans-
formation*

1. Specify desirable business model. The BPR notation is translated into the notations of the business modeling methods
   used by the IS department.
2. Transform to object model. Assuming that object technology
   is used to implement the applications, the business model has
   to be transferred to an object model so that object-oriented
   analysis and design methodologies can apply.
3. Create prototype. In modern software development, prototypes are often created to verify the assumptions made in the
   design and analysis stages.
4. Simulate result. The prototype developed in Step 3 can be

used to simulate the result of the end system. Data are collected and analyzed. Any needed change is fed back into earlier steps and the iteration starts again. For the sake of simplicity, Figure 13-7 uses feedback into Step 1 to represent feedback into all the steps.

5. Pilot test of executable model. With a working prototype, end users can be brought in to verify the system. This enables the system designers to examine its correctness and usability. The required changes discovered can be fed back into previous steps.

6. Transform to traditional application. This is the traditional application development step, in which the code for both client and server is written and tested. This step also includes legacy system integration.

7. Roll out the business system. After the new application is developed and the users are trained, the business system can be deployed to the enterprise. Many issues arise during the deployment stage (for instance, how to scale up to all the users in the business). Again, change requirements are fed back into the previous steps to restart the iteration.

Note the large number of transformations required to get the new information system deployed. It takes time to go through the transformations, which makes it difficult to address frequent requirement changes in today's dynamic business world. In addition, the transformations create many opportunities for miscommunication and errors. The relationship between requirements and implementation often vanishes in this translation process. Feedback also comes later than is desirable. As Figure 13-7 shows, a flaw in the business process that was overlooked in the BPR stage might not be caught until Step 4. It might take six to twelve months for a significant business system development project to reach that point. As in any other kind of project, late changes can be costly, assuming they are even possible.

This process has many opportunities for miscommunication and error

In this traditional way of building the system, a little change in the business requirements can often result in big changes to the information system. The more desirable effect would be that small changes to a business model should result in correspondingly small changes to the information system.

Simulation and Execution of Business Models

One alternative is to combine BPR and AD into a single integrated process

A person familiar with the software development process might point out that the above way of developing a business system is too much a traditional waterfall process and involves too many transformations. One way to address this issue is to combine the currently disjoint BPR and application development (Figure 13-8 a) into an integrated activity (Figure 13-8 b). This is still a vision, and realizing it will take a great deal of thought and effort. We see it as a critical movement that can change the shape of business system engineering, address the business system backlog, and shape the future of object-oriented enterprise computing.

During BPR, some modern tools can create an executable business model

Tools like Visio Professional help business reengineering participants design and capture new business processes in graphical representations, such as network diagrams and process flowcharts. Instead of just keeping the information on paper or in an electronic paper format, tools like Gensym's ReThink support simulation capabilities that allow their users to explore alternative process designs. Other modern tools, such as the Enterprise Engine developed by Enterprise Engines, Inc., move even further to capture the business and its processes in an executable model. The result is a software environment that directly implements the abstract business model of an enterprise. When object technology is used to create such a model, the business processes, tasks, roles, and domain entities (such as orders and bank accounts) become objects in the system.

(a)

Change
requirements

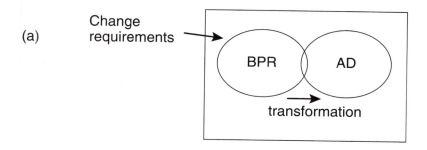

Figure 13-8 Two
ways that business
process engineering
and application de-
velopment can re-
late

(b)

Change
requirements

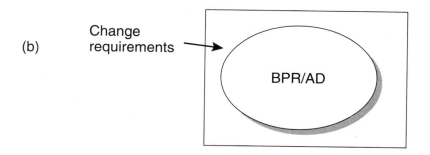

The short-term objective of this executable business model is to
provide a good simulation environment in which business analysts
can address what-if questions. This increases the chances of designing the new business system correctly to begin with. Remember,
the earlier a flaw is uncovered, the cheaper it is to fix. The executable model also serves as a live application specification (vs.
paper documentation) for application developers. The long-term
objective, however, is to produce executable business systems directly from the modeling exercise.

*This model provides
a simulation envi-
ronment and live
application specifica-
tion*

Let's examine the key long-term benefits that can arise from the
OO executable business model.

Benefits

*Problem domain
and solution domain
are nearly the same*

- The problem domain and the solution domain start to converge. This is one of the key promises of object technology. Analysts can think in terms of concrete objects rather than abstract programs and procedures. By making the information system object-oriented and by modeling the business entities with objects, the gap between the real world (the problem domain) and the software world (the solution domain) is minimized.

  Minimizing the gap can significantly reduce the number of transformations needed to go from the requirements to a solution. It's useful to have a system in which analysts and programmers all use the same terminology—that is, for objects such as *account* and *customer* that inhabit both the problem domain and the solution domain.

Application development is redefined

- Application development (AD) takes on a new meaning. Traditional AD takes the requirements that emerge from the BPR and delivers individual applications that implement the respective processes. With the new approach, AD's task is to incrementally refine and extend the executable business model created during BPR. AD becomes the extension of the modeling activities. Traditional AD disappears because there are no individual applications to deliver any more. Instead, business functions are delivered through the extension of the executable model. The new AD focuses on tasks like connecting the model to the legacy system or refining the system's user interfaces to make them more user friendly. (UIs can be generated automatically from the business model, but they are not necessarily user friendly.)

*Business processes
become more explicit*

- Business processes become more explicit. In the traditional method, the transformation between BPR and AD buries the business processes in the code of the resulting applications.

This makes the business processes difficult to maintain. Suppose there is a need to change a business process. Before the application could be modified, the code that corresponds to the process would have to be studied to understand how the old process is encoded.

The encoded business processes would also be very difficult to reuse because of the way the processes and application code are coupled. There is no way to reuse just a single process outside the context of its container application. When business processes are represented as objects, the processes become explicit. As first class citizens of the OO world, they enjoy benefits, such as ease of maintenance and reuse.

- Simulation and analysis are easier. As discussed, the executable model allows simulation and analysis of the business process to be deployed and provides rapid and early feedback to the business analysts.

Simulation and analysis are easier

- The advantages of OO are present. Because it is object-oriented, the executable business model enjoys the benefits of OO. The business processes, being explicit, are easier to maintain and reuse. In addition, it is relatively easy to wrapper the legacy system, as well as to manage change and complexity.

The advantages of OO are available

Let's use an example to illustrate these key characteristics of the executable business model. XYZ bank has an existing loan approval process, shown in Figure 13-9. A customer submits the loan application to the system. The branch manager (first level) needs to approve it and forward it to the underwriter (second level). After the underwriter approves the loan application, it is processed by the payment system, which releases the payment to the borrower. The process, represented by the arrows and boxes in the diagram, is captured explicitly as an object.

Example: A bank changing its loan application process

Figure 13-9 An existing loan approval process

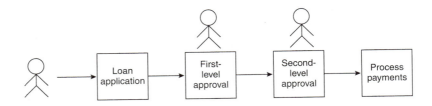

First, the improved
process is identified

Now assume that through business process reengineering, the bank finds that it can increase its competitiveness and revenue by shortening the wait time for a loan. One way to shorten the wait time is to change the sequential approval process to a parallel process, as shown in Figure 13-10. Because the bank already has an executable model of its business, which includes the existing sequential loan process, it decides to test out the new parallel process on the executable model first.

The bank can use
object technology to
access and modify
existing processes

Because the processes are explicitly identified as objects, the bank is able to quickly locate the original process and create a derivative of it to represent the new parallel process. Note that most of the building blocks from the old process are reused. Because most of the user interfaces and back-end processing functions remain the same, only minor changes to the UI and the code are required. Object technology also insulates the modules

Figure 13-10 A proposed improvement to the loan approval process

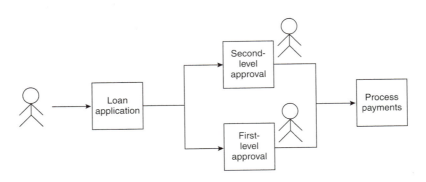

from one another so that the changes can be localized in just a few modules.

The scale of change to the software is proportional to the scale of change in the process. Most of the change consists of creating the new derivative process object. The more different it is from the original process, the more changes are required. However, the code supporting the process does not have to be changed. In contrast, if we were to create a new process in the traditional way, it would require us to create a new application. Some code from the original application could be reused. However, the new business process embedded in the code could require modification of many modules.

The change in the software is proportional to the change in the process

Because its business model is executable, the XYZ bank decides to exercise the new process with a set of typical input collected during normal day-to-day operations. The simulated result is analyzed and shows that the new process cuts the wait time by 30 percent. This reduction of wait time can be projected into a 50 percent increase of revenue in six months, which makes the new process very attractive.

The executable model enables simulation with operational data

Before committing itself to the new process, the bank asks a few of its branch managers and underwriters to sit in front of the new business model and exercise it. Some minor problems in the model are uncovered and fixed. All pilot participants are happy about the new processes. Now the bank is ready to deploy the new business process. Because the bank's operations are driven from a production executable business model, the changes can be propagated from the test business model to the production model. The streamlined loan process is now in effect.

The new process is easy to test and deploy

Figure 13-11 Information system development using an executable business model

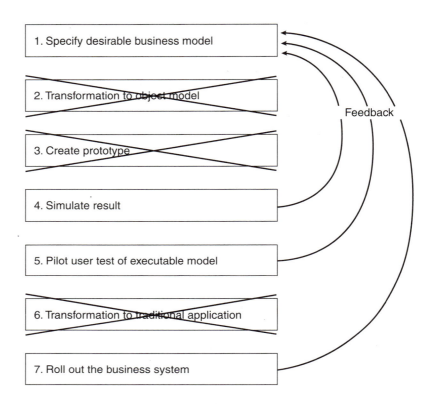

1. Specify desirable business model

2. Transformation to object model

3. Create prototype

4. Simulate result

5. Pilot user test of executable model

6. Transformation to traditional application

7. Roll out the business system

Feedback

The executable business model reduces the transformations required

As shown in Figure 13-11, business system engineering using an executable business model removes or significantly reduces the required transformations. By eliminating the transformation work, businesses can move faster and get earlier feedback to correct potential problems.

The new process can be reused for similar business cases

As we mentioned before, structuring business processes as objects also makes them reusable. The loan approval process can be abstracted into a generic approval process. By subclassing the generic approval process, the bank can create an approval process for travel expense accounts that reuses most of the loan approval process. Any improvements to the loan process may also be applicable to the new process. The inheritance hierarchy of the processes can help to identify additional candidates for improvement, as well as the locations in the processes in which to make improvements.

Executable Business Models
and OO Enterprise Computing

The executable business model must sit on top of an execution platform, as shown in Figure 13-12. This platform must be able to run on top of a variety of hardware and operating systems and span network and enterprise boundaries. It needs to provide strong data and transaction processing, as well as workflow and system management. It also needs to integrate well with the existing systems. Finally, it needs to be integrated with the business process engineering tools.

The executable model needs to integrate with existing system infrastructure

No existing system can satisfy all of these requirements. This means that a gap currently exists between the model and the infrastructure. Organizations must bridge this gap manually (one reason why practices include so many transformations). The challenge is to narrow the gap. OO client/server systems are an attractive start-

Currently, a gap exists between model and infrastructure

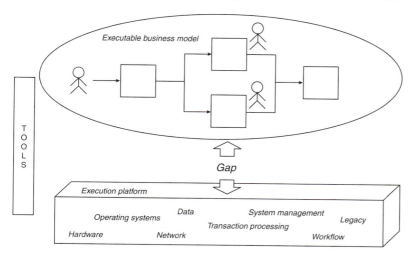

Figure 13-12 The gap between executable business model and existing infrastructure

ing point because, with them, the gap is not as wide as with other systems (either centralized or non-OO systems).

The gap can be closed from the top down or bottom up

The gap can be closed either from the top down (from the perspective of the business model) or the bottom up (from the perspective of the execution platform) or from both directions at once. From the top down, the requirements are for further development of reusable components and frameworks, an execution engine for the business model, and business engineering tools.

Closing the gap from the top down requires further development in several areas

- **Reusable components and frameworks** need to be developed and maintained. The need is for both generic components, such as *person* and *customer,* and domain-specific ones, such as *insured* and *beneficiary* (to use examples from the insurance domain). Note that the reusable components are not restricted to concrete objects. You can also capture and reuse more abstract objects such as business processes. For example, a generic approval process can be reused for bank loan approval and travel expense approval.

A way to execute the model

- **A model execution engine** is needed, which would treat the executable model as input and execute it on top of the IT infrastructure. The term *engine* is conceptual. Business models are not executed by any single entity, and we do not propose creating a new runtime environment. What is needed is runtime integration between the frameworks that contain the objects and the underlying IT infrastructure.

Scaled-up business engineering tools

- **Business engineering tools** need to scale up to handle complex models, team development, versioning and change control, testing, documentation, support, and maintenance. There is also a need for high-level visual builders, which can make it easy to construct the business objects and use the frameworks. All this should be fairly familiar to the application development community, in which hundreds of programmers typically collaborate on complex programs that have to remain operational and maintainable for many years. We need to leverage this team development experience in providing business engineering tools.

The business engineering tools would also have to integrate well with existing AD tools because the new executable business model will have to interface with existing applications in the foreseeable future. Information systems that efficiently serve businesses require a combination of the old and the new.

From the bottom-up perspective, two types of technology are important in filling the gap: distributed objects with transaction support and workflow management.

From the bottom up, two technologies are important

- **Distributed object technology** can enable the higher-level business model software to treat the lower-level infrastructure as a set of objects. Using this technology, the business model can treat the entire network as a single computer and manage the resources as objects. (The system management community has long used a similar approach.) Instead of having to deal with the complexity of low-level communication and hardware boundaries, the executable business model can focus on issues related to the business.

Distributed object technology masks the low-level communication complexity

Distributed transactions ensure the integrity of the objects supporting the business system. By supporting transaction coordination across the network and distributed recovery, distributed transactions further support the perception of the network as a computer.

Workflow management can be more than what is discussed in groupware

- **Workflow management** is another key to closing the gap. When we discussed workflow in the context of groupware, we presented it as mainly people-oriented. In the context of business systems engineering, a broader definition of workflow is useful.

Workflow Requirements

A workflow process is a collection of activities executed by tools

The Workflow Management Coalition (WfMC), a nonprofit international body for the development and promotion of workflow standards, defines a workflow process as a collection of activities. An activity is a logical step that contributes toward the completion of a workflow process; it is executed by a "tool," which is an application outside the workflow system. For example, a tool can be a spreadsheet program or a client/server application. The workflow engine controls the flow of work and the input and output between the workflow system and the tools.

Workflows that help close the gap have several requirements

Such a definition enables us to consider workflows more formally and to apply them to more business systems. The workflow support becomes part of the platform on which the business model executes. When we look at workflows in this way, we can see several requirements that will be useful in closing the gap between the business model and the execution platform.

Non-human services can act directly on items in a workflow

Workflows with Nonhuman Actors In a people-oriented workflow, users collaborate by acting on the forms that the workflow service circulates. In a business system, system services that are not human beings can also act directly on the work items flowing through the system.

A business-system workflow can exist even for a single user. For example, a travel agent who wants to reserve hotel and airlines tickets from two reservation systems can use a workflow service to coordinate the two systems. When no airline ticket is available to reach a location, the hotel reservation should be canceled automatically.

A workflow system can have no human user at all. For example, a fully automated manufacturing production line can involve no human user but has strict workflow.

Workflows Supporting Real-Time and Long Transactions Because people-oriented workflow servers are often database servers, they often do not support transaction coordination outside the resources they control. In a business system workflow, the workflow engine needs to support transactions that coordinate multiple resource managers.

The workflow engine must coordinate resource managers over longer periods

The transactions can also be long-lived. The travel reservation example can be represented as a long-lived transaction that involves updates to multiple resource managers (for example, the reservation databases) and eventually involves payments from the accounts of various parties.

Workflows that are Better Integrated with Distributed Object Technology The business-system workflow service needs to integrate closely with a distributed object infrastructure. It needs to leverage services provided by the distributed object systems, such as distributed transaction services. It also needs to extend workflow control to individual objects. To better support the business engineering activities, workflow services need to be able to schedule and route information among objects instead of among application-level tools. Activities such as the development of the OMG's workflow management facility can potentially lead to a standards-based solution.

Workflows must also leverage a distributed object infrastructure

A Vision

*The vision of an OO
business system can
serve as a beacon*

We close this chapter with a vision of what business system engineering could be, based on current technological trends. This vision can serve as a beacon to technology providers as they move OO enterprise computing into the future.

*Such a system provides a number of
advantages*

In our vision, the business system closely models the real world and can quickly react to a change in business requirements. Little transformation is necessary between the problem domain and the solution domain. Once a new business system is proposed, it can quickly be turned into an executable model. This model enables simulation, analysis, and even end-user pilot testing early in the cycle, which ensures not only that we can implement the system quickly but also that we implement the right system.

Once the executable model has been refined, it can be deployed to execute in the real world. During execution, the flow of the business processes can be monitored and logs of execution characteristics can be captured (by observing the running business model) to guide future enhancement.

*For business system
users, daily operations are fully automated.*

For business system users, daily operations are fully automated. Each employee receives a personalized to-do list, and the right objects are automatically available on the user's workstation for the tasks on the list. Completed tasks are forwarded to the person or computer handling the next step. Tasks for absent employees or unavailable system components are automatically routed to substitutes. Workloads are balanced among available resources.

*OO client/server systems provide a good
start for achieving
this vision*

The achievement of this vision requires hard work. Practical issues, such as performance, reliability, and system management, still need to be addressed. We believe OO client/server systems provide a good starting point in the direction of this better future.

Summary

A business system is the combination of three critical elements: business processes, people and organizations, and the information system. Two important enterprise factors beyond the information system are groupware and business systems engineering.

Groupware supports the use of nonstructured information in support of collaborative activity. It generally includes such functions as e-mail, shared document databases, schedule and calendar applications, Internet access, and Web capability. It can also include workflow applications, discussion groups and conferencing, and telephony applications.

Groupware products are client/server applications, and groupware systems face many typical client/server issues. The groupware trend is toward object technology and better integration with the Internet and AD tools.

Business system engineering means creating and operating a system to achieve the goals of an enterprise. Traditional business-systems engineering separates process reengineering and information systems development. The IS development requires numerous transformations, which can lead to miscommunication and error.

One alternative is to combine business process reengineering and application development into one integrated process. This leads to the vision of an executable business model, which could provide a simulation environment and even live execution, which would significantly reduce the required transformations and offer additional benefits, such as the advantages of object technology.

Currently, a gap exists between the executable business model and the existing system infrastructure. Closing this gap from the top down requires further development in several areas.

- Reusable components and frameworks
- A model execution engine
- Business engineering tools

Closing the gap from the bottom up can involve distributed object technology, as well as workflow management that goes beyond its groupware implementations. The executable business model offers a vision of an enterprise in which daily operations are fully automated. Object-oriented client/server systems provide a good start toward this vision.

14

Some Conclusions and Predictions

To conclude, we return to our three-part view of the client/server system (client, server, glue). Because the topic of object-oriented enterprise systems is so complex and dynamic, we have taken a structured approach to it. In this way, we have emphasized what we see as the perennial architecture principles that are not likely to vary drastically over time. It seems to us that understanding these principles is a better way to cope with the rapid evolution of technology than simply knowing the details of existing products and technology. The principles also help to distinguish reality from commercial hype.

We expect this book's architecture principles to remain stable

Objects in the Three-Part Model

Figure 14-1 summarizes the three parts of a typical client/server system. The client (or desktop) is where the system meets the user. This part of the model historically makes extensive use of object technology, particularly in graphical user interface construction and compound desktop architecture. Because the adoption of object technology for clients started early, it has progressed further

Clients are evolving toward pure object technology

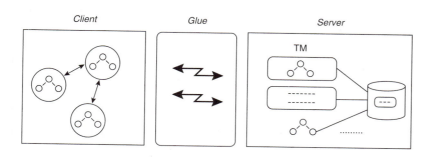

Client   Glue   Server

Figure 14-1 The three-part client/server model

than for the glue or the servers. We expect clients to be entirely OO in the near future.

Server adoption of object technology is progressing

Servers come in many types. They mainly fall into the major categories of transaction server, database server, and native server. Server technology providers are evolving their non-OO servers into a variety of OO servers, with corresponding benefits and drawbacks. Server adoption of object technology has lagged behind the client, in part because organizations responsible for the servers are necessarily more conservative. However, significant progress is occurring in this area.

The Year-2000 problem may provide a boost for server object technology

Interestingly, the so-called Year-2000 problem may provide a strong push toward the adoption of server object technology. Because so many existing legacy applications store dates in a two-digit format, many critical calculations based on the year number will produce the wrong results when the last two digits of the calendar year turn to zero. This will render many existing server applications nonfunctional. Corporations facing the choice between patching the existing system and rewriting it with objects may decide to make the jump to object technology. In this way, they can both solve the Year-2000 problem and establish a system that is more adaptable and easier to maintain.

Many types of client/server glue are available

As long as client and server need to communicate with each other, some form of glue is needed. The glue provides a transport mechanism between client and server, a programming model for using such a mechanism, and tools supporting the programming model. Depending on communication styles, many types of glues are available, with different messaging models and levels of services. The choice of server and client often narrows down the choice of glue you have, and vice versa. Within the glue, we discussed the three communication levels: common buffer, common middleware, and common language. These levels apply equally well to procedural and OO systems. We expect glues supporting different levels to continue to co-exist and complement one another.

Objects Across the Enterprise

The destination of object technology is the end-to-end client/server system. When objects are pervasive on both client and server, the maximum benefits of object technology are available. At the same time, we realize that the push to make objects pervasive across the enterprise is evolutionary. Overnight conversion simply cannot happen.

The destination of object technology is the end-to-end enterprise system

Even if the changeover to object technology occurs gradually, much work can start right away. The sooner developers start training and becoming proficient with object technology, the better equipped they will be to take advantage of advances in the technology and turn them into business advantages. (For example, while waiting for OO language support to be available on the server, an organization can start working with the same language on the client.)

Much of the work of introducing objects can start right away

The modularity of the object-oriented approach makes it possible for organizations to start on a modest scale and expand as they gain expertise. Starting small also enables an organization to test the waters before jumping in. With object technology, as with all new technologies, the possibilities are very real for getting locked into tools and approaches that don't work for your organization. For example, a company could invest in a new OO server technology, only to find that it has dependencies (for example on a proprietary objectified stored procedure architecture) that prevent their new applications from scaling in the way they expected as their system becomes larger and more heterogeneous.

Organizations can start with objects on a small scale

Modularity enables organizations to move forward piece by piece

Development teams can convert an existing system piece by piece, encapsulating applications and system components and reengineering them from the inside. As organizations gain confidence and master the necessary skills, they can increasingly use object technology for application development and convert larger, enterprise-critical applications.

An Ever-Evolving Technology

OO client/server technology is evolving as we speak. This is a trait of any vibrant technology. We expect this evolution to continue in the years to come.

Many elements are in place for OO client/server technology to "leap the chasm" to the mainstream

In his book *Crossing the Chasm,* Geoffrey Moore discusses the typical stages of technology adoption, from experimenters to early adopters to the mainstream.[1] OO clients have already entered the mainstream, and many server and glue implementations that we discussed are poised to "cross the chasm." Certain elements are necessary for this to happen, and we have seen that many of these elements are falling into place. The need exists, the technology continues to evolve, reports from the early adopters are good, and standards are forming rapidly. In the years to come, we anticipate that continued evolution and enhancement will push the use of object technology for servers and glue increasingly toward the mainstream.

New areas of applicability continue to emerge

It is also interesting to consider the continuing emergence of new areas to which OO client/server technology can apply. The obvious example is the World Wide Web. Instead of having to invent a whole new paradigm, Web architects and developers can leverage

---

[1]Geoffrey Moore, *Crossing the Chasm: Marketing and Selling Technology Products to Mainstream Customers* (New York: HarperCollins, 1991).

the more mature OO client/server experience and architectures from the IS arena. In this way, they can minimize their own risk and move forward faster. (Of course, along the way, they add new technological twists to reflect the new circumstances.) We can reasonably expect this pattern to continue. OO client/server technology will adapt to new problem domains as they emerge.

This kind of adaptation implies a synergy. OO technology has proven that it can combine with existing and emerging technologies to suit new purposes. The successful merger of object technology and client/server computing gives evidence of this. However, the trend doesn't stop here. As soon as the synergy between OO and client/server technologies was apparent, people started to look for other technologies that can be combined into the OO client/server base to create new synergies. A good example is business systems engineering, discussed in Chapter 13. OO client/server techniques combine with BPR techniques to create a new vision of the executable business model. (As another example, we are also seeing the infusion of design pattern techniques into OO client/server computing to help capture and apply the best application coding and design practices.)

Technologies continue to combine and create new synergies

We've discussed before how objects make it easy to wrapper existing code, from single procedures to legacy systems. The existing code can operate intact as the end-to-end OO enterprise system emerges around it. This makes it easy to infuse new technologies. In a sense, object technology is like an enzyme that attracts and adapts new technologies to enterprise systems.

Objects make it easier to infuse new technology into enterprise systems

All these factors point to a dynamic future for OO enterprise computing. The precise terms of that future and the uses to which the technology can be put will continue to unfold. We anticipate its further evolution and its emergence as a dominant paradigm in the

The future looks bright for OO enterprise computing

world of computer systems. Given the progress made on OO servers, glues, standards, customer applications, languages, and tools, the goal is already within sight—seamless, high-quality, easily maintained OO enterprise applications. These applications can bring order and simplicity to the complex systems of today's computing environment.

Abbreviations

3GL Third-generation language

4GL Fourth-generation language

ACID Atomicity, consistency, isolation, durability

ACL Access control list

AD Application development

ANSI American National Standards Institute

API Application program interface

APPC Advanced Program-to-Program Communication

ATM Asynchronous Transfer Mode

BMS Basic Mapping Support (CICS screen mapper)

BPR Business process reengineering

CAD Computer-aided design

CAM Computer-aided manufacturing

CASE Computer-aided software engineering

CGI Common Gateway Interface

CICS Customer Information Control System

CMIP Common management information protocol

COM Component Object Model

CORBA Common Object Request Broker Architecture

CPU Central processing unit

DB2 Database 2 (an IBM database management system)

DCE Distributed Computing Environment

DCOM Distributed Component Object Model

DBMS Database management system

DDL Data Definition Language

DEC Digital Equipment Corporation

DES Data Encryption Standard

DML Data Manipulation Language

DRDA Distributed Relational Database Architecture

ECI External Call Interface (used in client/server CICS environments)

FTP File Transfer Protocol

GUI Graphical user interface

HTML Hypertext Markup Language

HTTP Hypertext Transfer Protocol

IDL Interface Definition Language

IIOP Internet Inter-ORB Protocol

IMS Information Management System (an IBM hierarchical database)

IMS/TM IMS Transaction Manager

IS Information systems

IT Information technology

JDBC Java Database Connection

LAN Local area network

MFS Message Format Service (IMS screen mapper)

MVS Multiple Virtual Storage (IBM mainframe operating system)

NT New Technology (the Microsoft Windows client/server operating system)

OCS Object Concurrency Service

ODBC Open Database Connectivity

ODBMS Object database management system

ODL Object Definition Language

ODMG Object Database Management Group

OLE Object Linking and Embedding

OLTP Online transaction processing

OMG Object Management Group

OO Object-oriented

OOUI Object-oriented user interface

O-R DBMS Object-relational database management system

ORB Object Request Broker

OTS Object Transaction Service

RC Risk cost

RDB Relational database

RE Risk exposure

RMI Remote method invocation

RP Risk probability

RPC Remote procedure call

RSA Rivest-Shamir-Adleman (a common public key encryption algorithm for security)

SAA Systems Application Architecture (an IBM client/server architecture)

SAP Systems, Applications and Products (a software vendor)

SATAN Security Administrator's Tool for Analyzing Networks

SDK Software development kit

SMTP Simple Mail Transfer Protocol

SNMP Simple Network Management Protocol

SQL Structured Query Language

SSL Secure Sockets Layer (a widely available network privacy mechanism at the TCP/IP socket level)

TCP/IP Transmission Control Protocol/ Internet Protocol

TOOL Transactional Object-Oriented Language (a proprietary language of the Forte application development tool suite)

TRPC Transactional remote procedure call

UI User interface

UIMS User interface management system

UNIX A common workstation operating system

URL Uniform Resource Locator (also called "Unified Resource Locator")

VSAM Virtual Storage Access Method

WAN Wide area network

WfMC Workflow Management Coalition

Glossary

The glossary includes terms that are essential for understanding enterprise computing with objects, key terms that may be unfamiliar to the general enterprise computing community, and terms that are the subject of extensive discussion in the text. The definitions are our own.

ACID properties Atomicity, consistency, isolation, and durability—four properties essential to transactions and ensured by transaction processing systems.

ActiveX component Executable code that conforms to the COM standard and can run on a Windows platform. An ActiveX component can be downloaded from a server and executed on a client.

agent/manager architecture In system management, the client/server architecture for implementing the system management software. Agents represent the subjects to be managed. Managers monitor and manipulate the subjects through agents.

aggregator A person, service, or process that makes a wide range of information or services available from a single source, such as an online service or a reference book.

applet Executable Java code that can be downloaded from a Web server and executed on a client.

asynchronous messaging Communication between two threads of execution in which the calling thread does not need the response to the message before continuing to process.

availability A measure that is a function of the mean time between failures and mean time to restore after failure (the time to respond, isolate, correct, and verify). Availability is an effective measure of *reliability*.

business system engineering The activities involved in creating and operating a business system to achieve the goals of an enterprise.

business system A system that enables an enterprise to successfully carry out its everyday activities. Business systems involve three principal elements and their interactions: business processes, people and organizations, and information systems.

bytecodes The machine language used by the *virtual machine* in certain object-oriented language implementations, such as Java and Smalltalk.

class hierarchy A tree structure defining the inheritance relationship among classes. A class can have subclasses down the hierarchy from itself and superclasses up the hierarchy. A class inherits the methods and variables of its superclasses. In systems supporting multiple inheritance, the inheritance relations can form a lattice instead of a tree.

class A template for defining an object, with its attributes defined as variables and its behavior defined as methods. A class can be used to create instances of itself, all of which have the same methods and instance variables, but they can have different variable values.

client In common usage, the front end of the client/server system, the component with which a user interacts. In the *logical client/server model*, the client is the system component that requests a service.

common buffer approach A communications approach in which client and server agree on a buffer format and the communications middleware ships the buffers back and forth between them. The application code takes care of low-level duties, such as data marshaling and data conversion, between the client/server platforms.

common language approach A communications approach that takes advantage of a client and a server that are implemented in the same language. This approach can provide high local/remote transparency that masks the existence of underlying middleware as much as possible.

common middleware approach A communications approach in which the client and server are connected by a middleware service, such as an object request broker. Data conversion and marshaling are done by the middleware, and interaction across languages is possible.

compound document A software document consisting of portions that are managed by different types of applications, such as a word processor and a spreadsheet program.

compound object An object composed of one or more other objects. For example, a dialog box is a compound object made up of text entry fields, buttons, list boxes, labels, and so on.

concurrent computing Computing in which several elements of a program execute at the same time.

content authoring tool In Internet application development, a tool used to create and manipulate content for Web-based applications, typically including a variety of text and multimedia types.

conversational communication Communication between two programs in which a network connection is established and kept open for the duration of the communication.

data extraction Copying all or part of a database for use on a read-only basis. Compare with *data replication.*

data partitioning Storing certain database records on one machine and certain others on one or more different machines. No piece of data is stored in more than one place.

data replication Copying all or part of a database in such a way that the replica can be updated. Any data partition can have many replicas; it is necessary to ensure that updates to a data element are eventually applied to all replicas. Compare with *data extraction.*

data schema The definition of the structure of stored information in the data store.

database server A server is based on a database management system, often relational. Currently, the most pervasive server type in client/server computing.

defect An error in a product's requirements, design, implementation, or documentation. Contrast with *error, fault.*

disintermediation The process of removing middlemen, such as *aggregators,* from an activity so that participants have direct access to a source of service and information.

distributed computing Computation on multiple machines using computing resources that are distributed across a network. A general category, of which client/server computing forms a subset.

distributed debugging Support for debugging an entire client/server system as a single unit. See also *remote debugging.*

encapsulation The practice of hiding and protecting an object's data and internal implementation details. Another object can access the data only through methods available from the object's interface and cannot access the private methods used in the internal implementation.

enterprise computing The development, deployment, and maintenance of the information systems required by businesses.

error In system reliability, a human mistake, such as an operational problem, missing functionality, or a mistake in programming. Contrast with *defect, fault.*

executable business model A software business model of an enterprise that can provide simulation or even live execution.

failover The process of switching over to an alternative service provider when a service becomes unavailable because of a fault. Failover is a way of enhancing system *reliability.*

fat client A client that contains a large amount of functionality. Usually refers to first generation client/server computing, in which all business logic and UI reside on the client.

fault In system reliability, the failure of a component to function as designed or required. Contrast with *defect, error.*

firewall A system element that protects a private network from intrusion. Firewalls normally have two principal functions: to block traffic from accessing the protected network, and to allow certain classes of traffic through.

framework A set of protocols or interfaces, along with their corresponding code, that define the interaction among objects or components in a system.

garbage collection The process of reclaiming the space an object instance occupies when the instance no longer has any references to it (although its actual physical removal may be delayed until an appropriate time).

glue The means by which a client and a server communicate with each other. Glue includes three aspects: low-level "plumbing" (TCP/IP, for example), a programming model, and application development tools that support the programming model.

groupware Software that supports the creation, flow, and tracking of nonstructured information in direct support of collaborative group activity.

GUI Graphical user interface. An end-user interface to a computer system in which the end user communicates with the system by manipulating graphical objects. See also *OOUI*.

inheritance A mechanism that enables one class to share the methods and variables of another. A subclass inherits from its superclasses in the class hierarchy. Some OO languages, such as C++, have multiple inheritance, which enables a class to inherit from two or more superclasses.

instance variable A container for data within an object.

instance A single object that is defined by a particular class. One class, such as Customer, can have multiple instances in a single OO program.

Internet A network of networks, based on a common communications protocol, TCP/IP (although capable of operating with other protocols).

JavaBeans A component standard for Java objects. JavaBeans are specifically designed to be manipulated by software development tools.

lazy fetching A way of optimizing performance when using persistent objects. The persistence mapping mechanism brings objects into the application only as they are needed.

legacy A computer program or system that is still required by an enterprise but may be based on technology or architecture that is no longer current.

load balancing Spreading the system workload among the available resources so that the job can be done faster. Load balancing can occur between client and server or among servers.

logical client/server model A paradigm in which elements of a computing system request services from each other in order to complete one or more tasks. The requesting element is the client, and the elements that provide services are the servers. In this model, the roles of client and server are not fixed.

logical three-tier architecture A client/server model in which user interface, logic, and data are seen as separate logical entities. The three tiers may be partitioned differently between the physical tiers (hardware) of the system.

message A request from a sending object for the receiving object to perform a behavior. Normally, a message consists of the name of the receiver's method that calls the desired behavior and can include a set of parameters and return value.

message latency A measurement of the delay introduced by the glue on message sends.

method A defined behavior that an object can exhibit, given a name on the object's interface by which other objects can request that behavior. Also referred to as a member function.

native server A server that runs directly on top of the operating system.

network computing A style of computing in which most of the functionality occurs on servers and the client is limited to the role of network access device. Also known as thin-client computing.

***n*-tier architecture** Client/server architecture with multiple system partitions inside the logic or data portion of the application. Physically, the application can run across four, five, or even more machines (tiers), hence the name *n*-tier.

object database management system (ODBMS) A database management system designed for object-oriented programs. An ODBMS can often store the code, as well as the data, for the objects. It organizes objects in terms of composite structures that "contain" objects by means of referencing them.

object implementation The code that implements the methods defined by an object's interface.

object interface The interface through which an object allows other objects to interact with it. It contains the declarations of a set of methods and their semantics.

object schema The definition of the structure of the objects in an application. See also *data schema, schema mapping.*

object scraper A tool that "scrapes" legacy screens into objects. See also *screen scraper.*

object The basic building block of object technology. A self-contained software component that includes variables for storing data and methods that can act on the data.

OLE Object Linking and Embedding. A *compound document* architecture that enables a desktop program to seamlessly link to and activate different applications from within the same document.

OOUI Object-oriented user interface. A type of GUI in which the graphical elements of the interface represent objects so that the interaction is object-centric rather than application-centric. Users interact with the objects themselves rather than with the applications that underlie them.

OpenDoc A *compound document* architecture that enables a desktop program to seamlessly link to and activate different applications from within the same document. (Note that vendor support for this architecture has diminished in favor of OLE and JavaBeans.)

O-R DBMS Object-relational database management system. A database management system that combines elements of object database management systems and relational database management systems.

plug-ins Software executables that can be "plugged into" a Web browser and interpret data received from the Web server. Plug-ins can come packaged with the Web browser or can be downloaded from servers across the network.

polymorphism The ability for a message to invoke different behavior (methods) depending on the class of the receiver. Because of polymorphism, a sending object does not have to know the implementation details of the behavior it requests.

pre-fetching A means of moving persistent objects from an object store to an application. When a persistent object is invoked by the application, the mapping mechanism brings in additional persistent objects referenced by the initial persistent object in expectation of a future need for them. Contrast with *lazy fetching*.

principal A human user or an object that accesses services in a computer system. Client and server applications can also be considered principals. Every principal has at least one, and possibly several, identities, depending on the roles it assumes.

private key encryption An encryption method that requires both sender and receiver to know a single key that is private to them. The key is typically a large number carefully selected to conform to the requirement of the encryption algorithm used.

pseudo-conversational communication Communication between two programs that does not maintain the connection between them. The connection is released after each request and reestablished when the next request comes. System support enables the applications sitting above the communication layer to behave as if they are having conversational communication.

public key encryption An encryption method in which every principal has two keys: a private key known to no one else, and a public key available to everybody. Data sent to a recipient is encrypted using the recipient's public key.

push model See *webcasting*.

record mapping service A service that maps the data types between objects and the data in the data store—for example, mapping a database string to a string object representing a customer name.

reliability A quality generally associated with a system's *availability* but also indicative of other things in specific contexts, such as having a system operative at the scheduled time, having system failure occur gracefully, and having a quick recovery time.

remote debugging Support for debugging a piece of code that resides on a remote machine. See also *distributed debugging*.

response time A measure of how quickly a system responds from the user perspective. The amount of time a user perceives between the initiation of a request and the rendering of the system response. It includes client processing time, network time, and server processing time.

schema mapping A mechanism to transfer objects between the schema by which they are represented in the application and the schema by which they are represented in the data store. See also *data schema, object schema.*

screen scraper A tool that provides a new GUI interface to a *legacy* application without changing the legacy code.

security boundary A delimitation in a computer system by which security functions can be implemented to protect system assets. Security boundaries can exist on a number of levels: physical, system, application, data, and object. Also known as security perimeters.

server In common usage, the back end of the client/server system, the component that provides shared resources, such as a database, that can be connected to multiple clients. In the *logical client/server model,* the server is the system component that provides any requested service.

sniffing A system security threat characterized by programs that monitor network traffic in order to illegitimately collect security information, such as user IDs and passwords.

spiral model An iterative application development model in which design, development, integration, and testing occur throughout the development cycle, enabling regular feedback to occur.

spoofing A system security threat characterized by fake *principals* that collect critical information. For example, a fake server could collect client authentication information intended for a real server.

stored procedure A frequently used extension to a database management system that stores and executes application logic in a database on the server side for better performance.

subclass A class that inherits its methods and variables from a class above it on the class hierarchy. A subclass can define additional methods and variables of its own, or it can override the inherited methods from the superclass.

superclass A class whose methods and variables are inherited by a class below it in the class hierarchy.

three-tier hardware architecture Client/server architecture that involves three classes of machines: the client is usually a PC; the middle tier is usually a workstation server or a mini computer; the back end is usually a mainframe. See also *logical three-tier architecture.*

throughput In system performance, a measure of the amount of work done in a unit of time. Throughput is often a server-oriented measurement.

TP monitor The component of a transaction processing system in which the transactions run. Although TP monitors vary widely in functionality and scope, they all support two important functions: transaction management and resource management.

TP-heavy server A server that runs TP monitors.

TP-lite server A database server that can provide some basic transaction processing functions, such as commit and rollback of changes, to a table. However, it does not provide full transaction services, such as transaction coordination across multiple programs and resource management.

transaction server A server that is built around a transaction processing (TP) monitor.

trigger Generally, a stored procedure that is invoked automatically by a database event.

two-phase commit A protocol that synchronizes updates to the various system resources involved in a transaction so that they all either succeed or fail. If they succeed, they are committed; if they fail, they are rolled back. The two-phase commit protocol is a common method of maintaining the *ACID properties* in transaction processing.

two-tier hardware architecture Client/server architecture that generally involves only the client and either a middle-tier server or a mainframe.

virtual machine A mechanism that supports portability of object-oriented programs. Virtual machines are implemented in such a way that they present the same functionality and system interfaces to the programs no matter what operating system the virtual machine actually runs on. Also known as the *bytecode* interpreter.

visual programming A programming technique in which programs are created by manipulating objects rather than by writing code. The visual specification and the connections among the objects are used to generate the code.

vulnerabilities System weaknesses that leave the system open to one or more types of security threats (definition from the Object Management Group).

waterfall model An application development model in which all the stages are carried out in sequence: requirements gathering, application specification, analysis, design, coding, testing, and maintenance.

webcasting The process of automatically sending information from a server to a client that fits the interest profile of the client's user.

Web site development tools Tools that support content assembly and content management in developing a Web site. The content assembly tools take active contents and compose them with static contents to form a cohesive Web application. The content management tools provide the ability to identify and manage the resources that make up the Web site, dealing with such issues as broken links and site structure visualization.

workflow management The routing and coordination of the events/work from one principal to another to complete a process. The principals involved can be human users or system components.

World Wide Web A means of accessing information over the *Internet* by using graphically oriented browsers. Specifically, the Web is a networking application supporting a protocol (HTTP) that runs on top of the Internet. To some users, *Internet* and *World Wide Web* have come to mean the same thing. However, other applications also run on top of the Internet that are not part of the Web.

wrappering Encapsulating a conventional program with an object interface. Although the program's internals remain unchanged, the system can view a wrapped program as a single object.

References and Further Reading

For the convenience of readers seeking further information, these references are organized according to the topic areas addressed in this book. The topics are presented in the following order.

- Business Engineering
- Client/Server Computing
- Concurrent and Distributed Computing
- Development Models and Risk Reduction
- Glue
- Groupware
- Internet and Web
- Object Technology
- Persistence
- Queuing Theory and Operations Research
- Scaleability and Reliability
- Security
- Transaction Processing

Business Engineering

Andrews, Dorine, and S. Stalick. *Business Reengineering: The Survival Guide.* Englewood Cliffs, NJ: Yourdon Press, 1994.

Berztiss, Alfs. *Software Methods for Business Reengineering.* New York, NY: Springer, 1996.

Gelernter, David. *Mirror Worlds.* New York, NY: Oxford University Press, 1992.

Hammer, Michael. *Beyond Reengineering.* New York, NY: HarperCollins Publishers, 1996.

Hammer, Michael, and J. Champy. *Reengineering the Corporation: A Manifesto for Business Revolution.* New York, NY: HarperCollins Publishers, 1993.

Harrington, James H. *Business Process Improvement.* New York, NY: McGraw-Hill, 1991.

Jacobson, Ivar, M. Ericsson, and A. Jacobson. *The Object Advantage: Business Process Reengineering with Object Technology.* Reading, MA: Addison-Wesley, 1995.

Moore, Geoffrey. *Crossing the Chasm: Marketing and Selling Technology Products to Mainstream Customers.* New York, NY: HarperCollins, 1991.

Tapscott, Don, and Art Caston. *Paradigm Shift: The New Promise of Information Technology.* New York, NY: McGraw-Hill, 1993.

Taylor, David A. *Business Engineering with Object Technology.* New York: Wiley, 1995.

Client/Server Computing

Berson, Alex. *Client/Server Architecture.* New York: McGraw-Hill, 1996.

Dhumne, A. "Multitier Application Benefits," *Application Development Trends,* June 1996, 52–56.

Dickman, A. "Two-Tier Versus Three-Tier Apps," *Information Week,* November 13, 1995, 74–80.

Dixon, Rand. *Client/Server and Open Systems: Technologies and the Tools that Make Them Work.* New York, NY: Wiley, 1996.

Hart, Johnson M., and Barry Rosenberg. *Client/Server Computing for Technical Professionals: Concepts and Solutions.* Reading, MA: Addison-Wesley, 1995.

Kara, Daniel. "Client/Server Development Tools: A Taxonomy," *CASE Trends,* December/January 1993, 12–21, 64–66.

Lewis, T. "Where is Client/Server Software Headed?" *IEEE Computer,* April 1995, 49–55.

Lowe, Doug. *Client/Server Computing for Dummies.* Foster City, CA: IDG Books, 1995.

Orfali, Robert, Dan Harkey, and Jeri Edwards. *Client/Server Survival Guide, 2nd ed.* New York, NY: Wiley, 1996.

Renaud, Paul. *Introduction to Client/Server Systems: A Practical Guide for Systems Professionals.* New York, NY: Wiley, 1993.

Schlack, M. "The Key to Client/Server OLTP." *Datamation,* April, 1, 1995, 53–56.

Shafe, Laurence. *A Manager's Guide: Client/Server.* Reading, MA: Addison-Wesley, 1995.

Tibbetts, John, and Barbara Bernstein. *Building Cooperative Processing Applications Using SAA.* New York, NY: Wiley, 1992.

Vaskevitch, David. *Client/Server Strategies: A Survival Guide for Corporate Reengineers.* Foster City, CA: IDG Books, 1993.

Concurrent and Distributed Computing

Andrews, G., and F. Schneider. "Concepts and Notations for Concurrent Programming," *ACM Computing Survey* 15:1, (March 1983), 3–44.

Coulouris, G., and J. Dollimore. *Distributed Systems: Concepts and Design.* Reading, MA: Addison-Wesley, 1994.

Development Models and Risk Reduction

Boehm, B. W., and T. DeMarco, Eds. "Software Risk Management," *IEEE Software,* May/June 1997. Special issue includes many articles on managing risk.

Booch, Grady. *Object Solutions: Managing the Object-Oriented Project.* Reading, MA: Addison-Wesley, 1996.

Brooks, Fredrick P. Jr. *The Mythical Man-Month.* Reading, MA: Addison-Wesley, 1995.

Cupparo, John A. "Iterate Applications Not Just Prototypes," *Addendum to the Proceedings of the ACM Conference on Object-Oriented Programming Systems, Languages, and Applications* (OOPSLA) 1993, 35–36.

Fichman, Robert G., and Chris F. Kemerer. "Adoption of Software Engineering Process Innovations: The Case of Object Orientation," *Sloan Management Review,* Winter 1993, 7–22.

Goldberg, Adele, and K. Rubin. *Succeeding with Objects: Decision Frameworks for Project Management.* Reading, MA: Addison-Wesley, 1995.

Guttman, Michael, James A. King, and Jason Matthews. "A Methodology for Developing Distributed Applications," *Object Magazine,* Jan.–Feb. 1993, 55–59.

Jones, C. *Assessment and Control of Software Risks.* Englewood Cliffs, NJ: Prentice-Hall, 1994.

Karolak, Dale W., *Software Engineering Risk Management.* Los Alamitos, CA: IEEE Computer Society Press, 1996.

Love, Tom. *Object Lessons: Lessons Learned in Object-Oriented Development Projects.* Roxbury, CT: SIGS Books, 1993.

Glue

Adler, R. "Distributed Coordination Models for Client/Server Computing," *IEEE Computer,* April 1995, 14–22.

Amaru, C. "Building Distributed Application with MOM," *Client/Server Today,* November 1994, 83–93.

Dolgicer, M. "Unmasking the Mysteries of Message Queuing," *Application Development Trends,* June 1996, 57–67.

Evans, E, and D. Rogers. "Using Java Applets and CORBA for Multi-User Distributed Applications," *IEEE Internet Computing* 1:3, (May/June 1997), 43–55.

Kador, J. "The Ultimate Middleware," *Byte Magazine,* April 1996, 81–83.

Orfali, Robert, Dan Harkey, and Jeri Edwards. *The Essential Distributed Objects Survival Guide.* New York, NY: Wiley, 1996.

Roy, Mark, and Alan Ewald. "Distributed Objects: Interworking COM with CORBA," *Object Magazine* 6:3, (May 1996).

Ruber, Peter. "Hitting the Mark—Thanks to CORBA Compliance, Better Tools and More Portability, Object Technology IS Starting to Live Up to its Promise," *Communications Week,* February 28, 1996.

Shan, Y. P. "Building True Distributed OO C/S Application with VisualAge Smalltalk," *Proceedings of the IBM International Conference on Object Technology,* June 1996, 52A.

Shan, Y. P., J. DeBinder, R. DeNatale, C. Krauss, and P. Mueller. "A Multiple-Platform Multi-Language Distributed Object-Oriented Messaging System," Addendum to the Proceedings, OOPSLA 1993, 27–29.

Whiting, R. "Turning to MOM for Answers," *Client/Server Today,* November 1994, 76–81.

Groupware

Hills, Mellanie. *Intranet as Groupware*. New York, NY: Wiley, 1997.

Khoshafian, Setrag, and M. Buckiewicz. *Introduction to Groupware, Workflow, and Workgroup Computing*. New York, NY: Wiley, 1995.

Marshak, David. "Competing (Groupware) Platforms," *Byte*, August 1995, 84–85.

Simon, Alan R., and W. Marion. *Workgroup Computing: Workflow, Groupware, and Messaging*. New York, NY: McGraw-Hill, 1996.

Sinclair, Joseph T., and D. B. Hale. *Intranets vs. Lotus Notes*. Boston, MA: AP Professional, 1997.

Trammell, Kelly. "Under Construction," *Byte*, August 1995, 93–101.

Woodcock, JoAnne. *Understanding Groupware in the Enterprise*. Redmond, WA: Microsoft Press, 1997.

Yavin, David. "Replication's Fast Track," *Byte*, August 1995, 88A–90.

Internet and Web

Baentsch, M., L. Baum, G. Molter, S. Rothkugel, and P. Sturm. "Enhancing the Web's Infrastructure: From Caching to Replication," *IEEE Internet Computing* 1:2, (March/April 1997), 18–27.

Bernard, Ryan. *The Corporate Intranet*. New York, NY: Wiley, 1996.

December, J., and N. Randall. *The World Wide Web Unleashed*, 2nd ed. Indianapolis, IN: Sams.Net, 1995.

Hoff, A., S. Shaio, and O. Starbuck. *Hooked on Java: Creating Hot Web Sites with Java Applets*. Reading, MA: Addison-Wesley, 1996.

Kaiser G., and J. Whitehead. "Distributed Authoring and Versioning," *IEEE Internet Computing* 1:2, (March/April 1997), 76–77.

Nwana, Hyacinth S. "Software Agents: An Overview," *Knowledge Engineering Review* 11:3, (September 1996).

Robicheaux, Michael. "Client/Server/Web: Extending Your Reach," *Object Magazine*, July 1996, 50–53.

Umar, Amjad. *Object-Oriented Client/Server Internet Environments*. Englewood Cliffs, NJ: Prentice-Hall, 1997.

Umar, Amjad. *Application (Re) Engineering: Building Web-Based Object-Oriented Applications and Dealing with Legacies.* Englewood Cliffs, NJ: Prentice-Hall, 1997.

Vadhol, P., and V. McCarthy. "Who Wins the Web Server Shootout?" *Datamation,* April 1996, 48–53.

Object Technology

Booch, Grady. *Object-Oriented Analysis and Design with Applications.* Redwood City, CA: Benjamin/Cummings, 1994.

Forrester Research. *The Object Voyage.* Cambridge, MA: Forrester Research, Inc., 1992.

Fowler, Martin, with K. Scott. *UML Distilled.* Reading, MA: Addison-Wesley, 1997.

Gamma, Eric, Richard Helm, Ralph Johnson, and John Vlissides. *Design Patterns: Elements of Reusable Object-Oriented Software.* Reading, MA: Addison-Wesley, 1995.

Jacobson, Ivar. *Object-Oriented Software Engineering: A Use Case Drive Approach.* Reading, MA: Addison-Wesley, 1992.

Shan, Y. P., R. Earle, and S. McGaughey, "Rounding out the Picture: Objects Across the Client-Server Spectrum," *IEEE Computer,* October 1995, 60.

Shan, Y. P., R. Earle, and S. McGaughey, "Objects on the Server: A Natural Evolution," *Object Magazine,* May 1995, 49–53.

Taylor, David A. *Object-Oriented Information Systems: Planning and Implementation.* New York, NY: Wiley, 1992.

Taylor, David A. *Object-Oriented Technology: A Manager's Guide.* Reading, MA: Addison-Wesley, 1990.

Vlissides, John, James Coplien, and Norman Kerth. *Pattern Languages of Program Design 2.* Reading, MA: Addison-Wesley, 1996.

Persistence

Bukhres, O., and A. Elmagarmid. *Object-Oriented Multidatabase Systems: A Solution for Advanced Applications.* Englewood Cliffs, NJ: Prentice-Hall, 1996.

Cattell, R.G.G., Ed. *The Object Database Standard: ODMG-93 Release 1.2.* San Francisco, CA: Morgan Kaufmann, 1996.

Kemper, A., and G. Moerkotte. *Object-Oriented Database Management: Applications in Engineering and Computer Science.* Englewood Cliffs, NJ: Prentice-Hall, 1994.

Kleindienst, J., F. Plasil, and P. Tuma. "Lessons Learned from Implementing the CORBA Persistent Object Service." *Proceedings of the ACM Conference on Object-Oriented Programming System, Languages, and Applications (OOPSLA),* 1996, 150–167.

Loomis, Mary. *Object Databases: The Essentials.* Reading, MA: Addison-Wesley, 1995.

Martin, James, and Joe Leben. *Client/Server Databases: Enterprise Computing.* New York, NY: Prentice-Hall, 1995.

Nigam, Subhash. "ODBMSs: Rationale, Advances, and Challenges to the Current State of the Art," *JOOP,* June 1996, 21–24.

Pitoura, E., O. Bukhres, and A. Elmagarmid. "Object-Orientation in Multidatabase Systems," *ACM Computing Surveys,* June 1995, 142–165.

Vermeulen, Robert. "Object Relational Databases: Is the Combination Stronger?" *Object Magazine,* August 1997, 31–65.

Queuing Theory and Operations Research

Gross, D., and C. M. Harris. *Fundamentals of Queueing Theory.* New York, NY: Wiley, 1974.

Hillier, Frederick S. *Introduction to Operations Research.* New York, NY: McGraw-Hill, 1990.

Kleinrock, Leonard. *Queuing Systems,* 2 vols. New York, NY: Wiley, 1975.

Nelson, Randolph. *Probability, Stochastic Processes, and Queuing Theory: The Mathematics of Computer Performance Modeling.* New York, NY: Springer-Verlag, 1995.

Phillips, D., A. Ravindran, and James J. Solberg, *Operations Research: Principles and Practice.* New York, NY: Wiley, 1976.

Scaleability and Reliability

Abdel-Ghaly, A. A., P. Y. Chan, and B. Littlewood. "Evaluation of Competing Software Reliability Predictions," *IEEE Transactions on Software Engineering* 12:9, (September 1986), 950–967.

Hwang, Kai. *Advanced Computer Architecture: Parallelism, Scaleability, Programmability.* New York, NY: McGraw-Hill, 1993.

Leon-Garcia, A. *Probability and Random Processes for Electrical Engineering.* Reading, MA: Addison-Wesley, 1989.

Lyu, Michael R. *Handbook of Software Reliability Engineering.* New York, NY: McGraw-Hill, 1996.

Musa, J. D. "A Theory of Software Reliability and its Application," *IEEE Transactions on Software Engineering* 1:9, (September 1975).

Shan, Y. P. "Scaleability Issues in OO Client/Server Systems." *Proceedings of the IBM International Conference on Object Technology,* June 1997.

Security

Bishop, Matt, S. Cheung, and C. Wee. "The Threat from the Net," *IEEE Spectrum,* August 1997, 56–63.

Cheswick, William R., and Bellovin, Steven M. *Firewalls and Internet Security.* Reading, MA: Addison-Wesley, 1994.

Diffie, W., and M. E. Hellman. "Privacy and Authentication: An Introduction to Cryptography," *Proceedings of the IEEE* 67:3, (March 1979), 397–421.

Garfinkel, Simson L. "Public Key Cryptography," *IEEE Computer,* June 1996, 101–104.

Hutt, Arthur, Seymour Bosworth and Douglas Hoyt. *Computer Security Handbook.* New York, NY: Wiley, 1995.

Popek, G. J., and C. S. Kline. "Encryption and Secure Computer Networks," *ACM Computing Surveys* 11:4, (December 1979), 331–356.

Siyan, Karanjit, and Chris Hare. *Internet Firewalls and Network Security.* Indianapolis, IN: New Riders Publishing, 1995.

Stallings, William. "Internet Armor," *BYTE,* December 1996, 127–134.

Voydock, V. L., and S. T. Kent. "Security Mechanisms in High-Level Network Protocols," *ACM Computing Surveys* 15:2, (June 1983), 135–171.

Transaction Processing

Bernstein, Philip A., and E. Newcomer. *Principles of Transaction Processing.* San Francisco, CA: Morgan Kaufmann, 1997.

Cobb, Edward E. "Objects and Transactions: Together at Last," *Object Magazine,* Jan/Feb 1995.

Gray, Jim, and Andreas Reuter. *Transaction Processing: Concepts and Techniques.* San Mateo, CA: Morgan Kaufmann, 1993.

Gray, Jim. *The Benchmark Handbook: For Database and Transaction Processing Systems.* San Mateo, CA: Morgan Kaufmann, 1993.

Kramer, Mitchell I. "Microsoft Transaction Server: A General Purpose Infrastructure for Multitier Applications," Boston, MA: Patricia Seybold Group, November 1996.

Shan, Y. P., B. Barry, J. des Rivieres, J. Duimovich, D. Lesage, J. Lord, B. Nuechterlein, and T. Wolf. "Smalltalk on the Big Iron," Poster, ACM Conference on Object-Oriented Programming, Systems, and Applications (OOPSLA), October 1995.

Index